EX LIBRIS
TSM

THE
ULYSSES FACTOR

The exploring instinct in man

An early representation of Ulysses blinding the Cyclops Polyphemus, on a black-figured amphora dated about 530–510 BC

THE
ULYSSES FACTOR

The exploring instinct in man

For Tom, who
— "omnibus e meis amicis
antistans mihi milibus trecentis..."

by

J. R. L. ANDERSON

A full North-Easter's blowing up.
Just listen til it roar, now —
Lord help them, how I pities them
unhappy folks on shore now

J. Anderson

HODDER AND STOUGHTON

Printed in Great Britain
for Hodder and Stoughton Limited,
St. Paul's House, Warwick Lane, London, E.C.4,
by Richard Clay (The Chaucer Press), Ltd.,
Bungay, Suffolk

It would seem to be a fact that the remotest parts of the world are the richest in minerals and produce the finest specimens of both animal and vegetable life.

— HERODOTUS *(tr. A. de Sélincourt)*.

Preface

Between the idea
And the reality ...
Falls the shadow.

T. S. ELIOT has expressed the writer's dilemma for all time. If the reality here created from my conception of the Ulysses factor has any substance it is due primarily to the criticism and encouragement of Robin Denniston and my wife Helen. Others, living and dead, who have helped me are so numerous that I can but say how conscious I am of the debt that all men owe to their fellows. I have drawn deeply on the works of other men over some three thousand years of human history. I have tried to acknowledge my drawings scrupulously. But the mind's furniture (my mind's, at any rate) has untidy cupboards, and I fear that I do not always know whence some piece of knowledge has come. May its rightful owners forgive me. I owe particular thanks for time and learning ungrudgingly given to Mr Alan Cooke, Curator of Manuscripts at the Scott Polar Research Institute, Cambridge, and to Mr Graham Harrison and my son Richard, both of St John's College, Cambridge. Family catalogues are tedious, but I must acknowledge a considerable debt to my younger sons David and Timothy for help in transcribing bibliographies and the lists I needed for the statistical work in Chapter XXII. I should like to put on record my thanks also to Mrs A. F. Tschiffely and to the staffs of the Embassies in London of Argentina, France, Germany, Switzerland, Japan and the United States. I owe the splendid representation of Ulysses in the frontispiece to Dr Ann Birchall, of the Department of Greek and Roman Antiquities in the British Museum.

In my quotations from Homer I have turned to E. V. Rieu's splendid translation, published by Penguin Books. Occasionally I have used a word or phrase of my own, but Rieu's great work can scarcely be bettered and (as I would recommend to all readers of Homer in English) I have followed him with humility—and delight.

The passages from *A World of my Own* by Robin Knox-Johnston are reprinted by permission of Messrs. Cassell & Co. Ltd., and the poem by William Scawen Blunt on page 75 is reprinted by permission of the Fitzwilliam Museum, Cambridge.

J. R. L. ANDERSON

Contents

Illustrations

Key to Acknowledgements

[1] By courtesy of the Trustees of the British Museum
[2] Photo: Bassano and Vandyk
[3] By courtesy of George Allen and Unwin Ltd
[4] Eileen Ramsay
[5] London Express
[6] Foto Leon; by courtesy of David Lewis
[7] By courtesy of Robin Knox-Johnston

I

The anthropological approach

IT comes to most of us to be brought up wondering sharply, 'What on earth am I doing here, anyway?' This question struck me with force in the cockpit of a small boat in the Davis Strait between Greenland and Labrador. It was a horrible night, with low cloud seeming to meet the sea and a wind that whipped spray from the wave tops to fling it stinging in your face. We worked single watches on that trip, and I was alone at the wheel, my five mates sleeping, or trying to sleep, below. I had an hour or so of my watch to go, and my hands were brutally cold. What on earth was I doing there and why?

I was there by my own volition, my own act, but could I help it? Of course I could help it, I need not have been there at all. My mates were there because I had asked them to come, but equally their response had been voluntary. So. One can help getting married, or joining the Army. But is either an entirely voluntary act? Man is an animal species, belonging to his particular herd: unless enough men marry, and at times of need become soldiers, the herd dies. Was this relevant to my being in a small sailing boat in the Davis Strait attempting to rediscover America, or at least to cast some light on how America was discovered by the Norseman Leif Eiriksson roughly a thousand years before we sailed? I thought perhaps it was relevant.

Since the ending of the Second World War in 1945 the world has been much entertained, and a little excited, by the exploits of individuals in undertaking self-imposed tasks that require coming to terms in rather special ways with the elemental forces of nature. Thor Heyerdahl and five companions crossed the Pacific in or on a raft of balsa-wood. Edmund Hillary and the Sherpa Tensing climbed Everest. Men did not exactly begin to cross oceans in small boats, but did begin to do so rather frequently, and in very small craft. In 1951 Stanley Smith and Charles Violet sailed the Atlantic by the stiff northern route in the 20-ft yawl *Nova Espero*. Between November 1951 and February 1952 Patrick Ellam and Colin Mudie crossed from Casablanca to Barbados in *Sopranino*, an even smaller boat. In May 1952 Ann Davison left Plymouth singlehanded in the 23-ft sloop *Felicity Ann* and after calling at various ports in France, Spain and North Africa reached Dominica on the other side of the Atlantic in January 1953. In 1960 H. G. Hasler and Francis Chichester laconically challenged one another to a *race* across the Atlantic, and the Singlehanded Transatlantic Race was born.

In these same decades less dramatically publicised people undertook many exploits requiring at least equal determination and endurance. That great mountaineer H. W. Tilman, who, after climbing Nanda Devi with N. E. Odell, for a time held, with Odell, the distinction of having reached the highest summit yet attained by man, decided to go to sea. At an age when most men think of retirement, he sailed an old Bristol Channel pilot cutter, *Mischief*, to Patagonia. Husband and wife teams, the Hiscocks, the Pyes, the Smeetons adventured in small boats in some of the most inhospitable seas in the world. Why?

I began to think rather deeply about this when I was myself in a fairly inhospitable sea in 1966. Since then the exploits have increased both in number and intensity. John Ridgway and Chay Blyth *rowed* an open dory across the Atlantic. Chichester *raced* himself, or the ghosts of the masters of the old clipper ships, singlehanded round the world. Alec Rose took a twenty-years-old boat singlehanded round the world. Robin Knox-Johnston sailed singlehanded round the world without putting into port or taking on supplies. Sheila Scott flew a single-engined light aeroplane round the world. Men, and a few, a very few women continue such undertakings. Why?

Love of adventure, money (sometimes), desire for fame—the obvious and easy explanations seem to me not enough. They add words to things without explaining them—it is like 'explaining' that a man has a pain in his hip because he has sciatica, which does nothing to indicate why he has sciatica, nor what it is. Human exploits accepting physical challenge *because* of the challenge have increased in number in recent decades, but in terms of the world's population the individuals who undertake them form a percentage so minute that it could reasonably be ignored as having any kind of significance. Yet trace elements in animal and plant growth, in proportions so tiny that sometimes their existence can only be inferred, are now known to be of vital importance to survival. Is there here a genetic factor of importance to human development, or even survival?

There are two forms of adaptation in the evolutionary process to which man, with all other living things, is subject. They are known as *general adaptation* and *special adaptation*. General adaptation is the ability of a species to acquire characteristics that assist survival over the whole range of conditions in which it lives—in man, for instance, the ability to communicate by speech, to make tools, to be more or less omniverous. Special adaptation is defined by Professor Carleton S. Coon in *The Origin of Races* as involving 'the acquisition of a new trait, or trait complex, that is useful in a single environment, under special circumstances'. He adds:

> It is the process which enables an animal to resist heat, cold, or bright light, to see well in dim light, to run faster or swim better than its fellows, or to live without water in deserts.

Man has lived in communities from the beginning of the human story, and as communities have grown they have required more food, wood that would float better, or split more readily than the trees in their immediate environment, new needs in almost infinite variety. Most can be met in fairly obvious ways: food by the improvement of techniques for hunting and growing things, or by the sadly simpler method of attacking neighbours and taking their land and sources of food supply; better timber, new materials of all sorts, can be found by experiment, by looking for new kinds of trees, by digging into the earth. Every now and again, however, something so novel that its existence could not even be guessed has been brought into communities to give them a wholly new rung on the ladder of development. Someone has looked at a range of mountains regarded as an absolute barrier to the territory of his tribe and decided to climb them, to find out what is on the far side. Someone has looked at a sea known to everyone as marking the end of the world and set out with a raft or log of wood to discover if it really *is* the end of the world.

All very well, but is this any more than a love of adventure? Most healthy human beings have a spice of adventure in them, that sends little boys up trees, makes people want to change their job, or even to move house. But this explains the *how* rather than the *why* in the achievement of scaling unclimbable mountains or crossing—from choice—an ocean in a rowing boat. You use your arms and legs as you have been taught from infancy, and without an innate sense of adventure the teaching would not have got far. The normal man or woman enjoys a good country walk, a scramble over rocks or a sail, but does not particularly *want* to climb an ice face or to tackle an ocean in an open boat. Some force other than mere adventure must be looked for to discover what prompts a man not only to feel that it would be nice to know what is on the far side of the hills but to contract a fever of desire to know, and then an absolute determination to find out.

Men do extraordinary things in the hope of gain: a love of adventure coupled with a desire to make money may be explanation enough for all these feats of human endeavour. To write this is at once to dismiss it, for it is patently untrue. Men have beggared themselves, and done so coldly and deliberately, to build boats to cross an ocean for no apparent purpose, or to finance an expedition in search of no tangible treasure. Sometimes they have come across treasure, and have been glad enough, no doubt, to find it, but treasure-seeking in the ordinary sense cannot be the driving force I mean. Nor can that almost equally powerful motive, the lure of fame. Men like to be famous, and publicity of one sort or another has often been sought in connection with some enterprising feat. But sometimes the proposed feat is in itself an effort to attract notice to some project or manufacture, in which case it comes under quite another heading. Sometimes, particularly in recent years, publicity has been a method of trying to finance an expedition, but that does not make it necessarily the object of it. Sometimes a man dominated by the need to climb his mountain or to cross his unknown sea may have a considerable distaste for publicity at all. Of course, in some circumstances to shun publicity or to play hard-to-get is a method of courting notoriety, but certainly not always. Tilman, for example, any one of whose exploits could have made the name of a lesser man into a household word, has been content to be known to those who care to read his books. Adrian Hayter, whose remarkable first voyage in *Sheila* has never had the recognition it merited, is another who has sought no popular reputation for himself.

Neither gold nor fame will do. They may be won by a successful endeavour, but they do not explain this particular kind of endeavour. The anthropological approach remains: there is some factor in man, some form of special adaptation, which prompts a few individuals to exploits which, however purposeless they may seem, are of value to the survival of the race. I call this the Ulysses factor. But, if so, why is it manifest now; how, when the terrestial globe is mapped and explored, its resources known, can there be any survival-value in crossing an ocean by the primitive means of sail or oars?

We can look back over the evolution of man, and we can see plainly how special adaptation to heat or cold has helped communities to survive in the tropics and the Arctic. We cannot see forward. We can see why a tail is now useless to man, but we cannot say why he retains certain other attributes from his remote physical past. There are no seas left to be crossed for the first time, and the discovery of a new source of food will be the outcome of patient work in the laboratory rather than of finding fertile new land on the far side of an ocean. But adaptation takes many forms, and since we cannot see the end-product of human evolution, we cannot know to what new strains and stresses man may have to adapt. We can guess some. In human evolution *crowding* has been one of the forces to which man has had to adapt, by which, without successful adaptation, he has been destroyed. Primitive man lived in communities, but they were very small communities, often no more than one or two families. Ability to live in larger communities has been a potent factor in helping some of the races of man to prosper, inability to do so has led others to decline. Crowding is, or seems to be, an inescapable accompaniment of advanced civilisation, and it can be inimical to

B

survival. There *must* be human adaptation here, and in wholly new ways, for although man has crowded into communities over thousands of years, the *degree* of modern crowding is something quite new in human history. Here the Ulysses factor in him may be important. So far I have discussed it crudely, in physical terms. But the factor is complex, and it has psychological, even spiritual, implications. In these may be, indeed, man's hope of surviving as an individual in a mass society.

A genetic factor exists potentially in all members of a given race, but its manifestations are Protean, it may be dormant over long periods, and its emergence in individuals may be idiosyncratic. Changes in environment may repress it, or intensify it. The Ulysses factor has been exceptionally manifest in different peoples at different times in history, profoundly influencing history. It is discernible in the Phoenicians around the tenth century BC, in the Greeks about the eighth century BC, in the Persians of the sixth century BC, the Arabs of about the same time, or perhaps earlier. In more recent history the factor was a powerful driving force in the Scandinavian peoples of the eighth to the eleventh centuries AD, in the Portuguese and Spaniards of the fourteenth and fifteenth centuries, the British of the sixteenth century, the Dutch of the seventeenth, the British again and the French in the eighteenth century. At all these periods there were direct personal and national gains to be looked for in exploration, and it is impossible to disentangle the exploring factor in *man* from the commercial motives of the *men* who sought to profit from it. But it is hard to believe that Eiriksson, Vasco da Gama, Magellan, Drake, Davis, Cook, Bouganville and their peers were animated solely by commercial motives. They could not have been: and although they served many different interests, they shared certain human characteristics, which indicate a common driving force, deep seated in all of them.

In the nineteenth century the factor underwent some degree of mutation. It was less obviously necessary for national survival to extend physical horizons, but the compelling need to extend horizons still manifested itself in individuals. In a letter to Monckton Milnes (Lord Houghton) in 1863, when preparing to adventure up the Lower Congo, Sir Richard Burton wrote:

Starting in a hollowed log of wood some thousand miles up a river, with an infinitesimal prospect of returning, I ask myself Why? And the only echo is, 'damned fool—the devil drives'.

The devil? Burton's devil here was clearly an irresistible manifestation in him of the Ulysses factor. Livingstone and other great missionaries turned the factor to the service of religion. The missionary element in the religions of the world is, itself, a manifestation of this deep need in man to explore. To say this is not to decry the religious motive: God may use the obscure functioning of some human gland as readily as the work of human hands. The Ulysses factor was strong in St Paul—had it not been, the Christian Church might have been markedly different. It was strong in St Francis Xavier, and has been so in many of his followers.

With the dwindling scope for physical exploration of the world men invented new goals. Mountaineering for its own sake was a nineteenth-century invention. Travellers have always climbed mountains when they had to, but if there was a pass to the far side they took it thankfully. Edward Whymper looked to the great peaks of the Alps and felt that they had to be climbed because they were there. This ideal inspired first the English and very soon the French and the Italians: the Alpine Club was founded and mountaineering was born. After the Alps men looked to the greater peaks of the Himalayas and the Andes. Few people can hope to make money out of climbing mountains: most mountaineers spend money in order to climb. Theirs is another manifestation of the Ulysses factor. Its philosophical implications I shall discuss later.

At the turn of the twentieth century the Poles had still to be reached, and to get to them became in individuals an intense physical desire, stimulated by intense national rivalry. Peary (American) achieved the North Pole in 1909, Amundsen (Norwegian) the South in 1911, beating Scott (British) by a few weeks. Shackleton (British) attempted to cross the Antarctic Continent in 1913: heroic failure put him with the immortals.

The war of 1914–1918 called on every faculty in man. In war there is manifold activity for the Ulysses factor, but it is confused in the herd instincts of fighting nations. I shall touch upon some aspects of the factor in war, but this is a special side of the subject.

After the war Everest remained as a kind of special challenge to human endeavour, inspiring attempt after attempt to climb it. Irvine and Mallory died on the mountain in 1924: whether either reached the summit is unknown. In 1936 Tilman and Odell climbed Nanda Devi (25,645 ft), then the highest mountain in the world to have been climbed. In 1950 Maurice Herzog and Louis Lachenal climbed Annapurna (26,492 ft). Other great peaks felt the foot of man, but Everest (29,028 ft) remained the final challenge (unless either Irvine or Mallory had won an unknown victory) until 1953, when Hillary and Tensing climbed it, in the expedition led by John Hunt (Lord Hunt).

Final challenge? No sooner was Everest climbed by one route than men began to study other, perhaps more difficult, ways of getting to the top. The Ulysses factor is Protean. Thoughts returned to the Alps, to the North face of the Eiger and other routes once considered impossible to summits already reached. And new challenges appeared at sea.

The Ulysses factor appears to be unique to man. Other animals have a sense of adventure and certainly enjoy hunting, but deliberate risk-taking in pursuit of a goal of no apparent practical value is not the habit of any animal other than man. In man the factor can be an urge as compelling as sex. Like sex, indeed with all other human attributes, the Ulysses factor can be exploited and abused; it can take a psychological wrong turning and become inimical to survival. That is one reason why it should be studied. Again like sex, manifestations of the factor in individuals may stimulate powerful mass excitement: the crowds assembled to greet Chichester or Rose tingle with a sort of static electrical excitement not dissimilar to that felt in a crowd gathered to see an exceptionally beautiful film-star. This is because the factor is present in mankind as such, and although it may be dormant in the great majority of individuals, it will respond unconsciously to some exploit that excites it.

Historically, the factor has appeared most strongly in communities either dominant or about to become dominant—in the Scandinavians at the peak of Viking expansion, in the British in the sixteenth to the nineteenth centuries. Up to this century there is a distinct relationship between the occurrence of the Ulysses factor in the people of a nation and that nation's position in the world: when the factor is strong in individuals it assists national dominance. But there seems to have been a mutation here. In the decades since the Second World War, when Britain's power as a nation has been declining, the factor has been more strongly apparent in the British than in any other national community. Other outstanding manifestations have been in the Norwegians and the French, neither now a great power in the old sense. But what is national greatness?

I I

The type-figure

IN any study of human behaviour it is necessary to reach far back into the past, to discover as nearly as one can the roots, or springs, of action. You know before you start that the task is impossible of fulfilment, for history has no beginning. Very early man left few traces of his bones, and none at all of his thoughts. But he did leave some record of his actions, and his thoughts can sometimes be inferred. Teeth are all-but indestructible, and expert dental study of the remains of early man can indicate the sort of food he ate, which is a starting-point of fact in working out how and where he got it, and the kind of life he led. More important for my own study is where he left his bones, for location in death is the outcome of action in life. Fossilised human bones of similar racial characteristics have been found over widely separated parts of the earth's habitable surface, which implies the certainty that our remotest ancestors could and did travel, that they could cross mountains, rivers and, perhaps, seas; though here one must be careful not to draw too firm conclusions, for half a million years ago there were land bridges connecting Asia with Europe across the Bering Strait, Britain with the Continent across what is now the English Channel, and other places now needing boats where man once could walk. But method of travel is not here our concern: the certainty remains that by foot on land, by raft or log of wood on water, the most primitive of men wandered far. And from this comes the further certainty that some individual pointed the way, for although there can be mindless group migration when a pack of animals flee in terror, man's early travels, or some of them, at any rate, were not mindless, but deliberate attempts to seek a favourable new environment for the development of his culture and the practice of his skills. The distribution of the culture patterns of primitive man cannot be wholly chance. The Ulysses factor manifested itself early in human history.

We can say surely that some ancestor with the Ulysses factor strong in him brought Swanscombe Woman and her family to the Thames Valley some 235,000 years ago. We know nothing whatever about him. We can infer his existence, that is all.

With the beginnings of recorded history there is strong evidence of the Ulysses factor. Ancient Egyptian inscriptions record a remarkable voyage led by one Hannu from Egypt to the Land of Punt (probably Mozambique and the Zambezi valley) about 3000 BC. It took four years. Another great voyage to Punt, with better ships, and taking three years, is better recorded from about 1493–1490 BC. That was in the reign of Queen Hatshepsut. The leader of the expedition was a man called Nehsi, and he returned in triumph with a fabulous cargo of gold and incense.

If one knew more about Hannu or Nehsi either would have a good claim to be the type-figure of the exploring factor in man. But from that time past, 5,000 years ago for Hannu, 3,500 years for Nehsi, neither has left more of his personality than a name cut in stone inscriptions. To discover a type-figure one must move on in time to about the eighth century BC. If Ulysses left no log, we have a record even better—a vivid description of his character and personality by a great poet.

Modern scholarship, greatly assisted by the late Michael Ventris's decipherment of the Linear B tablets in Crete in 1952, suggests that Homer lived during the eighth century BC. The *Iliad* and the *Odyssey* are epic poems describing a heroic age at some time in the past—the past from Homer's time that is. Their setting is the Late Bronze Age, with iron known, but still scarce and valuable. The society depicted in the poems is not that of Homer's own day, but it was real enough, for all its portrayal as a Golden Age when men were heroes on speaking terms with gods. It cannot be dated exactly, but to put it at some time around the twelfth century BC will not be far wrong.

It was a real world, and the heroes, or their prototypes, were real people, as Arthur and his knights have a basis of historical reality underlying all the myths of the Round Table. The forerunners of the people who later created

Greek civilisation were expanding in the Eastern Mediterranean, establishing the settlements (small kingdoms still
under tribal leaders in the heroic period) which grew into the
splendid City-States of the Greek world. To secure themselves
and to prosper, these ancestors of the Greeks needed above all
two human qualities: fighting ability and the enterprise to
find and settle new land. They had both, and the Ulysses
factor which led to Greek expansion ultimately in colonies
throughout the Mediterranean world is personified in the
figure of Odysseus. He is better known by the latin version of
his name, Ulysses.

He is not the hero of the *Iliad*, though he has an important
place in that first of Homer's works. The *Odyssey* is entirely
concerned with him and his adventures over ten years between the fall of Troy and his homecoming in Ithaca, an
island off the west coast of Greece. In the story, Ulysses angers
the sea-god Poseidon, who sends a gale to wreck his ship and
besets him with troubles on his journey home. He is, however,
befriended by the goddess Athene, who in the end persuades
Zeus, the most powerful of gods in the Greek pantheon, to
permit him a safe homecoming. The *Odyssey* is one of the
best adventure stories ever written: it is also a case study by a
writer of the keenest psychological insight of a man powerfully affected by the Ulysses factor.

Homer provides us with a study of Ulysses over twenty years,
ten years with Agamemnon's allies besieging Troy, and ten
years of adventuring on the way home. It is not a continuous
study. The *Iliad* deals with but one episode, covering a few
days, in the long Trojan war, and the *Odyssey* is directly concerned with events in the last year of Ulysses's journey back to
Ithaca. But the *Iliad* tells us that Ulysses was with the Greek
forces throughout the ten-year siege of Troy, and provides a
number of glimpses of his life. In the *Odyssey* Ulysses himself
relates the narrative of his adventures over the whole period
from leaving Troy, telling the story one evening at the court
of a king who befriends him. There are also descriptions of his
home, his wife Penelope, his father and mother, his son and
some of his faithful old servants. Between them, the *Iliad* and
the *Odyssey* present a rounded picture of Ulysses as a full
man.

Homer was a poet, reciting sagas to audiences who knew or

half-knew the outlines of his stories. He omits many details which modern scientific study would like to have; but his poet's vision often presents an action or a quirk of character with a sharpness of insight that no science could match. The picture of Ulysses both gains and loses from its setting. On the whole, it gains.

Homer omits his age, as, indeed, he omits all passport particulars. But the age of Ulysses can be determined within fairly narrow limits. Although his father was still alive, Ulysses was himself ruling in Ithaca before he left for Troy, and he was old enough to have acquired a considerable reputation for subtlety and courage. His first child, however, had only just been born when he left for Troy, and twenty years later his wife was still young and attractive enough to be besieged by suitors. She need not have been more than seventeen or eighteen when Ulysses left her. He was obviously a good deal older than his wife. In the *Iliad* he is regarded always as among the senior captains, men sought his advice and deferred to his experience. But his physical performance in the Trojan war suggests the prime of life. He could have been forty or thereabouts when he left Ithaca, but he was more likely to have been around thirty-five. Another thing that suggests that he was probably still in his thirties is that both his parents were living. His mother died while he was away, his father was in Ithaca to greet him twenty years later.

The picture, then, is of a man between thirty-five and forty-five in the *Iliad* and between forty-five and his mid-fifties in the *Odyssey*. At the end of the *Odyssey*, when he slays his enemies against enormous odds, he must have been over fifty, perhaps several years older. This is important. Fifty was a considerable age for a man three thousand years ago, more like seventy now. A characteristic of the Ulysses factor is that it is retained in age, and some of its most interesting manifestations have been in men at ages which, even today, are regarded as late in the human span, when active life is over. Ulysses had this characteristic in a marked degree.

He had immense strength in his arms, back and legs, but he does not seem to have been of particularly noticeable stature. Had he been a giant of a man, Homer would have said so. Nausicaa, who was in love with him, called him 'tall and handsome', but the Cyclops, an enemy, described him as 'a puny little runt'. The eye of love and the eye of rage (which Ulysses had just blinded) may discount both descriptions, and there is no evidence to suggest that he was in any way exceptional in size. At the Phaeacian Games no one took him for an athlete, and his prowess caused surprise. He probably stood about 5 ft 8–9 ins, well built, but wiry rather than big. Women found him very attractive.

The qualities that Homer stresses in him again and again are resourcefulness, courage and cunning. Among the epithets used to describe him are 'man of many resources', 'of the nimble wits', 'crafty', 'shrewd', 'of the many wiles', 'wise', 'who knew all the tricks'. An enemy called him 'arch-schemer, arch-adventurer'. There is no doubt of his courage, in the most difficult circumstances. Homer calls him 'man of iron', 'stedfast', 'excellent', and of an 'indomitable soul'.

It is a personality attractive, but not wholly so. Ulysses was determined to get his own way. If not exactly selfish, he was intensely self-centred. He knew the value of a gift, and he was not above asking for one. The various women who fell in love with him on his travels he left without regret. True, he was married to Penelope and he wanted to get home, but some of these women were extremely good to him. He took what they offered, and apparently thought nothing of it. There was not much romance about him: he was hard.

Yet he was a man whom other men followed. He had occasional difficulties with his crew, but he settled them quickly, and though men sometimes grumbled at him, they continued to accept him as a leader. He had a strong sense of duty to those under his command. When some of his band were bewitched by Circe he set off at once to try to rescue them, although his lieutenant implored him to stay and it seemed highly probable that in fact all he could achieve would be to fall victim to Circe himself. The passage in the *Odyssey* describing this incident is moving. The lieutenant, Eurylochus, has come back to tell Ulysses of the disaster. The narrative continues:

> When I heard this story I slung my bow over my shoulder, and my big bronze sword in its silver scabbard, and I told Eurylochus to take me back with him by the way he had come. He threw his arms round my knees in supplica-

tion and broke into a pitiful appeal.

'My king,' he said, 'leave me behind, and don't force me to go back with you there. You will never come back yourself, and you won't rescue a man of your crew. I am certain of it. Let us get away quickly with those that are left here. We might still save our skins.'

'Very well, Eurylochus,' I replied, 'stay where you are, and eat and drink by the black ship's hull. But I shall go. It is my plain duty.'*

It would be hard not to follow a man like that. In the event, Circe fell in love with him.

Attempts to reconstruct the voyages of Ulysses have been made many times, never wholly convincingly. He certainly went through the Straits of Messina, and wandered far in the Western Mediterranean, an immense voyage from Troy, located on the coast of Turkey, some three miles inshore from the Dardanelles. But details here do not matter. What is certain is that Ulysses opened the way to later Greek expansion in the Western Mediterranean.

In Homer's story Ulysses did not sail voluntarily: he was trying to get home to Ithaca from Troy, and was driven off course by the anger of Poseidon. In the setting of its time any incident in the Ulysses story would be put down to the intervention of some god, malevolent or beneficent. If Ulysses had enemies among the gods he had also friends. Ulysses may well have started his adventures by being driven off course, but what stands out in the story is his 'adventure-proneness', as it were, and his sheer ability as an explorer. We know next to nothing of the methods of navigation used by these very early Greeks, but Ulysses seems never to have had the least doubt that given a ship which did not founder, he could get home. Moreover, although he may have started by being driven off course, he kept a sharp eye open for the advantages and disadvantages of the islands and coasts he met, a good harbour here, a dangerously exposed anchorage there, land suitable for pasturing flocks or growing vines. An example of this economic alertness is his assessment of the possibilities of colon-

---

* This, and other quotations from Homer, are from E. V. Rieu's translation, published by Penguin Books.

ising an island off the Cyclopean coast. Ulysses found it uninhabited, but noted that it had plenty of level land suitable for
cultivation, that the soil seemed rich and that there was a
secure anchorage with easy access to fresh water. He concluded that the island could be turned into a fine colony. Describing the position of the island, he says that it is not very far
from the harbour of the Cyclopean coast, but adds 'and not so
near, either'. An element of secrecy, of putting off possible
competitors, is a typical Ulysses characteristic.

He was practical, and extremely competent. Given an axe,
an adze and some trees, he built himself a boat in four days,
taking care to raise the topsides with plaited osier twigs reinforced with brushwood to give his craft extra freeboard and
additional protection against heavy seas, a sound and seamanlike job. He kept his head. When his boat was dismasted in a
storm and his steering-oar swept away he was tempted to
abandon ship and swim for it, to try to make a shore line that
at least he could see. This, indeed, was the advice given to him
by a friendly sea-nymph who came on board in the guise of a
seamew, leaving behind a veil with the promise that if he
wound it round his middle he would escape death. In spite of
the magic veil (though it came in useful later), Ulysses decided against the nymph's advice, arguing to himself:

> No, I shall not leave the boat at once, for I saw how far
> the land is where she promised me salvation. Instead I shall
> do what I myself think best. As long as the joints of my
> planks hold, I shall stay where I am. When my boat breaks
> up, I'll swim for it.

This was certainly the right decision: to stay with your
boat as long as you possibly can is nearly always the best form
of self-help in such circumstances.

When he did have to swim for it, because the boat broke up
under him, he still kept his head. After being buffeted about
for forty-eight hours he was swept inshore, but exhausted as
he was, he worked out calmly in his mind how best to make
land. He was being carried towards a reef, and an exhausted
man might have tried thankfully to grab a rock in the hope of
being able to scramble ashore. Not Ulysses. He decided that if
he let himself be carried on to the rocks the chances of being
dashed to pieces would be high, so he swam outside the

breakers until he came to the mouth of a river where there was a gap in the reef and he could get through to the beach.

Analysis of the character of Ulysses is complicated by the constant intervention of gods and goddesses in Homer's story. One cannot throw out the gods. But one can see them in modern terms, as the constant prompting and counter-prompting that influences action within a man himself. Homer's audience expected gods to walk with men. Perhaps they still do. Most of us at intense moments of our lives have felt love, anger, courage, envy, malice, kindness, almost as something outside ourselves, compelling us to action. A primitive audience expected such emotions to be personified: we may have made a mistake in depersonalising guardian angels and the devil. Be this as it may, the essential understanding of humanity in Homer is brought out even more sharply by translating him into our own idiom and seeing his gods and goddesses as facets of man himself. The wrath of Poseidon that sends Ulysses on his travels can be seen as something in the character of Ulysses which drives him to sail where men have not sailed before, which makes it imperative for him to *know* what is beyond the next horizon.

This is the analysis of Ulysses by another poet, Tennyson, who turned to him nearly three thousand years after Homer, to make Ulysses the subject of another great poem. Tennyson envisages him in old age, after some years of administering the petty kingdom of Ithaca. He is bored and restless. He says:

I cannot rest from travel: I will drink
Life to the lees: all times I have enjoy'd
Greatly, have suffer'd greatly, both with those
That loved me, and alone; on shore, and when
Thro' scudding drifts the rainy Hyades
Vext the dim sea: I am become a name;
For always roaming with a hungry heart
Much have I seen and known; cities of men
And manners, climates, councils, governments,
Myself not least, but honour'd of them all;
And drunk delight of battle with my peers,
Far on the ringing plains of windy Troy.
I am a part of all that I have met;
Yet all experience is an arch wherethro'

Gleams that untravell'd world, whose margin fades
For ever and for ever when I move...

This is an acute analysis of the Ulysses factor. Tennyson's
Ulysses is not driven about the world by the whims of gods.
He drives himself: he has *got* to *know*. He is not greatly concerned with *what* he wants to know, he is not looking for anything in particular. Wealth, position in life, fame after death
—all very well, and nice to have, no doubt, but not in themselves important. The compelling need is to *know* what is
across the sea, over the range of hills, perhaps in himself in
circumstances of difficulty or danger. It is a physical as well as
an intellectual need: to read, to listen to other men, is not
enough. He must go himself, see for himself, find out for himself.

He is equipped for all this. Tennyson sees him as having
aged, as having suffered some of the inevitable loss of physical
capacity that comes with age. This does not matter. Ulysses
addresses his men, the remnants of his old crew, who have
sailed with him before.

... You and I are old;
Old age hath yet his honour and his toil.
Death closes all: but something ere the end,
Some work of noble note, may yet be done,
Not unbecoming men that strove with gods.

The poem concludes with a lovely passage describing
Ulysses at the moment of departure:

The lights begin to twinkle from the rocks:
The long day wanes: the slow moon climbs: the deep
Moans round with many voices. Come, my friends,
'Tis not too late to seek a newer world.
Push off, and sitting well in order smite
The sounding furrows; for my purpose holds
To sail beyond the sunset, and the baths
Of all the western stars, until I die.
It may be that the gulfs will wash us down:
It may be we shall touch the Happy Isles,
And see the great Achilles, whom we knew.

Tho' much is taken, much abides; and tho'
We are not now that strength which in old days
Moved earth and heaven; that which we are, we are;
One equal temper of heroic hearts,
Made weak by time and fate, but strong in will
To strive, to seek, to find and not to yield.

Homer and Tennyson were not students of comparative anthropology, nor were they professional psychiatrists. In understanding of humanity, however, they may achieve more than such modern disciplines, for they shared the ability of the poet to *be*, at times, all men. Between them they composed a portrait of a man strongly endowed with the Ulysses factor sharper in psychological detail, perhaps, than if either had used psychological terms. It is a type-figure remarkably complete, larger than life because it embodies *every* characteristic of a complex human attribute which manifests itself in individuals in many different ways, but intensely living because each facet of the attribute is shown by its effects on a man's life.

By examining the type-figure a list of the qualities that go with the factor may be made. These include:

Courage
Selfishness
Practical competence
Physical strength
Powerful imagination
Ability to lead
Self-discipline
Endurance
Self-sufficiency
Cunning
Unscrupulousness
Strong sexual attraction.

This is a basic list. Every one of these qualities can be subdivided into many others, and each requires qualification. The typical Ulysses courage is not the hot-headed sort, oblivious of danger, but the cool taking of calculated risks. It will rush to a comrade's help, but not blindly: it will try to be sure that the method of help is effective.

Selfishness is not quite the ordinary form of selfishness. Ulysses was ready enough to leave his wife and abandon administrative duties to go off on an expedition; but when some of his men were in danger he let no thoughts of his own safety stand in the way of going off to rescue them.

Practical competence and physical strength are self-evident. But they are relative. The Ulysses factor requires physical ability, but not Samson-like performance. It requires the ability to make-do and mend, but not universal mechanical skill. More important than putting a fine finish on a boat's timbers with an adze is the ability to construct a serviceable boat quickly, and to use whatever comes to hand (twigs and brushwood).

Imagination is inherent in the Ulysses character, but it is a *driving* rather than a *contemplative* imagination. It is the imagination which crosses bridges before it comes to them because it is thinking ahead to be sure of having at least a bridge-project in mind if there happens not to be a bridge.

Leadership, self-discipline and endurance go together. They are distinct qualities and may be manifested in isolation, but each is needed to reinforce the others. All can be defined only to some extent. Some of the qualities that make a man a good officer can be defined, but *why* some men can inspire others to follow them through thick and thin can never be wholly explained.

Self-sufficiency is an important element. It does *not* mean self-satisfaction. It means readiness to go it alone, and to rely on one's own efforts, but not to the exclusion of working with other people. It can manifest itself, however, in impatience when others do not at once understand something that seems crystal-clear to the Ulysses mind. It is an admirable quality, but also a dangerous one.

Cunning is the ability to think quickly, and also to think obliquely, to see round the corners of other people's minds. It is a valuable quality in self-preservation, but it is not a wholly pleasant quality to live with, or even to look at. It is highly important in the Ulysses make-up.

Unscrupulousness has a general meaning to be understood fairly easily, but it is less easy to define its implications. Ulysses, the type-figure, had no qualms about turning pirate and sacking a town for what he could get, though in recounting the incident he was at pains to say that he divided the plunder fairly among his men. He had no hesitation in accepting the first prize for a race which he won only because the leading runner slipped on a piece of cow-dung. But one must be chary of judgment here. Unscrupulousness in one breath can be called determination in another. It is also a question of standards. The Ulysses type is self-centred, convinced of the rightness of the task in hand. What may assist that task must be obtained somehow: if somebody else gets hurt it's a pity, but it can't be helped. You are out to win.

Sexual attraction may be no more than a part of virility. The attraction of Ulysses is not crude, and he is certainly not coarse. He is intensely virile, quick-witted and ready with a compliment. He is an exciting person, and not merely physically exciting. You can sense that he had a quick, delightful smile, you want to talk to him, and you want him to talk to you. Women were strongly drawn to him, perhaps a little wanting to mother him, as well as to sleep with him. He enjoyed women, but was ready enough to leave them, and sex does not seem to have been a powerful motive in his own life. If the Ulysses factor is important to human survival, one would expect it to be accompanied by sexual attraction. In the highly developed forms in which the factor drives men to outstanding feats of exploration and endurance, it is rare in individuals: it is seldom directly inherited. It is all the more important, then, that it should be transmitted.

To find these qualities in the type-figure is not to imply that they are necessarily all to be found to the same extent accompanying every manifestation of the Ulysses factor in individuals. All will be there in some degree, but the Ulysses factor is only one gift in man's complex inheritance, and its manifestation in individuals will be modified by all sorts of other individual characteristics. Where the factor is dominant the type-qualities may be expected to show themselves in fairly marked ways, but not necessarily in the same ways. They will be modified, too, by the behaviour-patterns of an individual's own time. Ulysses thought nothing of turning pirate, nor did Drake. In modern forms this manifestation is unlikely to appear.

C

Can a purely intellectual search for knowledge be put down to the Ulysses factor? It demands similar type-qualities: Newton, Einstein, Fleming, all who have crossed the frontiers of existing knowledge by sheer intellectual capacity have manifested a compelling driving force requiring self-dedication, self-discipline, endurance, a restless need to *know*, many of the qualities inherent in Ulysses. But to be similar is not to be the same. The factor in man that makes for intellectual exploration is related to the Ulysses factor, but it is different in that it does not require personal, physical action. The Ulysses type cannot find fulfilment without personally being *there*: your *own* foot must tread the mountain top, your *own* eyes see the waves, your *own* hand be on the tiller. This is a fundamental difference.

Can individuals strongly influenced by the Ulysses factor work as a team? This is a difficult question. *Leadership* is inherent among the type-qualities, and the Ulysses man can certainly *lead* a team: manifestations of the factor which have produced some of the greatest of human achievements have required the leadership of others, crews, companions on a mountainside, expeditionary forces. But this is to *use* a team for one's own purposes; it is not the same as being *in* a team. Yet when a handful of men set out to climb an all-but inaccessible Himalayan peak, or deliberately drift together in a raft across an ocean, it is likely that, as individuals, *all* will be influenced by the Ulysses factor. And such teams have lived and worked together splendidly: one man is accepted as the leader, but the achievement is the work of the whole team. I think that the conclusion here is that the Ulysses factor enables men to work in *small* teams, but that it is not the motive for *large* collective performance. A general may be motivated by the Ulysses factor, but not his army. The ability of man to undertake big collective actions is due to other factors. A community may use the results of Ulysses-type exploration by sending out groups, or other individuals, to colonise new land, or to exploit newly discovered resources, but this is not a manifestation of the Ulysses factor. The Ulysses team must be small enough to remain a group of individuals. Each must have enough self-discipline to subordinate himself to the purposes of the leader and the needs of his companions—self-discipline is one of the type-qualities. But the individual must be able to feel that he *is* an individual, that *his* hand on the tiller or *his* work on a rope has a direct part in whatever is being done. Unless he can call on other qualities to suppress his Ulysses inclinations, the Ulysses-type is unlikely to show the dog-loyalty of accepting orders without asking why. He is capable of intense loyalty to others, but he must understand what is going on, and feel part of it.

The factor can be seen clearly in single-handed exploits. Self-sufficiency is a type-quality, and the type-figure was always ready to go it alone. But the Ulysses man is not essentially a loner. He may be at his best alone, equally he may be at his best as a member of a small team. The type-qualities vary in their intensity in individuals. Francis Chichester is at his best when utterly on his own. Maurice Herzog, who led the French expedition to climb Annapurna, the first summit of over 26,000 ft to be reached by man, felt intimately bound up with his companions. He wrote of them:

> They all put themselves completely in my hands... There is no feeling to equal this complete confidence of one man in another, because it is the sum of so many other feelings put together.*

The rider here is that this inter-dependence must be capable of being felt individually. The Ulysses type may be independent or inter-dependent, but he must remain a *person*.

Cunning and quick-wittedness bespeak intellectual ability, but the Ulysses intellect may be wide-ranging rather than deep. It may be impatient of formal instruction, preferring to learn at first hand for itself. This is another difference between individuals in whom the Ulysses factor is strong, and individuals moved by the related factor which prompts intellectual search. The pure intellectual concentrates his study. The Ulysses type is interested in everything. The factor may promote intense concentration in action, and the preparations for action, for the purpose in hand, but the next purpose may be something quite different. It will always be related to the need to *know*, but it may be knowledge in a variety of fields. *What* lies over the hills does not matter: the urge in the Ulysses factor is to cross those hills to find out. Ulysses was

---

* Maurice Herzog, *Annapurna*. Cape 1952.

a clever man, able in all sorts of ways, and perpetually interested. He was articulate and capable of vivid description, but he would not have been happy in a study.

In action, the factor can drive a man to keep going far beyond normal limits of human fatigue. Ulysses was rebuked by his lieutenant, who complained to him:

> You are one of those hard men whose spirit never flags and whose body never tires. You must be made of iron.

Yet it is not a question of the body's being tireless. These are mental qualities. All human bodies tire, all men feel fatigue. The quality in the Ulysses factor which promotes apparent tirelessness is a combination of self-discipline, courage and determination which enables a man to go on driving himself when others are compelled to rest. It is a strongly noticeable characteristic.

Among less readily definable mental or spiritual characteristics is a sense of humility in the face of nature, of religion in some contexts, of awe, in a meaning which implies fear touched by reverence, not physical fear. Ulysses was devout in sacrifices and services to his gods. He was conscious always of the littleness of man, and of the need for help outside himself, or, as some would say nowadays, of the need to call on inner reserves of strength which are beyond a man's own understanding. It is a matter of words, and comes to the same thing —consciousness of the helplessness of man in the face of great natural forces and awareness of power outside man, or at least outside everything that man is able to comprehend, which can be looked to for help. Adrian Hayter, writing of a bad time when he expected to be dragged to death on a coral reef, puts it plainly:

> In moments like this, when alone and untrammelled with ordinary logic, you feel that only belief can save you and your ship. This belief does not come because you want that which it will give; perhaps it comes only after you have done everything humanly possible to ensure by your own efforts that which you now need from a higher power.*

The famous prayer of Drake, almost another type-figure, is relevant here:

*Adrian Hayter, *Sheila in the Wind*. Hodder & Stoughton 1959.

O Lord God, when thou givest to thy servants to endeavour any great matter, grant us also to know that it is
not the beginning, but the continuing of the same until it
be thoroughly finished, which yieldeth the true glory.

Drake knew that no man can go on without the help of
God. The constant intervention of gods and goddesses in the
Ulysses story may be seen in modern terms as the promptings
of the unconscious or subconscious self, but beyond this
Ulysses had profound faith in the reality of a power outside
himself. As our type-figure Ulysses here is wholly typical.

The studies that follow illustrate the incidence of what I
have called the Ulysses factor in human society since the end
of the Second World War. They have been selected to show
various aspects of the factor as it has influenced individual
lives, modified by personality and circumstance. There is a
common thread, but a variegated pattern, as there must be,
for the factor is primarily an impulse to action, and the forms
and consequences of action differ with every individual. In
this is both the fascination and the importance to the future
of a common human attribute that sent Ulysses on his travels
some 3,000 years ago and Robin Knox-Johnston singlehanded
round the world in 1969.

III

Historical evidence

IN the opening chapter of this book I touched on some of the broad historical movements which seem to me to have been influenced by the Ulysses factor in mankind. The historical evidence must now be examined in more detail.

Identification of this Ulysses factor in man assists the interpretation of history. In very early periods of national or tribal development its influence may have to be inferred, but as the record becomes plainer the effects of the factor are manifest. They are clearly to be discerned in the biblical story of Abraham, and help to explain his towering importance as the founding father of the Jewish people.

Abraham, the son of Terah, was born in Iraq, at or near the ancient Sumerian city of Ur (Ur of the Chaldees). The family, however, were not city dwellers, but a pastoral community, wandering with their flocks from grazing ground to grazing ground. In Terah's lifetime they moved generally westwards, to the borders of Syria. The decisive moment in family—and Jewish—history came after Terah's death, with Abraham's decision to look for new land to the south-west. That this was a deliberate decision, and not a mere extension of pastoral wandering, is plainly recorded in Genesis xii. 1.

Now the Lord said unto Abraham, Get thee out of thy country and from thy kindred, and from thy father's house, into a land that I will show thee.

The direct prompting by God is in the idiom of the ancient world. Abraham showed typical Ulysses characteristics in his response, setting out to lead a small expedition through what was (to him) unknown country into Palestine. His followers

38

were few: in true Ulysses fashion he was content with a small band. He had with him his wife Sarah, his nephew Lot and a handful of family retainers.

He found good land across the Jordan and his flocks multiplied, but there was trouble a few years later either because of over-grazing or a crop failure. He did not think of going back, but went on southwards to Egypt. Here he profited by a piece of quick-wittedness that was also slightly unscrupulous. Sarah was an extremely beautiful woman, and when some officers of the Egyptian royal household saw her they were so captivated that they wanted to take her to Pharaoh. Abraham felt that a husband was an awkward, and as far as he himself was concerned, probably dangerous encumbrance. So he said that she was his sister. Sarah was duly taken into Pharaoh's court, and pleased the king so much that he showered riches on her 'brother'. But when the king wanted to marry her the story came out—one may imagine from the intelligent Sarah herself, though the record in Genesis tells of plagues that fell on the unfortunate Pharaoh to discourage him from pursuing her. She may indeed have found ways of plaguing him—her later history shows that she could be a Tartar. Abraham did well out of the affair. His stratagem had got Sarah to court, and she was well able to take care both of herself and him. Pharaoh sent them away, allowing them to keep the various gifts that he had made them. Boldness in risk-taking had succeeded.

The Egyptian adventure was the means of Abraham's transformation from a minor tribal leader into a rich and powerful chieftain. He came out of Egypt, as Genesis (xiii. 2) puts it 'very rich in cattle, in silver and in gold', and returned to Palestine. Lot was still with him as a loyal lieutenant, and both men prospered to such an extent that again there was danger of over-grazing as their herds increased. So they divided the land they had settled, Lot taking the plain of Jordan and Abraham the country farther west.

Then some of the neighbouring tribes raided into Jordan and Lot was captured. Abraham acted decisively. He raised a band of three hundred and eighteen men and went after Lot's captors. He took them by surprise, defeated them and recovered Lot and all his possessions. This sharp action established Abraham as a power to be reckoned with. He continued to prosper, and died full of years as the patriarchal father of his race.

Throughout this story there are clear indications of the influence of the Ulysses factor in Abraham's personality. Some outstanding quality set him apart from the shepherds and wandering pastoralists who were his stock. The rest of his family were content to wander on the borders of Syria and Iraq, following a pattern of life that was immemorial then and has not changed much among nomadic peoples even today. The boy Abraham looked across the desert hills and felt a compelling need to find out for himself what lay beyond the farthest horizon that he could see. The elders of his tribe no doubt thought him rash, and there were a hundred good reasons against going off into the unknown. The Ulysses factor in him was too strong to heed them. He had powers of leadership and inspired devotion, in his wife Sarah and in Lot. He took risks. His deception of the all-powerful Egyptian Pharaoh was an appalling risk, but it was calculated on his knowledge of Sarah and on a shrewd understanding of the personalities at the Egyptian court. He repaid loyalty with loyalty; when Lot needed his help he acted at once, without counting any risk to himself. Here are many of the qualities of the type-figure acting on human personality, influencing action, in a sharply defined manner. And here is an interesting early example of the influence of the Ulysses factor in an individual on the course of history.

This assessment of the personality of Abraham is not to discount the divine intervention in his affairs that is so important a part of the biblical story. Profound belief in a power outside man is characteristic of those influenced by the Ulysses factor, and here again Abraham was typical. The idiom of the Old Testament, as of Homer, is not ours, but whether a man be held to speak with God directly or to hear God through the voice of his own conscience is irrelevant if he acts in the conviction of faith. Robin Knox-Johnston, more than three thousand years apart from Abraham, wrote in his book on his lone voyage round the world, published in 1969:

Throughout the voyage I never really felt I was completely alone, and I think a man would have to be inhumanly confident and self-reliant if he were to make this sort of voyage without belief in God.*

At critical periods of his life Abraham felt that he was not alone. That his story became part of the fabric of three great religions, Judaism, Christianity and Islam, testifies to its inherent truth.

An Eastern Mediterranean myth, older than the earliest Greeks, tells of a demigod called Usoos who founded Tyre. He was one of a race of half-men half-gods who inhabited the earth soon after it was created, and he was particularly interested in the sea. Having discovered that tree-trunks float, he deliberately set out to sea on a tree-trunk. Whence he sailed is not clear, but his tree was carried to a little island off the coast of what was then Phoenicia (now Lebanon), where he built two pillars, one of gold, the other of emerald, and dedicated them to wind and fire. This was the first settlement of Tyre, which was situated on an offshore islet, although the later city was joined to the mainland by a causeway. Herodotus visited the place around 450 BC, and claims to have seen the pillars. He was told by the priests that they had already stood for 2,300 years.

The myth probably records precisely the origin of the seafaring Phoenicians, indeed of all seafarers, embodying folk memory of some prehistoric man strongly moved by the Ulysses factor who pushed out from shore on a log of wood to discover where the sea would take him. The Phoenicians, with the early Greeks, are historical examples of communities which owed their original survival and later rise to greatness to the strength of the Ulysses factor in their peoples. This concentration of the factor so that its influence pervades whole populations recurs, with decisive effects on history. It is to be seen again in Saxons, Norsemen, Portuguese, Spaniards and the English. Dr David Lewis's recent work on early Polynesian navigation suggests that the factor in certain Polynesian priests or chieftains contributed materially to folk-movements in the Pacific.

Of course there is no single cause for great historical move-

* Robin Knox-Johnston, *A World of My Own*, p. 173. Cassell 1969.

ments, or, indeed, for any human action. Over-grazing or a crop failure (described in Genesis as 'famine') may have been the direct incentive that sent Abraham on his southern journey into Egypt; population-growth straining local resources in Phoenicia, Greek islands, the estuary of the Elbe, Scandinavia, Portugal, Spain· and Elizabethan England was obviously a powerful force to encourage people to look abroad for sustenance at certain periods of their history. But in such situations some communities die out, or are reduced by disease to numbers that their land can support. Why do others thrive by exploration?

History is determined by the interaction of impersonal forces affecting mankind and individual response to them. The historical evidence shows that in some communities at certain times the Ulysses impulse has been particularly strong, and that this has been an important element in their survival. Can one isolate what I have called the Ulysses factor from other powerful human impulses that may drive men to cross seas or deserts—fear of enemies, immediate hunger, simple greed? I think one can. The Ulysses factor is a complex of impulses in an individual prompting him to seek firsthand physical experience of something hitherto unknown (to him) that has aroused his curiosity. It must include the impulse to learn at firsthand through physical action: what, is immaterial; it may be to discover what lies beyond a range of hills, to see new stars by travelling to some new part of the earth's surface to observe the heavens, to find the source of a river, to discover if there is a far side to an apparently limitless ocean. This is the main driving force—the physical satisfaction of man's curiosity. There may be secondary motives, perhaps many, that also influence an individual moved to some action by the Ulysses factor, but they will be secondary. Hope of gain is common to humanity, and certainly men adventure in the hope of gain. But economic pressure is not enough to explain the Ulysses impulse. The Ulysses qualities in a man also fit him for success in ways far easier than setting out to sail beyond the sunset, and perhaps for greater material success. Phoenician and Greek seafarers hoped to profit by their voyages, but the impulse that led them to seafaring in the first instance was something more compelling even than the hope of gain. Abraham sought a new country because God told him to, or, in a different idiom, because of some factor in his personality that impelled him to leave his known surroundings to see what he would come to.

An interesting early example of the influence of the factor is to be seen in one of the greatest voyages of antiquity—in relation to the maritime equipment available for it, one of the greatest voyages of all time. This was the voyage that first circumnavigated Britain, discovered Iceland and several other North Atlantic islands, and gave the ancient world its first knowledge of Arctic ice. It was made by one Pytheas, a Greek citizen of Marseilles (the Greek colony Massalia) over six years around the period 310–304 BC. It is poorly documented, for Pytheas's own books have perished, and all that has come down to us are quotations at second or third hand in the later writings of Strabo (c. 64 BC–AD 19), Pliny (c. AD 23–79) and a few others. Nevertheless, enough is known to authenticate the voyage, and some of Pytheas's place names remain on the modern map—Orcas in the Orkneys, Oxisama in Ushant and perhaps Ierne in Ireland. The derivation of Ireland seems to come from the same root as Iberia, from a prehistoric people who migrated to Ireland from what is now Spain. Pytheas picked up and recorded the name.

Something is known of Pytheas himself. He was a mathematical philosopher, and he made two major contributions to the science of navigation: he discovered that the Pole Star (Ursa Minor) is only an approximation to True North, which he located with remarkable accuracy, and he devised a practical method of reckoning latitude by the use of a gnomon or pointer on a sundial. Clearly the north fascinated him or even obsessed him to a point at which he felt that he must go himself to see how far north he could get on the earth's surface. We have no means of knowing how he financed his voyage. Conceivably he was able to finance himself, though this seems unlikely, for philosophers have seldom been particularly rich. Probably he found sponsors, in much the same way as modern expeditions find sponsors. There were no newspapers then, but he could turn to a variety of learned bodies and businessmen. Marseilles possessed one of the great libraries of the ancient world, and the library may have been willing to help. Then there were businessmen interested in amber, which found its way to the Mediterranean by land routes from the

Baltic; a northern expedition might hope to come across new sources of amber. There was keen commercial interest in tin, known to be found in some island in the northern seas, the route to which Phoenician traders tried to keep a closely guarded secret. Rich Massalian merchants may have been ready enough to contribute towards a voyage which might bring back information either on new sources of tin or on better routes to known sources. And in the fourth century BC, as now, there were wealthy men capable of responding to sheer adventure, who could be persuaded to help by giving supplies, or by putting up a little money. However he arranged things, Pytheas did succeed in financing his expedition.

Of his ship we know nothing, except that she was presumably a Greek trading vessel of the period, with a square sail and perhaps two banks of oars. Designed for the Mediterranean, she would have been an awkward craft in the Atlantic, her oars perilous in an ocean swell. Oars might have been useful for inshore work, but would have been useless in anything of a sea, a hazard rather than a help. Pytheas's ship, however, may have carried subsidiary lateen sails, which would have given her some ability to work to windward. Sailing ships of antiquity probably had more windward ability than the pictures that have come down to us suggest. Such pictures were mostly drawn by artists decorating pottery and were designed for decorative effect rather than nautical accuracy. They seldom show what subsidiary sails could be set; and they cannot show the skill of the men who sailed in those ancient ships. A sight of Pytheas's ship might make a modern seaman familiar with the North Atlantic tremble, but with Pytheas's crew she was probably a good deal handier than she looked. At any rate, she survived.

Pytheas's aim was to sail north, and he went north until the ice stopped him. How far he got one cannot say, but since he wintered ashore and sailed only in summer, he must have reached well beyond the Arctic Circle (66° 32′ N) to have been stopped by summer ice, perhaps as far as 70° N. He could have met ice a little farther south off southern Greenland, but there is nothing to indicate that he sailed so far west, and some positive indications that he did not. He recorded observations of the length of the longest day in various places at which he touched, and these authenticate his voyage and give some indication of his route. He appears to have landed in Cornwall to investigate the tin trade, and then sailed westerly up the coast of Britain to Scotland, the Hebrides and the Shetlands. He may have discovered the Orkneys, but his Orca which gives the Orkneys their name, was more probably in the Shetlands. From the Shetlands (or the Orkneys) he sailed on north, reaching an island he called Thule before being stopped by ice. Thule was probably Iceland, but it may just possibly have been Jan Mayen, even farther north. Returning from Thule, he sailed down the east coast of Britain, thus completing his circumnavigation.

Pytheas was the first literate man to set eyes on sea ice, and he extended knowledge of the northern hemisphere almost halfway to the New World. In the six years of his voyage he landed in various parts of Britain and he brought back the first recorded account of the British climate—'In consequence of the rain and the absence of sun the natives do not use open threshing floors, but thresh their grain in barns.' His own books—he is known to have written at least two—are an immeasurable loss. In his lifetime, while members of his crew were alive to bear out his statements, his discoveries seem generally to have been accepted, but his reputation suffered after his death. Later academic geographers, knowing only the Mediterranean world, could not accept his accounts of sea ice and of huge tides in the Bristol Channel. They quoted his observations as the tallest of traveller's tales and altered his maps. Fortunately they did quote from him, and modern knowledge shows that he was right and their scepticism wrong.

Pytheas's expedition has all the marks of Ulysses characteristics in origin, leadership and performance. His aim was to go north, to satisfy a personal need to see how far north a man could get. Like all good explorers, he kept a keen eye open for chances of economic advantage for his backers, but his voyage cannot have been planned as a trading expedition in itself. If so, having reached Cornwall and having obtained firsthand knowledge—very valuable knowledge—of the tin trade he would have hastened back to Marseilles to equip a tin fleet. Instead, he sailed on north, by coasts that grew poorer and poorer as he went north. They offered no trading opportunities, and yet he sailed on, wintering ashore in conditions that must often have been misery for a Mediterranean man. He must have had great powers of leadership. How did he hold his crew together through those northern winters, how did he persuade them to sail on into ever more inhospitable seas? All we know is that he did, that if there were mutinies he quelled them, that his crew took him as far as a ship could go, and brought him home.

Thanks to the small-mindedness of later commentators, much of the geographical knowledge that he brought back was lost. At least it was lost to academic learning, but there must have been shrewd Greek seamen who profited by it. And it was not all lost. His detailed observations may have been forgotten, or dismissed as travellers' tales, but the *fact* that he had sailed beyond the rim of the known world passed into contemporary consciousness and emboldened unknown men, who, perhaps, had never heard of Pytheas himself, to sail through the Pillars of Hercules into the Atlantic to add their bits and pieces to the sum of human experience. Secretive Phoenician traders before Pytheas had found their way to Britain, at least to the Cornish peninsula. Pytheas showed that a man might sail far beyond Britain, and return.

Certain Ulysses characteristics in Alexander the Great and Julius Caesar are discussed briefly in a later chapter on the influence of the factor in war. This is important to a full study of the subject, but the history of warfare is so vast, and influenced by so many other human hopes and fears and needs, that the part played by the Ulysses factor in war, although of great interest, cannot be more than touched on in this book. My main theme here is its identification in more general movements of human history. In these there is a constant recurrence of the qualities that caused the mythical Usoos to embark on his log and that inspired the type figure Ulysses to his adventures.

They may be seen in early English history in the first coming of the Saxons. There were economic pressures on the population of the Elbe marshes to turn to piracy in the North Sea, and the inviting coasts of England offered plentiful opportunity for raiding. With the collapse of Roman power in Britain the opportunities for plunder increased, and so did the chances of conquest and settlement for a land-hungry people. But some among those early Saxon raiders must have crossed the North Sea with more than hopes of plunder in mind. Why sail up unknown rivers into hostile country when there were slaves and grain and sometimes gold to be had nearer the coast? And 'sail' here is a misleading word. The Saxons worked their longships up the Thames and river systems of the Humber, but they could rarely sail up the winding streams and often could not row. Progress was constantly balked by shallows, over which boats had to be dragged, manhandled and shoved with the ever-present likelihood of attack by local people when concentration on boat handling might put the Saxon crew off-guard. The later Danish Vikings worked their ships up English rivers knowing what they would come to, knowing that it was worth pushing up the Thames to fan out into good country westwards up the Kennet valley from Reading, and north east into the rich Vale of Aylesbury through the gap in the chalk hills at Goring. The first Saxons did not. Not much is known of Saxon penetration inland in the fifth and early sixth centuries, except that it took place, and that it played a decisive part in the Saxon conquest. The impetus that took early Saxon crews up the Thames, the powers of leadership that held men together and persuaded them to go on when navigation became harder and harder and there was no apparent hope of plunder can have derived only from the Ulysses factor in individual chiefs. We know the name at least of one, perhaps of two. Some historians have doubted whether Hengist and his brother or half-brother Horsa ever existed, but *a* Hengist has left his name on the Upper Thames at Hinksey, the site of an early cattle-crossing by the ford that later came to be called Oxford. Hinksey means 'Hengist's island', and the name-form is an early one, not much used after the sixth century. There can be no doubt but that *an* early Saxon chieftain called Hengist, probably in the fifth or early sixth century, explored up the Thames at least as far as Oxford, and that he settled, or attempted to settle, one of the islands of firm ground in what were then the marshes of the Upper Thames Valley. It is possible, though less certain, that Horsa is recorded in the place name Horsted which occurs in Kent and Sussex and in a slightly different form in Norfolk, but these place names may have the more obvious derivation of a steading or farm for horses. The real existence of *a* Hengist on the Thames, however, must be recognised as historical fact, and the legends that have gathered round the name Hengist (and possibly Horsa) can reasonably be explained as folk-memories of inspired leaders who went where none had gone before.

The Norse discovery of America early in the eleventh century is a particularly interesting example of the driving force of the Ulysses factor. The first known European to set eyes on the mainland of North America was one Bjarni Herjolfson, an Icelandic merchant who was driven off course in a storm while attempting to sail to Greenland, and after some weeks of wandering in the North Atlantic made a landfall somewhere on the coast of what is now Nova Scotia. He was more merchant than adventurer, for although his crew wanted to land to see what this new coast offered, he would not let anyone go ashore and insisted on standing north for Greenland. Bjarni Herjolfson's accidental discovery of America was made about the year AD 986–987. The story of his voyage is recounted in the *Graenlendinga Saga,* one of the Icelandic sagas telling of the exploits of men and women who lived in the tenth and eleventh centuries. When Bjarni reached the Norse settlement in Greenland for which he was making he told people of his discovery, and among his listeners was a man in whom the Ulysses factor was strong. This was Leif Eiriksson, who became one of the greatest of medieval explorers.

Leif Eiriksson was haunted by Bjarni's account of a coast that he had seen but not visited, and determined to go there himself. Leif had to wait several years, for his father Eirik the Red was the leader of the Greenland Norse, and manpower was needed at home in those early Greenland settlements. Gradually they established themselves, however, and about fourteen years after Bjarni's arrival in Greenland Leif judged that conditions were settled enough to permit him to go adventuring. He bought Bjarni's ship, probably the best ocean-going vessel available in the Greenland colonies, got together a crew and set out to retrace Bjarni's voyage. These events are well recorded in the sagas, and were authenticated in 1965 by the publication by Yale University of the *Vinland Map.* This remarkable map, which gets its name from the

name Vinland or Wineland that Leif Eiriksson gave to his
new land in North America is so far the only known pre-
Columbus map showing an outline of the coast of North
America. It was copied from an early Norse original about
1440, nearly half a century before Columbus sailed.

There is a possibility that Leif Eiriksson took Bjarni Herjolfson with him on the voyage that led to the discovery of
America about the year 1000–1001. One account in the old
records suggests that he did, but most imply that he did not.
There is no reference to Bjarni in the saga stories relating to
the settlement of Vinland, and it seems more probable that
Leif sailed on his own. In any case, Leif was unquestionably
the leader of the expedition.

His great voyage of 1000–1001 gave European seamen the
first authentic account of Baffin Land, Labrador and New
England. Whether this knowledge was largely lost with the
collapse of the North Greenland colonies in the fourteenth
century or whether it remained in Iceland to influence
Columbus nearly five centuries later is still an open question.
Modern research makes it seem possible that knowledge of
America was by no means lost, and that Columbus, who is
believed to have spent some years in Iceland, drew on Norse
information in planning his own voyage of 1492. Whether or
not Columbus was influenced by these early Norse discoveries
—my own view is that he was—Leif Eiriksson's place in the
history of exploration is secure.

In the planning and execution of his voyage he showed
identifiable Ulysses qualities. He knew how to wait. This
characteristic is notable in the type figure: however much
Ulysses longed to escape from some captivity or to be on his
way to Ithaca, he was careful not to jeopardise his chances by
setting off before he had planned for every contingency he
could plan for. Leif Eiriksson must have been tempted to put
to sea as soon as he heard Bjarni's story. He did not. He
waited and nursed his project for years, gaining experience of
ice movements off Greenland, of currents in the Greenland
sea, of the prevailing wind system. He waited to be sure that
the settlement that was his family's home could sustain the
absence of his own and of his crew's manpower. When he
sailed he was ready to sail, his navigational planning and his
physical equipment as complete as he could make them.

D

All medieval seamen were accustomed to turn merchant or pirate as occasion might demand. Norse seamen had a long record of piracy, but by Leif's period they were becoming more interested in finding new land for colonies and in establishing long-term mercantile connections. Leif certainly hoped to profit by his voyage: he was interested particularly in finding reliable sources of timber, which the Greenland colonists needed and which they could not obtain in their settlements, in wine, which they liked but also had to import, and in furs, which they could send back to Norway to exchange for the products of the Baltic markets. Leif found all these things in the new world, but he was explorer first and merchant second. He studied the inhospitable coasts of Baffin Land, which he named Helluland, meaning 'land of flat stones', before sailing south for Labrador, which he named Markland ('forest land') and Vinland ('wine land'), which was almost certainly in what later became New England and the modern states of Massachusetts, Rhode Island, Connecticut and, perhaps, New York.

Leif's exploration of Vinland was exemplary. First he made his crew build log huts to secure a base for winter, and then he divided his men into two groups, one to hold the base, the other to explore. He noted everything—salmon in the rivers, the quality of fodder for cattle, the availability of trees for felling. He took observations of the sun, noting that on the shortest day of the year the sun was up before breakfast and did not set until after supper.*

Leif wintered in Vinland, and remained long enough into the next year to harvest the wild grapes which are still a feature of New England. He returned to Greenland with a valuable cargo of timber and of grapes, either dried or, perhaps, as wine. As far as is known, he did not himself see Vin-

---

* It is a pity that Viking timekeeping was not more precise. Breakfast was commonly taken at 9 am, supper at 3 pm, but we have no means of knowing how long before breakfast the sun rose on the shortest day, or how long it was after supper before it set. Leif must have taken more accurate observations for his own navigational purposes, but later saga compilers, alas, either did not know them or did not consider such details worth bothering about. Accurate knowledge of the times of sunrise and sunset on the shortest day of the year would determine the location of Leif's Vinland settlement beyond doubt. As things are, all one can say is that these rough timings indicate a location somewhere between New Jersey and southern Newfoundland. The location of Vinland in New England is suggested by other evidence.

land again, for he succeeded to the leadership of the Greenland Norse on his father's death, and he was needed at home.
But he encouraged other expeditions to go, and several of
which we have knowledge went. Leif Eiriksson's achievement
early in the eleventh century has been overshadowed by
Columbus's voyage at the end of the fifteenth—Leif lived on
the very edge of the known world, Columbus at the heart of
European power. It is probable that Leif lighted Columbus
on his way—a probability that I think will become a certainty
as research enables more to be learned of these early Norse
voyages.

From the beginning of the fifteenth century to roughly the
middle of the sixteenth, a period of some six human generations, there was an extraordinary flowering of Ulysses qualities in the people of the western Mediterranean, particularly
of Portugal and Spain. With their Atlantic seaboard, Portugal
and Spain were the leading nation-states in this age of discovery, but those who sailed under their flags were by no
means all Portuguese or Spanish. Christopher Columbus, who
sailed for Spain was Genoese. John Cabot, who explored in
the North Atlantic for Henry VII of England was a Venetian.
The impetus came from the western Mediterranean in
general, as if the heirs of Greek and Phoenician colonists had
suddenly remembered their birthright.

There have been many attempts to explain this concentration of the exploring instinct in man into a few generations in
a particular part of the world. It has been seen as the physical
expression of the Renaissance, the questioning of old beliefs
and quest for new knowledge which formed the intellectual
basis for the development of modern Europe. It has been seen
as the exploitation of new techniques in navigation, ship-
building, gun-casting—given new toys, men wanted to play
with them. It has been seen as a hunger for gold to sustain the
luxuries of courts demanding living standards higher than
their domestic economies could afford.

No doubt all these things came into it. But if the Ulysses
factor in man is considered primarily as a survival factor, a
necessity for its appearance at about this period of western
Mediterranean history can be discerned. The western Mediterranean was reaching a climax after some fifteen hundred
years as the centre of civilisation. There had been dark ages

and periods of barbarism, but the cities of Italy, Spain and Portugal, the successors to the civilisations of Greece, Carthage and Rome, and embodying much of Arabic learning and culture, led the world in culture and in the living standards at least of their upper classes. This was not merely a material leadership: in philosophy, in practical education, in civil and religious administration, leadership was in the western Mediterranean.

This chiefly affected the upper classes, but these covered a fairly broad spectrum of society, from petty squires to the great nobility, with important sections of scholars, lawyers and educated merchants. It was not difficult for an able poor boy to acquire an education. If he wished to enter the Church he had various avenues of advancement open to him. What if he did not wish to enter the Church? His father might have many sons, and his share of a patrimony was likely to be derisory. War in the retinue of some great lord offered occasional prosperity, but for western Mediterranean society as a whole such wars were self cancelling: the scale was too small, and the ambitious young man who profited from one squabble was as likely as not to be ruined by the next. The western Mediterranean world had become, in fact, too small to sustain its population of more or less educated men. They could take to drink and duelling. Or they could look across the sea.

Early in the fifteenth century one man in Portugal brought men's vision of the sea sharply into focus. This was Prince Henry the Navigator, a younger son of King John I of Portugal and grandson of John of Gaunt—Prince Henry's mother Philippa was John of Gaunt's daughter. The Prince, who was born in 1394, was obsessed by the sea. By the time he was 21 he had begun to establish a kind of marine university at Sagres. Here he assembled every scrap of maritime knowledge and tradition that he could buy, beg or persuade men to bring to him. From Sagres he financed and sent out expedition after expedition to explore the coast of West Africa or to sail northwestwards into the Atlantic to the legendary sea routes of the eleventh-century Vikings. He was related by the marriage of his cousin to King Erik II of Denmark, and it is probable that through this connection with Denmark he had access to the knowledge of the Norse voyages to Vinland.

Prince Henry's contribution to the opening of the Atlantic is unique. He made no voyages himself, but he inspired men who lighted the way to India round the Cape of Good Hope and who helped to bring about the re-discovery of America. The influence of the Ulysses factor on his personality raises some interesting questions. It is characteristic of the factor to prompt individuals to *physical* exploration at first hand: it is the impetus that impels a man to find out for himself what the horizon of his known world hides. Can the factor prompt action at secondhand? By definition, it cannot. Genetically it is a survival factor, acting on the individual to promote action of value to the survival of that individual and his immediate family or tribe. But of almost equal importance in group survival is human *response* to manifestations of the factor in others. (This will be seen more clearly when we discuss some later mutations of the factor.) Response, in admiration, eagerness to emulate, understanding of the opportunities created by one man's exploration or adventure, can be a powerful secondary motive to action, in some cases almost a primary motive in itself. At periods of national or tribal history when the impulse to explore is of particular importance to survival, response to the factor may take the form of a compelling desire to inspire others to further action. Prince Henry's lifelong work is an illustration of this. As a king's son and naturally accepted as a tribal leader, he was in a position powerfully to influence others, and he represented a kind of folk-impulse to respond to the Ulysses factor in the people who looked to him for leadership. A somewhat similar personal concentration of response, though in a different social setting, is to be seen 150 years later in Richard Hakluyt (*c.* 1552–1616), the English clergyman whose obsession with adventurous voyages led to the collection and editing of the famous narratives which inspired generations of later explorers.

The intense manifestation of the Ulysses factor among western Mediterranean peoples in the fifteenth and sixteenth centuries secured the survival of educated men who would otherwise have been unemployed. Columbus's voyages, Vasco da Gama's passage to India, Magellan's circumnavigation of the globe, Cortez in Mexico and Pizarro in Peru, opened a new world of opportunity for administrators, settlers, soldiers, sailors and the Church. As the opportunities were created the impulse to create them faded; businessmen and politicians succeeded the adventurers. The survival value of the factor, however, may be judged from just one example—the new life it gave to the Spanish language. Whole nations in Central and South America today are Spanish speaking, and have given work to generations of Spanish scholars, teachers and writers because of the impulse that sent a few Spanish-speaking individuals across the world five centuries ago.

The next folk-manifestations of Ulysses characteristics occurred in the English, and to a lesser extent (but lesser only because of a smaller population from which to draw) in the Dutch. Again the factor was inherent in survival, but it contributed to the survival of a rather different set of human values. The western Mediterranean need was to ensure the survival of a culture, an ancient culture reflected in the Roman Catholic Church and in the intense ancestral pride of the descendants (themselves by then often penniless) of once-great families. The English and Dutch need was for the survival of free-thinking men to whom the whole authoritarian concept of the Roman Church and its accompanying social hierarchy was hostile. These simplicities are, of course, overlaid by the developments of national power-politics. Spain (at this stage incorporating Portugal), newly rich from the discoveries in the new world, wanted a monopoly of her new possessions and to keep out trading interlopers. Since men naturally gravitate to sources of new wealth, defence of the Spanish monopoly required the subjugation of peoples that might infringe it. Using the institutions that Spanish rulers knew and understood, this meant in turn an attempt to defend the Roman Church against reformist thinking, to reimpose Roman Catholic administration on European nations which had revolted against domination from the western Mediterranean. In those nations which for various reasons had so revolted, survival required opposition to the Roman Church. This is not to say that men who fought for Rome or Protestantism were insincere. Deep religious feeling was characteristic of the age. The Spaniards who destroyed South American civilisations at least partly with the object of converting the heathen to Roman Catholicism believed that they were serving God. The English who fought Roman Catholic Spain equally believed that they were doing God's work. That these ideologies reflected national struggles for survival does not invalidate individual belief. Religious conviction is inherent in the Ulysses factor. The type-figure communed with his deities, Abraham called on his God, Leif Eiriksson was a devout convert to Christianity, Columbus and Drake were frequently at prayer. Their ghosts may agree that they all believed in one God whose power can make up for the littleness of man. As living men they served God in the form acceptable to their people in the setting of their time.

Drake is the prime example of the Ulysses factor in the sixteenth-century English, but it was manifest in John Davis, Raleigh, Frobisher and a host of lesser men. Drake's actions in his first independent command on the voyage of 1570–1571 are typical. He sailed to the isthmus of Panama, but he made no attempt to get rich quick and sail home. Patiently he explored the coast; the rivers and the mule-tracks of the interior, and he made friends with the community of escaped Negro slaves (the Cimaroons) who lived in the jungles of Panama and who were naturally hostile to Spain. He wanted knowledge, real geographical knowledge of this new corner of the world. He acted on this knowledge in his expedition of 1572–1573 when he returned to the isthmus and ambushed a mule-train of Spanish treasure. His great voyage of 1577–1580 in the *Golden Hind*, when he circumnavigated the world, is marked by Ulysses qualities. Faced with mutiny as he approached the Straits of Magellan, he showed superb powers of leadership. He could have made himself popular by turning round and sailing home, and his career would not necessarily have suffered much: he could have picked up prizes in the Caribbean or off the Azores which would have made the voyage profitable. He did not turn back. He landed on the desolate coast of Port St Julian, near the Atlantic tip of South America, where Magellan had had to deal with a rather similar mutiny some sixty years before. Drake held a trial (its legality can be questioned, its courage cannot) at which the leader of the mutinous faction was found guilty and sentenced to death. This man was beheaded. After this example of firmness, Drake offered anyone who wanted to go home a ship to sail in, saying that it was up to them to decide whether to sail on with him of their own free will or to go home and end 'as a reproach to our country and a laughing stock to the enemy'. An invitation in these terms was, perhaps, unlikely to be accepted. Still, it might have been: the crew had little to lose by going home, and a good chance of losing their lives by going on. But Drake knew what he was doing. No one opted to go home. And no one was offered an easy passage onwards. Drake's address to his crew—in a sermon that he preached at an open-air service on that remote South American coast— rings down the years with Ulysses's rebuke to Agamemnon when he suggested that the Greeks should withdraw before a massive Trojan attack. Drake said:

> I must have the gentleman to haul and draw with the mariner, and the mariner with the gentleman. I would know him that would refuse to set his hand to a rope.

That was the end of any questioning of Drake's command. His little fleet, the *Golden Hind, Elizabeth* and *Marigold*, sailed on. All got through the straits of Magellan. Then they were separated in a storm. *Marigold* was lost with all hands. *Elizabeth*, after various adventures, put back into the Straits and ultimately got home to England. Drake and the *Golden Hind* went on, to capture off Peru the richest Spanish treasure ship yet taken, and to complete a voyage round the world.

Drake's harassments of Spain in his voyages of 1585–1587 and his part in meeting the Armada in 1588 are in every English history book. He maintained the verve and imaginative courage characteristic of his earlier adventures, but his exploring days were over. By then he was England's greatest naval captain, and his exploits belong rather to the history of the Royal Navy than to a study of the Ulysses factor. In one aspect of his later years Drake was untypical of those in whom the factor is strong. It is characteristic of the factor that it remains alive late in individual life. In Drake's last years the vigour of the factor in him seemed to decline. He was not old by today's standards: in the year of the Armada he was only 45. But after that year something seems to have gone out of him. On his expedition to Portugal in 1589 he hesitated at critical moments in a most un-Drakelike manner, and his last voyage to the Caribbean in 1595–1596—the voyage on which he died—was mishandled sadly. He was not quite 53 when he died, and it is uncharacteristic that there should have been this relatively early waning of his powers. But men matured quickly and aged quickly in Elizabethan England. Moreover, in the last years of his life Drake was no longer an independent adventurer. He was an Admiral, exercising command through councils of his captains, harassed by political considerations. The Ulysses character is at its best in independent command. The type-figure, if Tennyson's assessment of him is correct, was bored by administration, and not particularly good at it. Drake was certainly no administrator. After the Armada his personal task in life was over. For his countrymen he had widened the known world, not so much by direct discovery as by showing that a little English ship boldly manned could go anywhere, and that Protestant England was not going to be hemmed in by the great power of Spain. His own major geographical discovery was that Tierra del Fuego was not part of a great southern continent, with the tortuous Strait of Magellan the only link between the south Atlantic and the Pacific. Drake found that there was open water south of Cape Horn. This discovery was kept secret during his lifetime, for it offered a route to the Pacific that Spain could not hope to shut. It is commemorated on the modern map by the name Drake Strait for the passage of open water between Cape Horn and the South Shetlands.

The Ulysses factor continued to be manifest in English and Dutch seafarers through the seventeenth and eighteenth centuries. In Dutch national history it was a major element in breaking Spanish attempts to control the Netherlands. As long as the Dutch could put to sea they could escape the Spanish net, and the adventurous voyages of such men as Le Maire, Schouten, Tasman and Roggeveen helped to create a powerful trading empire in the East Indies to sustain the economic strength of the Dutch people.

The English colonised North America and then turned to the Far East. Until the three great voyages of James Cook made between 1768 and 1769 there were huge gaps in western knowledge of the Pacific. The classical idea of a great Southern continent, *Terra Australias Incognita*, needed to balance the land masses of the northern hemisphere lingered.

That continent was shrunk a little by Drake's discovery, confirmed by Le Maire and Schouten, of open water south of South America, but it remained potentially enormous. The East Indies had been explored to some extent, first by the Portuguese then by the Dutch, and islands commercially valuable in the spice trade were well known. New Guinea was known, the north west and south coasts of Australia and the north coast of New Zealand had been glimpsed, but no one knew what sort of lands these were, whether they were separate from one another or parts of a vast continent. Cook added more to the knowledge of the southern hemisphere in ten years than the sum of all human experience before him.

Ulysses qualities are discernible in Cook from boyhood. He was the son of a farm labourer in Yorkshire, but his father was a man of some ability, for he rose to be steward or bailiff managing a farm. The boy learned reading, writing and elementary arithmetic at a dame-school, but there was no more that his schoolmistress could teach him, and when he was 11 or 12 he left school to start work with his father.

The family lived at Marton, on Tees-side, and young Cook wanted to go to sea. But he had the Ulysses quality of patience, and although there were jobs to be had for boys on local coasters, he stayed on the farm until he was 16. Even then he did not go to sea. He found work on the coast at Staithes, near Whitby, but it was in a grocer's shop. It was, however, in a seafaring world. Cook wanted an apprenticeship so that he could learn more about the sea than he could hope to as a deckhand. But he had no family influence, and his parents were in no position to help. He worked for his grocer and waited.

He did well, for he earned his master's respect—as he was to earn the respect of everyone he worked with. And the grocer was a man of substance in his town, with shipowning friends in Whitby. When Cook was 18 the grocer got him a seagoing apprenticeship with a family firm owning East Coast colliers. Cook was old for an apprentice, but he served his three years, learning all he could of navigation and mathematics in his spare time. When he came out of his apprenticeship he made some voyages as an able seaman and then his employers made him mate of a fine new ship. In 1755, when he was 27, he was offered command of her. This was a big step. It meant that

Cook was accepted as a captain in the East Coast trade, and that he could probably look forward to becoming a ship-owner. It was a fine prospect for the son of a farm labourer. Cook turned his back on it and joined the Royal Navy as a seaman.

Again he knew what he was doing, and he took a calculated risk in the Ulysses manner. The North Sea was his nursery school in seamanship—there is none better—but he had finished with the nursery. He had no influence to apply for a commission in the Navy, but he had confidence in himself. It was justified. After one month's service he was promoted master's mate, and within a year he was bo'sun of a sixty-gun ship. In two years he was master of a sixty-four-gun ship.

In the eighteenth-century Navy a ship's 'master' was not her Captain. He was not even a commissioned officer. He was a much respected chief petty officer, responsible for the general working of the ship, including navigation. Cook was not only an able navigator; his years in the North Sea coasting trade had made him a fine inshore pilot. War with France and the struggle for Canada took him to the St Lawrence. Cook's pilotage and charting of the dangerous waters leading to Quebec contributed materially to the capture of Quebec by General Wolfe in 1759. To consolidate victory in Canada the Navy needed accurate knowledge of the Gulf of St Lawrence and the surrounding coasts. Cook was employed to chart them. The accuracy of his charts of Newfoundland and Nova Scotia kept them in use for the next century.

Cook's opportunity as an explorer—the task for which he had been fitting himself all his life—came when he was 40. The Royal Society, in the heyday of the eighteenth-century spirit of inquiry, wanted to send an astronomer to the southern hemisphere to observe the transit of Venus, which would occur in 1769. The Navy, concerned with bases for the struggle at sea with France and Spain, wanted accurate knowledge of the South Pacific: if a great southern continent existed, it was imperative that Britain should have a footing there. To meet the combined need for scientific and strategical information the Navy mounted an expedition to sail to the south seas with a party of observers from the Royal Society. Cook was commissioned to command it. A Whitby collier, shallow-draughted and strong, the kind of vessel in which

Cook had served his apprenticeship to coastal pilotage, was bought by the Admiralty and fitted out for the job. She was originally the *Earl of Pembroke*, but on entering the Navy's service to take the expedition to the south seas she was renamed *Endeavour*.

Cook sailed for the Pacific in 1768. In 1769 he landed at Tahiti to enable the Royal Society's party to make their observations of the transit of Venus, and, this accomplished, went on to locate and chart the two islands of New Zealand, to discover New South Wales and the east coast of Australia, to discover and investigate the Great Barrier Reef and to prove New Guinea to be an island by sailing through the Torres Strait between New Guinea and Australia.* He returned to England in 1771, having proved that New Zealand, Australia and New Guinea were not parts of a southern continent; but there remained a possibility that such a land mass existed in the south Pacific farther west. He sailed again in 1772 to investigate the high latitudes of the southern ocean, made the first crossing of the Antarctic circle and proved that whatever land existed towards the South Pole was beyond the barrier of Antarctic ice. He removed the great southern continent as a land of legendary riches from the maps of the globe. He set out on his last voyage to the Pacific in 1776. This time he sailed north, to see if he could find a practicable route from the Pacific to the Atlantic. It was not then known whether Alaska was part of the North American continent or an island, and it was theoretically possible that a strait existed to link the North Pacific to the accessible Arctic ocean and the North Atlantic—the other end, as it were, of the North West Passage for which men were to go on searching for the next century.

On his way north Cook discovered Hawaii and the Sandwich Islands. He sailed up the Pacific coast of North America, proving that there was no strait to bisect the continent, and settling the question of Alaska—it was indisputably mainland. He sailed through the Bering Strait and coasted Alaska until he was stopped by ice—it was unlikely that there was a

---

* The passage between New Guinea and Australia was first made by the Portuguese navigator Luis Vaez de Torres, after whom the strait is named, a century and a half before Cook, but its significance was not appreciated. Cook had documents suggesting the existence of such a passage, but in his day many geographers held that New Guinea was part of a mainland. Cook settled the matter.

usable passage to the Atlantic that way. But his work was not finished: it was just possible that a practicable sea-route from the Pacific to Europe might be found to the north of Asia—a north east passage in European terms. It was too late in the season, however, to attempt more Arctic exploration that year, so he returned to Hawaii to winter and refit. There, in February, 1779, he was killed in a sudden skirmish with Hawaian natives. He was just 50.

Cook's importance was recognised by his contemporaries, but the full value of his life to his countrymen was not apparent until the next century. It was because of him that Australia and New Zealand became British, offering opportunity for a new life to British families whose prospects at home diminished as nineteenth-century industrialisation made men redundant. It was because of Cook that two great English-speaking nations took root in the southern hemisphere. And this is the briefest summary of his achievement. His contribution to geographical knowledge was immense, and his pioneering voyages played a large part in the development of later British commerce with the Far East. One of his biographers, Dr J. A. Williamson, calls him 'the greatest explorer of his age, the greatest maritime explorer of his country in any age'. It is a just summing-up.

Cook is a peculiarly exact illustration of the influence of the Ulysses factor on human personality and achievement. His impulse was *to know*, to discover at firsthand what lay beyond the mouth of the Tees, the North Sea, the Gulf of St Lawrence, Cape Horn and the horizons of the Pacific. He had one single purpose—to find out for himself. His whole life was subordinated to this purpose, his early years to fitting himself by self-education for his task, his late years to doing it. His impulse never wavered. After his second Pacific voyage he was given a sinecure at Greenwich Hospital, the kind of post that was the aim of most of his contemporaries with neither patrimony nor influence to provide a pension. He was then 47, verging on elderly in eighteenth-century terms of expectation of life. As soon as a third Pacific expedition was mooted he volunteered to lead it. Apart from his sinecure at Greenwich and the profits from a book which he did not live to enjoy and which went to his widow, he had little material reward in life—he sought none. He engaged in no personal commerce in his voyaging, sought neither gold nor gain. His purpose was exactly expressed in Tennyson's *Ulysses*:

... To follow knowledge like a sinking star.

This brief survey of the Ulysses factor in history both illustrates its continual emergence in man and raises some perplexing questions. My type-figure is from the eastern Mediterranean, and historical manifestations of the factor come overwhelmingly from the Mediterranean world and, later, from the peoples of north west Europe. A survival factor common to mankind might be expected to show a common pattern in history. Why is there this preponderance of Ulysses types in the Mediterranean and Europe?

An obvious answer is that the historical evidence is incomplete, and the picture, therefore, one-sided. If one knew more about the early history of the people of Africa and Asia there would be more examples of the influence of the Ulysses factor in their lives. What *is* known tends to bear out this. Chinese travellers visited India before our Christian era, and Arab seafarers reached the Far East centuries before any European seamen did so. In the Near East the factor undoubtedly influenced the early history of the Jewish people. In the unrecorded history of Central Africa many important movements of peoples may have followed manifestations of the factor in individuals.

But ignorance of world history at best gives only a partial solution to the problem. It was open to Africans, Chinese, Japanese, Polynesians, American Indians and all the rest to cross the oceans of the world and to follow exploration by settlement and trade. The prevailing winds and currents in the North Atlantic would have made it physically far easier for Western Europe to have been 'discovered' from North America than for America to be 'discovered' from Europe. If you throw an orange box into the sea on the eastern seaboard of America the chances that it will fetch up on some beach of western Europe are high. As far as we know, no such exploration was ever made from an indigenous North American people. It may be said that the North American Indians had no maritime tradition, but this is to beg the question. They had an immense seaboard. Why did not some American counterpart of Leif Eiriksson put to sea?

Prehistoric folk movements certainly took place over ocean distances. Polynesians reached, and settled in, New Zealand, and there may have been migrations from South America to Pacific archipelagos. Why did such voyaging stop?

In the next chapter I discuss a mutation of the factor which has had profound effects on western thought. It may be that other mutations in various peoples of the past have occurred to affect national history. In the west, diminution of the *primary* need of the Ulysses factor, the reduction or disappearance of any immediate physical necessity to find fresh resources for survival, did not diminish the power of the factor to influence individual action: a mutation took place giving new purpose to the physical instinct to explore. The factor has continued to find expression, with interesting differences in different national groups, and always with a bearing on group or national survival, not less important because it has become less direct. There may have been unknown mutations in which the factor has turned malignant: I shall present one case later in which it seems to me that some malformation in the factor had malignant effects on individuals. Other human traits can be malformed, or their development obscurely arrested. It may be that malformation or arrested development of the Ulysses factor is one reason why some human communities have remained backward, or have advanced less rapidly than others. This may help to explain, too, why some early advanced cultures, such as the Chinese and that of Hindu India, have remained inward-looking.

IV

Mutation

For the nations of Europe hopes of national benefit from primary geographical discovery began to decline in the eighteenth century. They revived in the nineteenth century with the struggle for territory in Africa, but by the end of the century such hopes had gone. Physical exploration is, of course, still of great importance in prospecting for oil and minerals, but it is not now primary exploration: modern prospecting is the application of technological skills to locate materials of value in areas geographically long mapped. In some parts of the Americas primary exploration continued to hold out hopes of direct economic benefit for another generation or so, but outside some localities in the basin of the Upper Amazon and its tributaries and perhaps in Antarctica the surface resources of the globe are all now broadly known. Modern political organisation inhibits direct benefit from geophysical discovery outside the tribe or nation already occupying territory: the days of claiming ownership of land by planting a flag are over (in this world, at any rate, whatever may be the legal situation on the moon). Wars to acquire resources in someone else's country are another matter.

Yet the impulse to physical exploration remains strong. With the cessation of its direct benefit, the factor in man making for this impulse has undergone a gradual mutation, substituting a philosophical driving force for what was once an economic compulsion. So far as I know, no one has hitherto applied a concept of the Ulysses factor in man to the history of philosophy, though Iris Murdoch, who studied philosophy before becoming a novelist, came somewhere near it by identifying among the terrors of Antoine Roquentin in Sartre's *La Nausée* a fear that 'there are no adventures'.* If the develop-

* Iris Murdoch, *Sartre*. Collins 1967.

ment of Western philosophy, particularly over the past two
centuries, is considered in relation to the Ulysses factor some
interesting things emerge.

After Cook's great voyages in the Pacific the broad pattern
of the earth was known: there was no longer any hope of
discovering a great Southern continent, *Terra Australis Incognita*, offering the vast access of new wealth brought by the
discovery (or re-discovery) of the Americas in the fifteenth
century. At about this time a new turn in philosophical thinking began to persuade men to see a kind of absolute value in
wild nature: mountains, rocks, the sea began to seem not
merely natural phenomena but to have, as it were, a moral
purpose, prompting the onlooker, especially when they were
difficult of access, to profound or noble thoughts. It is at least
significant that the end to primary exploration in the world
and the beginning of what is called the romantic movement
in philosophy should have been coincident.

The forerunner in this romantic movement was Jean Jacques Rousseau (1712–1778). It would be an over-simplification to call him the founder of romantic philosophy: rather,
his ideals of a return to nature attracted those who wanted to
feel that the natural world offered lessons of value to mankind, giving form and expression to their own vague feelings.
Rousseau's approach to nature was primarily political; the
embodiment of his ideas in philosophy came a little later. In
his *History of Western Philosophy*, Bertrand Russell
observes:

> The romantic movement is characterised, as a whole, by
> the substitution of aesthetic for utilitarian standards...
> The morals of the romantics have primarily aesthetic mo-
> tives. But in order to characterise the romantics it is neces-
> sary to take account, not only of the importance of aesthetic
> motives, but also of the change of taste which made their
> sense of beauty different from that of their predecessors...
> Dr Johnson preferred Fleet Street to any rural landscape,
> and maintained that a man who is tired of London must be
> tired of life. If anything in the country was admired by
> Rousseau's predecessors, it was a scene of fertility, with rich
> pastures and lowing kine. Rousseau, being Swiss, naturally
> admired the Alps. In his disciples' novels and stories we

E

find wild torrents, fearful precipices, pathless forests, thunderstorms, tempests at sea and generally what is useless, destructive and violent. This change seems to be more or less permanent: almost everybody, nowadays, prefers Niagara and the Grand Canyon to lush meadows and fields of waving corn.*

Bertrand Russell, writing of the romantic movement primarily in its political and social aspects, considers it to be essentially 'a revolt against received ethical and aesthetic standards'. This is true from Russell's standpoint, but it is only partly true of the movement as a whole. It was more than a revolt against anything. It was the creation of a new set of philosophical values. Most thinking about the romantic movement has been political, concentrating on its contribution to the chain of events which brought about the French Revolution, socialist theory, proletarian and 'National Socialist' dictatorships. Russell sums up Rousseau's thinking:

> Much of its philosophy could be appropriated by Hegel in his defence of the Prussian autocracy. Its first fruits in practice were the reign of Robespierre; the dictatorships of Russia and Germany (especially the latter)† are in part an outcome of Rousseau's teaching. What further triumphs the future has to offer to his ghost I do not venture to predict.

Russell was not surveying the whole historical landscape. It could be said that Nansen, Scott, Tilman, Shipton and Robin Knox-Johnston are in part 'tributes to Rousseau's ghost'.

As an individual Rousseau was an exceptionally unpleasant man, and some of his ideas on political organisation suitable to man in a 'natural' state seem now fairly weird. Worse, those ideas are capable of much distortion. But there was power in his thinking, and original vision. If politically much evil has flowed from his thought it also encouraged men to take a new look at the physical world. He was concerned mainly with

---

* Bertrand Russell, *History of Western Philosophy*. Allen & Unwin 1961.
† Germany in this context is Nazi Germany.

man in what he considered is, or should be, a state of nature, and in his concern with man in natural surroundings he saw those surroundings from a novel angle. The vision was exciting. Men began to consider forests, hills and seas not as stage-props in setting the human scene but as things with meaning in themselves. The romantic poets, Wordsworth, Coleridge, Byron and their school, all influenced to some extent by Rousseau and his followers, wrote of nature in an almost personal sense, seeing a new *kind* of relationship between man, the hills he climbed and the seas he crossed. Travel might be a purpose in itself: merely to look with one's own eyes on a waterfall or at the view from a hilltop justified a difficult journey. There need not be gold beyond the hills. It was sufficient to see beyond the hills.

This philosophical concept met a human need left by the diminishing returns from physical exploration. It is important to observe that it was a *philosophical* concept. Rousseau made no effort to go to the South Seas: he had little or nothing of the Ulysses factor in him; he was a tramp rather than a traveller. There were identifiable Ulysses characteristics in Byron, few in Wordsworth or Coleridge. They were attracted to the natural world intellectually and emotionally. But they gave expression to this attraction: they helped to create a climate of thought which appealed to the Ulysses factor in man, and which was favourable to the survival of the factor. Looked at another way, the emergence of this romantic movement in the eighteenth and early nineteenth centuries reflected the Ulysses factor in the process of undergoing modification: it may be seen as a biological mutation necessary to preserve a human attribute still important to the health of the species. There *had* to be a philosophy in mountains.

Having established a philosophical basis for continuing to explore, men rapidly undertook new forms of exploration. Mountaineering was invented as an end in itself, the achievement of a summit a goal as compelling as the quest in other ages for a route to India. The sea became an end in itself. Yachting, which had been a rich man's sport of racing large vessels with paid crews against one another for substantial wagers, changed to a delight in taking to the sea for its own sake. Joshua Slocum's singlehanded circumnavigation for no other purpose than to sail round the world alone was a turning-point at the end of the nineteenth century. It gave a permanent value to non-rational physical endeavour at sea.

As the scale on which new geographical knowledge could be acquired diminished, the impulse to physical exploration both benefited from philosophical reinforcement and contributed to the reinforcing philosophy. It is one thing to set off in search of a new continent, with all the hopes of national and personal advancement that such a search offered. It is another matter to attempt to reach the North Pole, a point on the earth's surface of no material significance and inviting danger and hardship to no very obvious end. Yet to reach the Pole became a compelling need, felt instinctively by whole nations. The form, or even the probable scientific content, of new knowledge ceased to count in the impulse to Ulysses-type adventures: there was no need for knowledge to be 'useful', it was sufficient that it should be new, or the re-discovery of the very old in man's past. This relative unimportance of material things in the purpose of exploration came to be felt alike by those moved by the Ulysses factor to personal endeavour and by the public in its response. The climbing of Everest was *felt* to be an achievement comparable with the discovery of a new continent. The philosophical thinking which made all this acceptable derived from the 'romantics' of the eighteenth and early nineteenth centuries, whose inspiration in turn derived from the continued need to find fulfilment for the Ulysses factor in man. In this sense the romantics were more practical than they themselves realised, or than many of those who studied them have realised. The Ulysses strand in romantic philosophy is wholly non-political. It is the collective expression of a deep human need, social thinking, but not political thinking. The political development of romantic thought was not exactly a side-issue, because to many of those influenced by it political reform was the main issue. But the relationship is complex. The end of primary geographical discovery coincided with the end of the medieval sense of wonder. The two are not directly related—in order to believe in angels a man does not have to think that an undiscovered country lies across the sea. But there is an obscure relationship: the emotional substitution of mountains for El Dorado is the same sort of substitution as the dictatorship of the proletariat for the companionship of angels. The sense of wonder which helped to keep man going from pre-history until about the eighteenth century derives from deep human needs similar to those promoted by the Ulysses factor. The romantic discovery of mountains was akin to the romantic discovery of the noble poor. Bertrand Russell may have the last word here.

> The poor, to the romantics, were never urban and never industrial; the proletariat is a nineteenth century conception, perhaps equally romanticised, but quite different.*

Romantic philosophy in itself is now old-fashioned. The idea of 'sermons in stones, books in the running brooks', which once seemed novel and enlightened, now seems slightly absurd. But it has done its fertilising work. Philosophical effort has now turned to mathematical logic and linguistic analysis. There is, however, a related body of philosophical thought which seems more typical of the common hopes and fears of the twentieth century. This is termed (badly) existentialism, and derives mainly from the thought of Søren Kierkegaard, Friedrich Nietzsche, Karl Jaspers, Gabriel Marcel, Martin Heidegger and Jean-Paul Sartre. Existentialism is impossible either to simplify or to define. H. J. Blackham suggests:

> Existence lies beyond thought, and beyond existence is possibly some form of transcendence; this is the field of personal venture and experience in which the manoeuvre takes place. The business of existential philosophy in helping the person to make himself and get his experience is to furnish analyses of the concrete structures of firsthand experience... If the speculative fantasies of the classical rationalist philosophies were true in principle, and the individual could be assigned an appointed place in a system, man as man would not exist. Man's separation is a malaise, but it is not nostalgia for the Great Chain of Being; it is a disorder which founds and refounds the human order of possibilities which are temporal and modest and never final. In this order the existing individual has no refuge from continuous responsibility. But why the anguished respon-

* Russell, *History of Western Philosophy*. Allen and Unwin. New Edition, 1961.

sibility of the existentialist? A certain anxiety in carrying out given tasks and duties, a fear of not being equal to the demands, is understandable enough; and normal people feel acute anxiety in the midst of the uncertainties which beset an original decision: but these are only echoes of the primordial anxiety felt by the man who knows that at every moment in absolute solitariness he is responsible for the fate of man. This absolute responsibility of the individual can be treated as a platitude, or it may be held to be the fundamental truth about the individual which he is most reluctant to face and accept, although he is only authentically man in so far as he lives and acts in the full consciousness of it.*

This is not easy reading, but it is worth persevering because it comes near to finding words to express the vague sense of personal dissatisfaction that is characteristic of the individual in the advanced communities of this century. Iris Murdoch's identification of the fear in Sartre 'that there is no adventure' is an important addition to expression. Why is there no adventure, no sense of responsibility, for the common man?

To attempt to answer this question at all fully would go far beyond the scope of this book. Man lacks, and becomes afraid of, responsibility because political and social systems discourage responsibility in the individual. The little daily excitements —the opening of a flower, a stoat scurrying to safety, the feel of raindrops—met in the life of the fields are gone from the repetitive work of factory or office. In insulated urban boxes for living rain is no longer an adventure: it is unnoticed, or a nuisance. There are no sermons in concrete or artificial stone (at least, none that one wants to listen to), no books in culverted brooks. Romantic philosophy has gone sour. There are ten thousand particular reasons for this. One general reason, however, can be identified in the unexercised Ulysses factor in man. We have seen that there are two aspects of the factor, impulse and response. The impulse prompting individuals to physical expression in major, Ulysses-type adventures may be rare, but the response of communities to such adventures is widespread, almost universal. The crowds that flock to Falmouth or Portsmouth to welcome a Knox-Johnston or Alec

* H. J. Blackham, *Six Existentialist Thinkers*, pp. 154–55. Routledge.

Rose probably do not know why they are there: they have gathered instinctively, and the instinct is sound. They may be excited by adventure at second-hand, but they are moved by adventure, every individual in the crowd responding to adventure in his private dreams, identifying himself with the adventurer. Crossing oceans in small boats has become almost commonplace; but let it be known that a small boat is about to make port after a long voyage, and a crowd will assemble. The existentialist fear 'that there is no adventure' underscores the importance of adventurers. Without adventure there is death.

Yet there must be a purpose in adventure. To reach the North or South Pole, to discover the source of the Nile, to make the first crossing of the Greenland Ice-cap, to climb Everest—these are all purposes with an understandable physical content. It may not be of practical value in the sense that seeking a new route to India was likely to be of practical value, but at least it is definitive. Before Robert Peary reached the North Pole in 1909 no human eye had seen this geographical point. Peary extended the vision of mankind. So with the other great goals of exploration. One by one they have been achieved. Just as the practical rewards of exploration diminished with discovery, so have the romantic rewards diminished. With the Poles achieved, earth's highest mountain climbed, what is left for the fulfilment of man's exploring spirit?

Again there has been a philosophical mutation. Adventure must have a purpose, but it may be a purpose wholly personal to the adventurer. Since man began to navigate, shipwrecked seamen have been compelled from time to time to attempt remarkable voyages in very small boats, or sometimes on rafts of spars hastily lashed together. Some succeeded, many were lost. When they succeeded such voyages were regarded with admiration, but it was admiration for professional seamen in the exercise of their profession; escape from shipwreck was looked upon, as it were, as an incident in life devoted to the sea. With the larger goals of navigation achieved, men began to see a purpose in deliberate attempts to cross oceans in ever smaller boats, to voyage singlehanded to circumnavigate the world alone. This is physical endeavour to explore an individual's own capacity to endure hardship or solitude as much as to explore the sea, but the Ulysses factor in humanity has come to respond to it as it responded to adventure with a wider purpose. In climbing there has been a similar progression—the peaks have, as it were, receded as they have been scaled. The achievement of each 'highest' summit, Nanda Devi, Annapurna, Everest is as definitive in its setting of time as Peary's achievement of the North Pole, but climbers have found new goals in tackling unclimbed faces of climbed mountains, in exploring new routes to known summits, in devising new techniques. Here, too, the exploration is primarily of man himself in exacting physical conditions. This field is limitless, and human response seems ever self-renewing.

The voyages of Chichester, Rose or Knox-Johnston may seem pointless in relation to the voyages of Nansen or Darwin, but neither the individuals themselves nor the millions who have been thrilled by them regard their adventures as pointless. And they are not. They have achieved a personal fulfilment, which can be communicated. Many people feel that their own lives have been enriched by a Rose or Knox-Johnston.

Much modern philosophy is not easily understood, and tends to be regarded as expressing the sense of despair in modern man. If it be considered in relation to the Ulysses factor in man it will be seen to express a despair for which there is a physical basis. If this physical basis can be identified by the individual in his own life despair ceases to be a forlorn heartcry and becomes a rational hunger. Perhaps some existentialist thinkers would deny this, and insist that their thinking concerns the physical merely to the extent that it reflects the philosophic 'ambiguity' in existence. I am not here concerned with any particular system, or even non-system, of philosophy. What seems to me both interesting and significant is the identification of a *general* malaise of lack of adventure and denial of responsibility in a *body* of philosophical thought peculiarly typical of the twentieth century. This is a physical basis of thought, similar to that which helped to bring about the romantic corrective to philosophy in the eighteenth century. If this identification be accepted it may promote new thinking on at least some of man's problems in existing.

It is desirable here to change the gear of this discussion to bring philosophy nearer to the man in the Mini or the Chevrolet. In terms of inarticulate urban living what is the philosophical manifestation of the Ulysses factor?

It is necessary to contemplate a world in which the man in the Mini may see hills personally only where a motorway cuts through them, and to whom the sea has become the seaside. The personal excitements in his life are few. Sex is his main chance of instinctive human fulfilment, and sex is liable to be distorted for him by commercial titillation which invites desire in order to frustrate it with soap or breakfast food, or, every four or five years, the supreme achievement of a new car. The effect on his wife is likely to be even more unhappy: she is encouraged to believe herself a cross between a siren and a reigning monarch, her husband's inarticulate lovemaking seeming a poor thing after what she has been led by women's magazines and TV to look for as her right. They may experiment with other partners at the cost of losing even what remains of domestic comfort for a brief illusion of excitement. Outside their sexual lives their world is deadly dull. The woman has a better chance than her husband of self-fulfilment through children, but after a few years of charming infancy, when maternal instincts are aroused and necessary, children too often tend to bring the weariness of more drudgery. How can children give much to their parents when parents have so little to give them? Daughter will soon join her mother in the synthetic excitement of the bingo session, and son follows father to the factory or office. The walls of concrete, steel and brick that cut off humanity from the natural world grow higher with each generation: and those who are cut off build their own prisons.

The odds are weighted against them, but vestigially each remains an individual, with the instincts of man from the beginning of time, among them the Ulysses factor. It may be dormant in communities for many generations, but it is not dead. Walter Mitty, the prototype of two-dimensional adventurers, lives in every man, and the fact that it is always *possible* that he may become three-dimensional keeps him alive. Every now and again a man *does* throw away his brief-case or his sandwich tin to sail an ocean. The millions who do not, meditate secretly as they sit in their cars at traffic lights that they themselves *might* one day do so. The most real part of a man's whole life may be in such daydreams.

This is commonly recognised. What is less widely recognised is the physical basis of Walter Mitty's dreaming. He is *not* seeing himself at the tiller of a cutter in a storm *because* he has seen such an adventure at the cinema or on television. He sees himself as a sailor on a wild sea because potentially he *is* a sailor on a wild sea. Cinema and television screens hinder his vision rather than induce it. Both are poor substitutes for human imagination left to itself, to feed on books or travellers' tales. The medieval sense of wonder provided a tapestry for the mind compared with the fustian of television. In spite of the claims made for the presentation of actualities by television, it is a rare programme which leaves people with any real sense of having participated in a great occasion. More commonly it leaves a vague feeling that the occasion was not, after all, so very great. Television as it is usually presented is another wall rather than a window in the wall.

Man must make his own windows and, sometimes, doors. It was easier in a primitive world, where there were fewer walls. But there are balances in life as well as checks, and although it is harder nowadays to sustain a sense of wonder in everyday living, in some ways the physical means of sustenance for wonder have increased. The man in his Mini *need* not see hills only from a motorway. If he is fortunate enough to fall in with the right friends in adolescence, or to have a grown-up relation or schoolmaster with undulled imagination, he may be encouraged to take to the hills or the sea. The reward for acquiescence in industrial society is a relatively high money wage, and money can be spent on climbing boots or a boat as well as in the bingo hall. It will buy books as well as lace-trimmed shirts, books that not only open doors to wonder but also tell you how to make the doors. The Mini will take a man to the sea as readily as to the seaside. Weekend sailing or climbing or canoeing is not the full expression of the Ulysses factor, but it is *some* expression of it, of vital importance as a physical response to a physical and emotional need. Sailing a dinghy on a reservoir is not a severe test of personal responsibility, but it does require personal decision to achieve a physical purpose, and it does bring moments at which an individual may feel that 'he is responsible for the fate of man'. The collective response to the exploits of a Knox-Johnston is deepened and made more real by the fact that in the responding community are a fairly large number of individuals with *some* firsthand knowledge of sailing a small boat. Most of them may have little idea of what it actually means to sail around the world alone, but they have enough firsthand experience to achieve an emotional understanding of the reality. The physical basis of their daydreams is not an atrophied physical instinct: it is a fact of their personal lives. What Knox-Johnston has done I could do, perhaps... Of course this is unlikely, for Knox-Johnston is an exceptional man. But it is not *quite* impossible. And what is not quite impossible may be possible. And for something to be possible makes it real. And that reality may save a soul from damnation.

> He who has once been happy is for aye
> Out of destruction's reach. His fortune then
> Holds nothing secret, and Eternity,
> Which is a mystery to other men
> Has like a woman given him its joy.
> ... He can bear to die.

This rather difficult poem by W. S. Blunt expresses an absolute truth if happiness (a subjective word) is considered as fulfilment. For most people the Ulysses factor will be dormant. That has always been so. The type-figure was wholly exceptional, necessarily larger than life, and those who are inspired by this human factor in them to prolonged personal endeavour are also exceptional. But if the factor is not to atrophy to the hurt of the individual and community it must be kept at least passively alive. Its sustenance is in a sense of wonder; not incomprehensible wonder, but wonder at experiences that can be felt and physically understood. In a good many individuals during the course of a lifetime it can stir actively to attain a momentary sense of fulfilment. If that fulfilment is complete, and it may be complete for a split second at the tiller of a dinghy or on some quite ordinary climb that individual is 'out of destruction's reach'. He may have to live a two-dimensional existence, but he will never again be quite a two-dimensional man.

Mutations in the Ulysses factor as human society has

changed have kept alive the exploring instinct in man and produced new philosophical values to replace its earlier practical value. It remains a factor important to man's survival on earth. But is man limited to earth? Mutations in the factor are directly relevant to his terrestial existence. What is the relation of the factor to exploration beyond the confines of earth, to lunar or stellar adventure? I consider this in the next chapter.

V

Cosmonauts

THE chief emotional *fact* in the world's response to man's landing on the moon in July 1969 is that nobody, from peasant to professor, felt any particular surprise. There was great interest and a feeling that technicians are really remarkably clever, but not much surprise. The weird pictures on television of ghost-like figures conducting a sort of stately dance on an awesome golf course brought no sense of comprehension. Men were on the moon, yes; it was an extraordinary technological achievement, yes. Those who believe in God prayed that they might get back safely to their families.

Some years earlier—in March 1965—when the Russian cosmonaut Alexei Leonov became the first man to take a short walk in space I had to write a leading article about it in *The Guardian*. It was a difficult subject: there did not seem much to say. I considered the impact of the event on minds conditioned by terrestial history and permitted myself the reflection, 'it is easier to believe in angels than in weightlessness'. This brought a letter from one reader expressing indignation that in this technological age *The Guardian* should employ a man who found it easier to believe in angels than in weightlessness. I accepted the rebuke, but remained unconvinced. Perhaps in the next century weightlessness will be an experience so general that it will be accepted as an incident of air travel, like the boiled sweets that are handed out to passengers on take-off. For humanity at least up to the eighth decade of the twentieth century it *is* easier to believe in angels. And conceivably, unless man can retain a capacity to believe in angels, it will not be worth living in a technological age.

At first sight a journey to the moon may seem a logical development of the Ulysses impulse. So it is. The moon is there, exciting shadows that look like seas and continents can be seen with the naked eye, and from the dawn of time men have looked and wondered at the moon, and pondered how to get there. But imagination here is more satisfying than reality. If man could climb or swim or sail to the moon it would be a wonderful physical journey, more wonderful by far than getting to the North Pole or reaching the summit of Everest. The reality is different. Man can get to the moon only by depersonalising himself to the extent of becoming an extension of the computer, and with the aid of a vast power-house of engines and instruments, collectively understood, of course, by the technicians who control them, but almost beyond individual comprehension. It is not a personal journey. It is more like a dream while under an anaesthetic.

Yet *men* have got to the moon, have walked in space—or swum or floated there, whatever may be the proper term for the mode of propulsion. For all the army of technologists who make space travel possible, the travellers are individuals. They must have Ulysses qualities developed to a high degree, courage, self-discipline, self-reliance, many different skills. In their selection they are typical of the best human product of the active Ulysses factor almost to perfection, mostly married, with strong family attachments, seasoned by living, nearer forty than youth.

Somehow they seem de-natured: not as individuals, but as explorers. They are the tools of an exploring organisation rather than men who set out to explore, used, one feels, because the human hand and human brain are still indispensable in the execution of the computer's plan. Of course it is not the computer's plan: behind the computer the planning is man's. But it is planning *through* the computer, and the human agents, though important, are in some sense less essential in the journey to the moon than the machines that calculate their flight and the rockets that drive their capsules. The very air they breathe they must take with them.

A sense of wonder does not require comprehension, but its object must be comprehensible. The medieval mind did not comprehend angels, but found no difficulty in regarding angels as comprehensible. The modern mind may not comprehend a Tilman or a Knox-Johnston, but can accept them as entirely comprehensible. Therefore they inspire. If Knox-Johnston can do this, I could do it, perhaps... The cosmonauts are an inspiration, but a collective rather than an individual inspiration. A boy's imagination may be fired by their example so that he decides that he must go to the moon. But he must first join the appropriate Service, spend years in dedicated training, and even then he can but hope that he *may* be selected (by someone else) for a space adventure. Unless he is an American or a Russian citizen, or can acquire such citizenship, he has little hope of personal adventure in space.

These are the reflections of 1970. Technological progress is incessant, within a few decades private space-ships may be available, as private aeroplanes are now. It may be possible for a Sheila Scott early in the next century to make a single-handed flight to Mars. Who knows? Science fiction has barely managed to keep up with science fact in this century. It may not be many decades more before a determined man or woman can plan an independent journey to the stars.

The Ulysses factor will require another mutation, but biological mutation is going on all the time. The change required here, however, will be a great one, the substitution of satisfaction from collective endeavour for satisfaction by personal effort. This change would be so great that the human impulse deriving from it would be different in kind, not merely in degree. A man or woman may sit alone at the controls of a space-ship, but the ship will demand a huge supporting crew on earth, perhaps manned space-stations scattered through the universe. Aircraft already demand an elaborate support organisation. The pilot of even a private light aeroplane needs fuelling points and maintenance facilities, and is subject to flight control from the ground. Man can still fly without radio and meteorological services, but this is becoming less and less practicable. In this *dependence* on ancillary support is the doubt I have on the extent to which even singlehanded exploits in the air nowadays can be regarded as manifestations of the Ulysses impulse and not of some other human factor. The Ulysses factor has undergone some modification to produce Sheila Scott. Whether it can mutate sufficiently to send Ulysses into space I am not sure. In theory it is certainly possible.

> To follow knowledge, like a sinking star,
> beyond the utmost bound of human thought—

This is a characteristic inherent in Ulysses, but it can and does inspire other types of man. The purely intellectual exploration of an Einstein or a Bertrand Russell is related to the impulse towards physical exploration, but rather distantly. All human qualities are related, but they do not necessarily go together. Moral courage and physical courage are not quite the same thing. The Ulysses factor is a complex of human qualities, very old in man, prompting the *individual* to action to satisfy a mixture of intellectual and physical curiosity *by personal physical effort*. It is of value to the survival of race, tribe and family within the human species, and while the species survives more or less as we know it, this factor must survive in one form or another. But there are limits, not definable, within which the factor can work. It *must* express itself in *personal* effort. Human history in other fields suggests that collective effort is *not* an emotional substitute for personal effort. Collective farms may be more efficient (though not always) than personal farms, and work on a collective farm may produce satisfactions that are not obtained by a farmer working his own land for himself. But there is plenty of evidence that the deep human satisfactions that *do* come from working one's own land do *not* come from collective agriculture. Collective farming may have all sorts of political, social or agricultural virtues, but it is *not* a substitute for all man's emotional needs in his relationship with the land. The same emotional lack is manifest in modern industry: the man working at an assembly belt does *not* obtain the emotional satisfaction of the individual craftsman. Man's history suggests, therefore, that voyaging in space, where the individual is merely a projection of collective endeavour, will *not* satisfy the Ulysses impulse in him. Space-travel has already come: there will be more and greater voyages than that to the moon. But these adventures will reflect other qualities in man than those which combine to create the Ulysses factor in him. Or they may reflect a combination of Ulysses qualities—all, individually, fairly general human characteristics—so different from the complex called the Ulysses factor that it will be not a modification of it but a sharply distinct variant.

If the factor is necessary to the survival of race, tribe or family it will continue to find expression. Is it a terrestrial factor, its limits of working, although indefinable, restricted to earth? There is no reason why this should be so. If man could exist on the moon, climb its hills and cross its deserts by his own efforts, the Ulysses impulse would surely send men exploring them. If such ventures on the moon were possible the means of getting to the moon would be no more relevant to the venture itself than travelling to India by steamer to the cimbing of Everest. Personal adventures in space-suits equipped with cooling systems and oxygen may one day be possible on the moon. If so, men will undertake them, and they will help to meet the Ulysses need in man. But again it is a matter of degree. Men have climbed Everest, but not quite by unaided human effort—they were assisted by oxygen. Men still have dreams of climbing Everest without carrying oxygen: indeed, the achievement of its summit with the help of oxygen may be considered one step on the way to getting there with unaided human lungs. It is doubtful if this could ever be felt about the moon, where not only lungs but every human attribute requires scientific aid.

There may be worlds in space where man can walk freely. If so, and if he can get there, the same impulse which has prompted physical exploration of the earth will impel him there. The Ulysses factor is not so much earthbound as limited by man's physical capacity. The limits of this are not definable in degree but are in kind. Thus one can say that man cannot live without food without being able to say precisely for how long without food a particular man may be able to live. So with air and water: an environment containing neither is so inimical to man that he cannot live, and he has therefore *no* unaided physical capacity.

The matter of aid is relative. Man cannot live without air, or rather, without the oxygen contained in terrestrial air, and in high climbing, where the air is tenuous, he takes oxygen breathing-apparatus for additional support. This does not reduce his physical achievement, though it may to some extent prevent *complete* satisfaction in it. Everest is not beyond earth's atmosphere; it would be a finer achievement, somehow, to climb its peak without the aid of oxygen apparatus. This is not wholly a logical feeling. Man cannot live without food

F

and water, so to cross a desert or the sea he must take food and
water with him. Likewise he must carry food if he attempts to
climb Everest at all, for the high slopes of snow- or ice-bound
mountains offer no sustenance. The margin of logic is perhaps
the dividing line between sustenance for normal living and
specially induced sustenance. The water a man drinks at sea is
ordinary water; it gives him no extra strength or staying
power; it confers no special advantage. Even this line is not
quite logical. A man may properly encourage himself with a
glass of wine or whisky, but to obtain abnormal staying power
by the use of more powerful drugs would demean physical
achievement. Athletes are not supposed to use drugs to improve, or to try to improve, their physical performance, but
no one (except, perhaps, his trainer, and then for different
reasons) would frown upon an athlete if he drank wine with
his dinner. Again it is perhaps a question of normality. The
world, or a large part of it, accepts wine as a normal form of
nourishment: drugs are abnormal. Human instincts here,
even if not very logical, are sound. The world would think
less of its explorers and adventurers if they tried to accomplish
their feats under the influence of drugs; and if they were drug-
sodden they would not accomplish them. Drugs, though they
may enhance performance for a time, are destructive. The
Ulysses factor in man is of value to survival, and it is bio-
logically important that the best Ulysses types should be
physically unimpaired for breeding. The instinct which
counters physical impairment from drugs is a good biological
precaution. It is inherent in the Ulysses complex and there is
an interesting manifestation of this instinct in the type-figure.
Having landed on one strange coast, Ulysses sent two men
inland to have a look at the country. They fell in with a tribe
of lotus-eaters and did not come back. Ulysses continues the
record:

> As soon as each had eaten the honeyed fruit of the plant
> all thoughts of reporting to us or escaping were banished
> from his mind. All they now wished for was to stay where
> they were with the lotus-eaters, to browse on the lotus, and
> to forget that they had a home to return to. I had to use
> force to bring them back to the ships, and they wept on the
> way, but once on board I dragged them under the benches

and left them in irons. I then commanded the rest of my loyal band to embark with all speed, for fear that others of them might eat the lotus.

Ulysses has no thought of experimenting with the lotus himself: he recognises it for the dangerous thing it is, and his concern is to rescue his men who have taken it before they become addicted, and to preserve the rest of his band from temptation to use the drug. The first Ulysses, however, evinced no reluctance to drink wine, a characteristic shared by most of those who have followed him—illogical, maybe, but good human sense.

The Ulysses factor, then, though it will certainly undergo further modification as time goes on, is likely to continue to seek expression in action within man's personal physical capacity. The excitements of space-travel are not a substitute for this: they may even intensify the need in man for activities to prove to himself that he can still live at firsthand, travel at firsthand, discover things physically for himself. Admiration for cosmonauts will not diminish admiration for a Tilman or a Ridgway. The sense of wonder these travellers on earth invoke will remain a human need, unlikely to be satisfied by the technological marvels of space-travel. To return to my angels, the medieval mind found no difficulty in accepting angels because they are beings who accomplish ordinary things in superhuman, but not non-human, ways. If you had to cross a ford in flood and were lucky enough to meet an angel he would not miraculously waft you across; he would put you on his shoulders and carry you across, striding through the flood with superhuman strength. St Frideswide, escaping from her pursuers at Oxford, fled to the Thames to find a boat with an angel at the oars. The boat did not glide miraculously over the water. The angel rowed her downstream to Abingdon, remarkably quickly, but still by the use of oars. Such things are outside the ordinary run of life, but still readily comprehensible.

Therefore they both evoke a sense of wonder, and satisfy it. There was little surprise in the world's response to man's landing on the moon because incomprehensible result followed incomprehensible cause with a sort of inevitability. The technologists had said that men would go to the moon, and men duly went, or were sent. The rockets and the weight-lessness and the systems that 'go' are non-human, miracles that are yet non-miracles because there is enough technology in the modern climate of thought for people to know that if the right chemicals are mixed, the right machinery constructed, the right buttons pressed at the right moment, then the planned consequences will follow. On a good railway system there is more surprise when a train is late than when it runs on time. In fact, it is much more remarkable for trains to be on time than to run late, but the technological success of run-ning to a timetable occasions no surprise because success is expected of technology. There is no emotional satisfaction in flicking a switch to get electric light: there is in striking a match to light a candle. *I* light a candle; the electric light that comes when I touch a switch is the product of collective in-genuity, clever, wonderfully well organised, an extraordinary achievement, but I do not feel that it is anything to do with me.

If Knox-Johnston can do this I could do it, perhaps... But rocketry is nothing to do with me. I am not diminishing the marvels of rocketry, nor the sheer brilliance of conception and execution in this advanced technology. What I am saying is that it does not satisfy, and will not satisfy, the personal need in man for physical adventure. A man making a landfall after a long voyage in a small boat, or standing on a lonely moun-tain top which he has reached by his own effort, will continue to evoke wonder, to excite and to inspire.

The story of the first Ulysses has been read and listened to for nearly three thousand years, and mankind will not tire of it. He may be larger than life, but he is never non-human. He meets gods and giants and ogresses, but he meets them on human terms. He adventures to Hades to meet the dead, but the ghosts are still vivid with the humanity they once wore.

> And now the souls of the dead who had gone below came swarming up from Erebus—fresh brides, umarried youths, old men with life's long suffering behind them, tender young girls still nursing this first anguish in their hearts and a great throng of warriors killed in battle, their spear-wounds gaping yet and all their armour stained with blood.

This is what we need to know. I am not suggesting that we need a conception of an after-life in which the stains of poor humanity remain visible. But if our heroes do extraordinary things we need to be able to feel with them, and we can accompany them in imagination only to the extent that they report the unfamiliar in familiar terms. The extraordinary journey of Ulysses to 'the deep-flowing River of Ocean and the frontiers of the world' would be as incomprehensible as rocketry but for the *ordinariness* of his description, and of his actions. When he left Hades:

> I made off quickly to my ship and told my men to embark and loose the hawsers. They climbed in at once and took their seats on the benches, and the current carried her down the River of Ocean, helped by our oars at first, and later by a friendly breeze.

These are actions as ordinary as setting off for a voyage down the Thames. They make real an incredible adventure and satisfy the sense of wonder which man needs to live.

Three thousand years or so later the extraordinary is made real by Chichester in precisely the same way. He is approaching the end of his first singlehanded crossing of the Atlantic:

> At 1.30 pm as I decided to eat lunch, a faint breeze livened up, and I did not get a meal till twelve and a half hours later.

Nothing could convey reality better than that. We can *hear* the splash of the oars 'helping the current' as Ulysses gets away from Hades; we feel hungry with Chichester over that missed lunch. We do not need to *believe* in Hades, but we have been there, too.

If space-travel extends the range of Ulysses type adventuring by providing a way to non-human worlds in which man can survive as an individual, what turn will the Ulysses impulse in man take then? We have the answer in Hades. As long as man can get somewhere by his own physical action, survive by his own physical effort, the Ulysses impulse will respond as it does on earth. A canoe voyage on Mars, the exploration of a Martian range of mountains, would be just as exciting, and emotionally satisfying as anything on earth. For the next few decades the space-journey to get to Mars would make an interesting first chapter, then it would be dismissed, 'I took the afternoon space-flight from Houston, arriving at the Earth Terminal on Mars without incident.'

As soon as Ulysses can go to Mars on his own he will go, and the rest of us will listen to his tales and read his books with the enchantment that we have always followed his wanderings on earth. He can travel in a non-human world, and still nourish our sense of wonder by the stuff of his own humanity. It does not follow that the impulse to adventure on earth will diminish because there is adventure to be found on Mars. If the impulse to adventure is true, and the eyes fresh, there is exploring to be done on the Berkshire Downs or the headwaters of the Thames. Ridgway and Blyth's achievement in rowing the Atlantic was not lessened by the fact that it had been rowed before. The crowds which flocked to Plymouth to welcome home Chichester were not concerned that Joshua Slocum had sailed round the world singlehanded before this century began. The impulse is in the man, and the response to the man. Obviously repetition stales. The once-great adventure of the Singlehanded Transatlantic Race has been organised into an event in the world's yachting calendar, a tough ocean race, probably still the toughest in the world, but now like the Fastnet Race—considered when it was mooted to be foolhardy almost to the point of meriting condemnation a respectable challenge to the enterprising sailor. Nevertheless, there will be other small-boat voyages in the Atlantic that touch the world's imagination. The Ulysses factor will continue to move man to exploits and expeditions in known seas, each adding something to physical knowledge and to knowledge of man himself.

There remains the unexplored half—or rather more than half—of this world itself. I have said that by the end of the eighteenth century the surface pattern of the globe was fairly well established. What of the world beneath the sea? Save for the shallower edges of the continental shelves, the sea-bed is as unknown still as it was a million years ago. It is curious to reflect that man has walked on the moon before he has walked on the sea-bed of the Atlantic a mere two miles down. In fact, it is more difficult to descend two miles at sea than to travel a quarter of a million miles through space: the pressure of water even a short distance below the surface brings problems of survival more severe than those in airless space. Weight-lessness can be endured: crushing cannot. Deep-sea diving, even to the relatively shallow depths so far reached, demands technological sustenance for man comparable to that needed to travel in space. Dr William Beebe and a few others have adventured to remarkable depths in immensely strong bathy-spheres, but man is still at the stage of studying the depths of his own world from the windows of capsules—he cannot yet walk on the ocean floor. The technological requirements of deep-sea exploration have inhibited the Ulysses impulse as they inhibit its expression in space travel: it is a collective adventure, not yet a personal one. But individual man is going deeper. The aqua-lung has given him a new freedom of underwater exploration, not yet very deep exploration, but it has opened a new world. The work of Jacques Cousteau and his disciples has made possible personal physical experi-ence of the hidden landscape beneath coastal waters and in shallow seas, a region rich in beauty and exciting in discovery. And in re-discovery—underwater archaeology is adding steadily to knowledge of man's past, of the ships he sailed two thousand years ago, of the cargoes he carried, of his ways as a merchant, of his way of life. There is a wonderful field here for Ulysses-type adventure, and it has already motivated the Ulysses impulse. Cousteau is clearly influenced by the Ulysses factor, and the strength of underwater appeal to the Ulysses instinct in man is shown by the numbers who join diving clubs to enter this exciting world. Women seem to be as strongly attracted to underwater exploration as men, an in-teresting example of the response of the female Ulysses com-plex to an activity in which muscular strength is less impor-tant than skill, cool-headedness and staying power. It is pos-sible to lift weights or to move with a heavy pack *in* water in ways that would be out of the question on land.

At present the deep sea-bed is as inimical to man as any-where on the moon: he can survive only by taking his own air or oxygen, his whole body enclosed in a pressure-resisting cover, not much less complex to design and make than the moon-suits woven for cosmonauts. But this is a technological challenge, and the technologist's record in meeting challenge is astonishingly successful. Although it may be as difficult to get man to the ocean floor as to get him to the moon—or perhaps more difficult—if the problem of survival can be overcome the journey will be a great deal shorter, and should be a great deal cheaper. The supporting army of technologists will be required primarily in design and experiment. If free-moving deep-sea suits can be developed, enabling man to explore the sea-bed without attachment to a diving vessel, as he can explore now in shallow waters, the field of new adventure on the terrestrial globe will be limitless. There are underwater mountains to be climbed—or descended—unknown creatures to be discovered, almost an unknown universe still to be explored on earth.

Space-exploration is a major human enterprise related to the Ulysses factor in man, owing something to it, but not itself —at least in its present form—a direct manifestation of the factor. Rather similar considerations apply to manifestation of the factor in the older human enterprise of war. When the history of space exploration comes to be written there will be incidents in which the Ulysses factor in individuals may be seen to have played a decisive part in determining an event. Military history offers many examples of this. But war is not an expression of the factor, though warfare has often been influenced by it. War both masks the emergence of the factor and creates opportunities for its emergence. This must now be examined.

VI

The factor in war

WAR is essentially a collective activity, whole nations being involved on one side or the other, but wars may be won or lost by individual performance. The type-figure was a splendid soldier in the Trojan war, loyal, brave, full of contrivance and a master of his weapons, particularly of the bow. He was always getting mentioned in dispatches. But War is not the natural setting for the factor to work in. Its motivation is to *individual* action, and although there are many individual missions in war, they cannot be wholly individual: those who take part in them are subject to command, not the self-imposed obedience that the member of a voluntary expedition gives to his leader, but a discipline external to a man himself. Instincts in war are often herd-instincts, and motives to action may be patriotism, hate, revenge and other such powerful human passions which have nothing to do with the Ulysses factor. Nevertheless, the fact can be manifest in war as in peace, prompting men to undertake commando raids, reconnaissance deep into enemy territory, small-boat missions from submarines and the like. The spy as such is not a Ulysses type, but there may be many Ulysses characteristics in the successful spy.

All really great soldiers must have something of the Ulysses factor in them, recognise it in other men and be able to use it in others. Wavell provides an interesting example of this in responding to Orde Wingate's unorthodox proposals for operations in Burma, and in the imaginative backing he gave to Wingate. But this is the factor as a secondary influence in great campaigns, itself influenced by many other considerations, political, military, naval and economic. Its more typical manifestation is in the incident in war, as this example from the type-figure shows.

The Greek forces besieging Troy had been badly mauled by a sortie from the city, and at nightfall had withdrawn to their ships in considerable anxiety. Their leaders were not sure whether the Trojans proposed to renew the assault next day, nor, if the Trojans did attack in force, whether the Greeks could hold their ships. The Trojans had recently been reinforced by the arrival of allies, particularly a strong contingent of Thracians. Agamemnon, the Greek Commander-in-Chief called a night council of his regimental commanders. A raid on the Trojan camp by a small force under cover of darkness was suggested, with the two aims of reconnoitring the Trojan positions and creating confusion. A man called Diomedes at once volunteered to go, and several others, including Ulysses, also volunteered. It was decided to limit the expedition to two, and Diomedes was invited to choose his companion. He picked Ulysses, observing, 'He and I could go through blazing fire and yet come home. He has the quickest brain of any man I know.'

Ulysses was slightly impatient at the speechmaking, replying that there was no need to sing his praises and that it was time they started or there would not be any night left. So they set off, both with a prayer to Athene.

The Trojans, however, were also planning a night-raid, and sent out one Dolon to make a surprise attack on Agamemnon's headquarters, offering him—somewhat rashly—the famous horses of Achilles as a reward. To obtain the horses the Trojans would have had first to deal with Achilles.

Diomedes was nominally in command of the Greek raid, but their plan of action was concocted by Ulysses. They saw a shadowy figure—Dolon—moving towards the Greek lines, and Ulysses persuaded Diomedes not to attempt to seize him at once but to let him pass. Then they would be between the raider and the Trojan camp and could cut him off. This they did. They allowed him to pass safely and then pursued him, so that he had to run *towards* the Greek camp. They captured and questioned him. Dolon broke down and poured out information about the Trojan dispositions, even specifying the exact location of the Thracian newcomers, in an attempt to save his life. This did not work. He was considered too dangerous to let go, and Diomedes killed him. Then Diomedes and Ulysses made their way to the Thracian encampment, where they found these valuable reinforcements to the Trojan army, tired after their march to Troy, sleeping unsuspectingly. They wrought havoc among them, killed their leader and got away with a particularly fine string of Thracian horses. In recounting this episode Homer says of Ulysses 'Adventure was always dear to him.'

That night-raid on the Trojan camp shows all the qualities of the Ulysses complex, daring, quick-thinking determination and faith in a divine power to help if they acted as well as they could themselves. It was essentially an individual mission. Ulysses and Diomedes were on their own. They were sent out at the instance of the Commander-in-Chief, but they had no specific orders, their sole instruction being to make themselves as much of a nuisance to the enemy as they could. How they were to make a nuisance of themselves was left to them. It was quick thinking by Ulysses that made a plan as soon as they spotted an enemy raider coming towards them. The interrogation of Dolon, described in detail by Homer, was carried out by Ulysses, and brilliantly done. The killing of Dolon strikes harshly across the centuries, but it was war: he would have killed Ulysses and Diomedes if he could. The decision to direct the raid against the Thracians was imaginative and bold. They were the latest arrivals on the Trojan side, and their discomfiture might deter other potential allies. They were the freshest troops, and therefore formidable, but they had only just arrived and might be caught while they were fatigued after their march—as they were. The raid paid rich dividends for no loss at all.

On another critical occasion Ulysses intervened decisively. A counter-attack by the Trojans under Hector had penetrated the outer defences of the beach on which the Greek ships were drawn up. This bridgehead was all important to the Greeks. The Trojan aim was to set the ships on fire: if it succeeded, then the Greeks were lost. Agamemnon felt that Zeus was against them and that it was futile to continue. He said to his captains:

There is nothing for it—you must all do as I say. Let us drag down the ships that were drawn up next to the sea, launch them on the good salt water, and moor them well out until the friendly night allows us to drag down all the

rest—unless the Trojans go on fighting even then. There is
nothing to be ashamed of in running from disaster, even by
night. It is better to save one's skin by running than to be
caught.

Ulysses, who had been wounded, turned savagely on the
Commander-in-Chief:

> My lord, this is preposterous... You had better hold your
> tongue, or the men may get wind of this idea of yours,
> which nobody with any sense in his head would even have
> put into words. You can have no brains at all to have made
> such a suggestion—to expect us, in the middle of a pitched
> battle, to drag our ships into the sea and put the Trojans,
> who have beaten us already, in an even better position to
> do exactly as they like with us and wipe out the whole ex-
> pedition. Do you imagine that our men are going to keep a
> steady front while their ships are being dragged down into
> the sea? They will do nothing, but look behind them, and
> lose all heart for the fight. That will be the disastrous effect
> of your tactics.

Agamemnon acknowledged the rebuke, and changed his
mind. It is a fortunate commander who has a lieutenant unafraid to speak out. In truth the plan would have been disastrous: it would have meant not defeat but rout. Ulysses
understood immediately that once the Greeks broke off the
action they were finished: his instinct to look over a hill
showed him what lay on the far side of that particular slope.
So the Greeks fought on, to hold their bridgehead, and in the
end to win the war. The incident—ultimately decisive to the
Greek cause—shows several Ulysses characteristics. One could
not convict Agamemnon of cowardice. He was hard pressed
and, as he put it fairly enough, there are times when it is not
ignoble to run away. He was thinking of his men as much as
of himself, and his thinking was dominated by fear for the
ships. But his plan was poor generalship: this was one occasion when the only defence of the ships was to go on trying to
hold the bridgehead. Ulysses was wounded but tired as he was,
he could still think quickly, and he saw beyond the order
to launch the ships to the disorder that would come as soon as

the Trojans threw themselves on men struggling to get their heavy boats into the water. Half the Greeks would not even have weapons: they would be holding ropes and gear. His rebuke to the Commander-in-Chief showed imagination as well as courage. More typical still, he showed his own quality of endurance and refusal to give up as long as there was *any* chance of coming through. He did not minimise the seriousness of their position—'The Trojans have beaten us already.' But he reckoned that there was still fight left in the Greeks and that it was the job of their leaders to encourage them to go on fighting. The event showed that he was right.

This, however, is an example of the Ulysses *character* in war rather than of the Ulysses *factor* at work: a mathematician may apply himself to the laying out of a tennis court, using his mathematical qualities, no doubt, but without acting in any special way as a mathematician. Survival in war, and the achievement, if possible, of victory, are demanding activities, calling for the use, if not for the special development, of most qualities in a man. It may be adventure of a different sort, but for a time there is enough adventure, and the Ulysses factor is likely to be quiescent. There is little scope for private activity in war, and men who might be moved to action of their own by the Ulysses factor in them have other work to do. Thus David Lewis served with the Airborne Division, Tilman in half a dozen different theatres of war, Heyerdahl trained to work with the Norwegian resistance, Manry was in the United States Army. The *special* activity of the factor in man almost requires peace, or at least conditions—which may sometimes occur in war—where a man may properly be on his own. Some of the finest manifestations of the factor in war have been in escape from captivity by prisoners of war. Again, however, other driving forces are at work as well.

On a grand scale, the factor in men who have also been leaders of nations has helped to determine history. Alexander the Great was moved by the Ulysses factor in him as well as by the desire for conquest. The driving force that took him to India was at least in part a compulsion to find out for himself what lay beyond each river to which he came. He commissioned exploration, sending his admiral Nearchus to investigate the sea route from India to the Persian Gulf. Of course he was concerned strategically as well, wanting as much geographical knowledge as he could get for the communications and defence of his empire. But he wanted to know for himself, too. He was the greater general for the strength of the Ulysses factor in him. So with Julius Caesar. There were sound military reasons for his invasion of Britain: the tribal leaders with whom he was engaged in Gaul were getting aid from across the Channel, and were finding refuge there when he made things too hot for them at home. The allies of Gaul in Britain needed a taste of Roman power; it was difficult to hold Gaul with an unsubdued Britain on his flank. Nevertheless, the invasion of Britain was a formidable undertaking. The Belgic tribes in Britain were a nuisance, but they could be contained on their own side of the Channel, and an intensification of his policy of reprisals and political alliances might work: it would be cheaper and less risky than a seaborne invasion of a scarcely known coast.

Caesar had good reasons for invading Britain, but reasons for not doing so that many military and political leaders might have found better. The Ulysses factor in him turned the scale and sent him across the Channel. History offers many more examples. Wolfe's capture of Quebec was almost pure Ulysses, and the factor was strong in British military leaders in India, particularly in Clive, Wellesley (later Duke of Wellington) and Lawrence. In the still greater sweep of history the Mongol invaders who came out of Central Asia to conquer northern India, much of the Middle East and eastern Europe were at least partly influenced by the Ulysses factor in man.

But the complex of human causes in such great historical movements is too vast for analysis here. One can identify the factor in individuals now and then, and one can say that it certainly influenced many of the men and some of the women, who have determined the political and economic history of mankind. But the degree of influence varies, and the Ulysses factor as a prime driving force in man is often lost in the immediacy of political opportunity, the pressure of expanding populations and the sheer lust for power and conquest.

The factor may be a component in military adventure, and in military success, but it is not itself a military attribute. Indeed, its greater importance to mankind is in prompting non-military alternatives to men's emotional need of adventure.

VII

Some Modern Explorers

HAVING identified the Ulysses factor in mankind and examined some of its historical manifestations, its appearance in men of our own time requires analysis. Who are the modern explorers? Words here need definition. Columbus was an explorer, and so was Galileo. In its deepest sense, man's instinct to *discover*, physically or intellectually, is one, but intellectual discovery may or may not require physical action. The Ulysses factor is the impulse to seek knowledge by physical experience at first hand, the impulse to go to look for something. The scientist in his laboratory may be concerned to find physical proof of his theories, but his voyages of discovery are in his mind. There is a related factor, perhaps it might be called the Archimedes factor, prompting man to scientific investigation, but it is not the Ulysses factor.

Opportunities for scientific discovery have multiplied with the centuries—there has been no need of mutation. The impulse to physical exploration has undergone mutation. Its power in man has not diminished. The modern explorer of the terrestrial world has no longer continents to find or seas to cross for the first time, but secondary exploration of man's behaviour or *capacity* to survive in a strange environment is an urge as compelling as that which sent the first seafarers to adventure in strange seas. Mountaineers, small-boat sailors, some fliers, some who force cars across roadless deserts are explorers in precisely the same sense as the explorers of antiquity: their instincts are the same, the Ulysses factor in them is the same. Great mountaineers or small-boat sailors, Shipton and Tilman, Knox-Johnston and Robert Manry, for instance, are explorers comparable with the great ones of the past, with Amundsen, Cook and Leif Eiriksson. If there had been a Pole left to discover, Francis Chichester would have driven himself to be the first to reach it. Lacking a Pole, his achievement in his own way is comparable with a series of great Polar journeys. So is Tilman's, and there are a number of other men whose individual exploits show the vitality and strength of the Ulysses factor in its modern forms.

Sometimes a scholar and a man of action have been combined in one individual, the Archimedes factor and the Ulysses factor both strongly influencing one man. Sir Walter Raleigh, Sir Richard Burton and the first Lord Wavell are examples of this. The mutation of the Ulysses factor may encourage this combination in ways that are both novel and valuable to mankind, particularly in the physical reconstruction of man's past. Thor Heyerdahl made his own great raft voyage because he wanted to reconstruct what he believed to have been similar raft voyages in the Pacific in the prehistoric past. In a minor way, we who sailed in a small boat to Green land and North America in 1966 in an attempt to reconstruct Leif Eiriksson's voyage of a thousand years before us were similarly moved.

The personal studies that follow are selected to illustrate particular manifestations of the Ulysses factor in individuals since the end of the Second World War. They imply no league-table of merit: I have omitted exploits as great or greater than those I have included. To some extent all selection must be arbitrary, but I have tried to select exploits which seem to me to bring out most clearly certain defined Ulysses characteristics in those who made them. I have not been much concerned with 'firsts', 'highests' and the like. It is interesting that Maurice Herzog's climb on Annapurna achieved the first summit over 26,000 ft to be reached by man, but the behaviour of Herzog and his companions on their mountain is more significant by far. Where superlatives are relevant I have recorded them, but these are not studies in superlatives. They are studies of an age-old exploring *factor* in mankind manifest in the actions of individuals of the middle twentieth century. I have included a note on my own voyage in *Griffin* not from conceit but because it has enabled me to write at firsthand of certain moods and feelings that are relevant to my study. Elsewhere I have done my best to be objective. I have been happy to know personally some of the individuals concerned in these studies, but except in writing

G

of David Lewis, where I have drawn on personal conversations directly concerned with the material of my study, I have been careful to quote only from published sources, so that judgments and inferences can be checked.

VIII

The adventurous scholar—Thor Heyerdahl

In most of the world in 1947 the dominant feeling was of relief rather than of hope. The war, or at least the major fighting, was ended, but the appalling destruction of it, physical, political and moral, remained visible everywhere. A rationed, greyish life could go on without much immediate danger: there was little to inspire confidence in man's capacity to do much better. In this setting a 32-year-old Norwegian with five companions succeeded in drifting across the Pacific on a raft of balsa-wood. They were not castaways; they launched their raft to drift across an ocean. Their voyage had a purpose: it was intended to prove the practicability of a theory of prehistoric migration from the west coast of South America to Polynesia. Its achievement showed a war-sickened world that men could cheerfully risk their lives without orders, for the simple reason that they wanted to try to find out something or other of no importance whatever to politics or economics.

Next to nothing is known of the relations between Ulysses and his parents, although there is much to indicate that these were unusual. A study of forebears is important to the understanding of any manifestation of a genetic factor in the individual. The Ulysses factor seldom manifests itself strongly in both father and son, and its transmission from one generation to the next is highly complex. But it *is* transmitted, and when an individual is powerfully affected by it its influence is strong from infancy. The parent–child relationship is likely to have a direct bearing on the forms it takes in the child as he grows up. Ulysses's mother, Anticleia, died while he was taking part in the Trojan war. His father, Laertes, was still living on Ithaca when Ulysses returned some nineteen or twenty years after leaving home. Ulysses seems to have been an only son, though he had a sister, Ctimene, and there may have been other children, for Ctimene is once referred to as Anticleia's 'youngest' child, which implies that she had more than two. But the reference is rather vague. Half brothers or sisters would have been common at that period in ancient Greece, for men naturally took concubines. But Laertes seems to have been high-principled in these matters, and he is recorded as having refrained from sleeping with a particularly attractive girl slave for fear of hurting his wife's feelings.

The sister, Ctimene, is not important in the story: she was brought up with a young slave in the household to whom Anticleia showed great kindness, and not, it seems, with her brother. She was married off young. Laertes, Anticleia and Ulysses seem to have been on good terms throughout their lives. But *why* did Laertes abdicate? He had been a warrior of note, and in old age was still capable of fighting gamely by the side of his son. But in his son's long absence from home he seems to have made little attempt to protect the kingdom from the depredations of the would-be usurpers who sought to marry Ulysses's wife Penelope and acquire his possessions with her. Ulysses himself was believed dead, but Laertes had his grandson's rights to protect, to say nothing of his own. Instead of putting up a fight, he retired to the life of a gentleman farmer, and after Anticleia's death he seems to have gone to pieces. Yet Ulysses retained respect as well as affection for him. One may speculate. The old man may have been pretty useless at administration, and he may have been glad enough to hand over the throne to a vigorous and able Crown Prince. Laertes had fought well in his time, but his personal interests seem to have been mainly with his garden. Ulysses respected good farming, and was proud of his own ability to plough a straight furrow. There must have been many qualities in Laertes to respect, although his spineless behaviour during his son's absence remains inexplicable. It also seems strange that he was not murdered: those who were after his son's throne would scarcely have wanted him around, even though he had abdicated. The fact that he was not murdered suggests either a general contempt for him as a sort of half-wit or that there was something in him to retain men's respect. Temporary insanity in Laertes would explain the assumption of kingship by

Ulysses, while remaining on good terms with his father, but although this is an attractive theory, there is no evidence to suggest it. Ulysses was an exceptionally able son, and there was some quality exceptional about his father: that is as far as one can go.

Study of the Ulysses factor in Thor Heyerdahl is of particular interest because his boyhood, and his relations with his parents, have been recorded at firsthand by a sensitive Norwegian writer, Arnold Jacoby, who was at school with Heyerdahl. Parent–child relationships emerge to some extent in autobiographies such as Chichester's *The Lonely Sea and the Sky*, but an objective study by a childhood friend who is both a good observer and a good reporter is of rare value. My study of Thor Heyerdahl owes much to Arnold Jacoby, although, of course, inferences and conclusions are my own.

Heyerdahl was born at Larvik in 1914, the youngest child of a complicated family, his father having been married twice, his mother three times. Heyerdahl senior was 45 when Thor was born, his mother 41. There were children by his parents' previous marriages, but they were considerably older than Thor, and he grew up almost as an only child. Neither parent could have been easy to live with, and when Thor was about 14 they separated. But it was a civilised separation, with no tussle over their son. He continued to live with his mother, but saw his father frequently. It is significant that he dedicated his book *The Kon-Tiki Expedition* to his father.

Heyerdahl senior was a prosperous businessman, who owned and ran the local brewery. He married Thor's mother, Alison, after divorce from his first wife. It required considerable social courage to remarry after divorce and to continue living in the same small town in Norway before the First World War. Both parents had such courage. They ignored gossip and lived as they wanted to live. Whatever may have been thought about his personal life, Heyerdahl senior had a good reputation as a businessman, and those who worked for him at the brewery considered him a good employer. In his business life he showed qualities of firm but unobtrusive leadership, qualities which certainly showed themselves again in his son.

Fru Alison Heyerdahl was an extremely intelligent and often extremely unhappy woman. Her own mother, a neurotic invalid, died when Alison was 6, and the rest of her childhood alternated between severe discipline under very strict aunts and freedom to do as she liked in the home of a pleasant and laughter-loving uncle. As a young woman she spent a year in England, where she was much influenced by the writings on evolution of Charles Darwin.

At some time in her early childhood she apparently heard her invalid mother invoking God to release her from a miserable and painful life, and this made an appalling impression on the child. When her mother did die she turned violently against the idea of God, an attitude reinforced by her later conversion to Darwinism. She grew up wilful, intolerant and full of fads, but also vivacious, attractive and with an abiding interest in natural history. In her forties, when Thor was born, she was a bewildering mixture of emotional intensity and free thinking. She combined severe household rules of physical behaviour with what she regarded as freedom to live one's own life. Physical cleanliness was a mania, and so were health rules. Thor was permitted only goats' milk, and there was an inflexible law that he must go to the lavatory the moment he got out of bed. When the household was roused in the middle of the night because of a serious fire in the street Thor—then 8—had to make a pilgrimage to the lavatory before there could be any thought of leaving the house. With all this she devoted herself to teaching her son about natural history and evolution, taking him almost as a baby to museums, and giving him models of prehistoric animals as toys.

Through this strange childhood Thor turned for affection to his father and to his elderly nurse, who was very good to him. For all his apparent worldliness, his father had a simple faith in Christianity, which, in a gentle, kindly way, he tried to share with his son. To the irritation of his wife, he taught Thor the Lord's Prayer and encouraged the little boy to talk over his hopes and fears with God. Thor's mother dismissed his father's teachings as so much nonsense.

A genetic factor cannot be inculcated, and this brief digression on Thor Heyerdahl's upbringing does not imply that the Ulysses characteristics so strongly manifested in him later were *due* to his somewhat peculiar childhood. But a human charac-

teristic can be much modified—even suppressed—by upbringing, and the *form* of Heyerdahl's later life was certainly
moulded by his childhood. A study of his parentage is also
interesting for the light it throws on the transmission of the
Ulysses factor. Neither his father nor his mother had that
compelling urge to physical discovery which motivated their
son, but both were unusual people, of marked individuality,
and with able, questioning minds. Within this human compound, which they, in turn, had inherited, going back, perhaps, to remote Viking ancestors, lay the germ which developed so remarkably in their son. There is not enough information on the boyhood of the type-figure to detect similar-
ities between Laertes and Anticleia and Thor Heyerdahl's
parents: there need not, of course, be any close parallel.
What is significant is that the little we know of Ulysses'
parents indicates that they were unusual people and that the
characteristics by which Ulysses has come to be identified
must have been influenced by an unusual boyhood. The
known facts of Heyerdahl's parentage and boyhood are a
striking illustration of an unusual childhood accompanying
development of the Ulysses factor.

The qualities that fit a man for physical exploration are not
necessarily helpful in coming to terms with the rest of life. In
the ancient world the Ulysses-characteristics of curiosity,
quick-wittedness and endurance were likely to be of direct
value to their possessor in achieving material success. In the
more complex society of the modern world the same qualities
may be inimical to material success, for the cost of direct
action for no obviously commercial purpose may exceed its
rewards. Moreover, the Ulysses mind is inclined to
impatience with formal study, and although a capacity for self-
instruction may be of the utmost value in a tight situation on
an expedition, it does not help to acquire the bits of paper
that are passports to academic recognition. Heyerdahl showed,
and suffered from, this impatience to get on with learning at
firsthand. His mother's interest in natural history and his
early introduction to museums determined his own bent, and
almost from infancy he showed a scientific interest in zoology.
This continued throughout his school life, and in 1933, when

he was 19, he went to the University of Oslo to study zoology. He did not find undergraduate study satisfying. He developed quickly, and his own preference was for long expeditions to the Norwegian mountains to study animal and insect life on the spot. He began to detest urban living, and his love of mountains and wild places prompted a somewhat juvenile 'Back to Nature' philosophy by which he concluded that happiness was to be found in the abandonment of all modern devices and a return to primitive life. He fell in love with a girl student at the university, and when he was 22 they married and went off to the South Seas to attempt a 'Back to Nature' experiment on Fatu Hiva, an island in the Marquesas.

The experiment was immensely important to them, but it was not in itself a success. They found that they did not greatly like eating sea-slugs raw. As Norwegian Protestants they fell foul of a Roman Catholic missionary on the island, who set the islanders against them. Their experiment required that they should take no medicines or medical equipment with them, and they became infected with serious tropical sores. They stuck it for just over a year, and then they had to make a hazardous small-boat voyage to another island in search of medical treatment. After this they came home.

Although, in a sense, this was a failure, it was the starting-point of Heyerdahl's personal mission in life. On Fatu Hiva he came across some old stone carvings, apparently unrelated to any known Marquesan culture. His interests turned from zoology to anthropology and ethnography, and he returned to Norway determined to find some explanation of Polynesian origins. He had first, however, to make a living. His wife was expecting their first child, and he had to have some sort of income. He contrived this by journalism and lecturing on life in the Pacific. After one of these lectures a man showed him photographs of some rock carvings in the Bella Coola valley, on the Pacific coast of North America. These struck him as remarkably similar to the carvings he had come across in the Marquesas.

From then on Heyerdahl became obsessed with his theories of ocean migration by primitive peoples. With kindly help from a Norwegian shipowner who had been a friend of his father's, he got cheap passages for himself, his wife and their infant son to Vancouver, and he set off for firsthand exploration of the Bella Coola valley. That was in 1939. Soon afterwards Norway was invaded, and he was cut off from his slender source of income from writing for Norwegian newspapers.

After much difficulty he was able to get a work-permit in Canada, and he became a manual labourer to support his wife and child. His aim, however, was to join the Norwegian Army, and after various adventures he managed this, volunteering for training as a parachutist for resistance work in his beloved Norwegian mountains.

As soon as he could get out of the Army after the war he set to work on a book outlining his theory on trans-Pacific migration, and in 1946 he went back to America to try to get support for his researches. He was not successful. His theories involved anthropology, archaeology, ethnology and the history of navigation, and he had no proper academic qualifications in any of these subjects. Experts regarded him as a crank, and when they bothered to see him told him firmly that his theories were impossible because prehistoric Americans had no boats conceivably capable of crossing the Pacific.

Ulysses challenged is a formidable figure. Heyerdahl's own studies had convinced him that it was entirely feasible for the Pacific to be crossed in the big dug-out canoes used by the Bella Coola Indians, or on the balsa-wood rafts used on the Peruvian coast before the Spanish conquest. Ocean currents went the right way, and provided that men could keep afloat, there was no natural obstacle to migration from the west coast of the American continent to Polynesia. He had become particularly interested in Peru, for he was convinced that the Peruvian sun-god Kon-Tiki was identical with Tiki, the ancestral tribal god of Polynesia. In Peruvian legend, Kon-Tiki and his followers were defeated in a battle on Lake Titicaca, after which they made their way to the coast and disappeared to the west. Heyerdahl believed that this legend recorded the departure of a body of people from Peru who ultimately reached Polynesia. If no one else believed that this was possible he would build a raft for himself, float off from the Peruvian coast and find out. Heyerdahl's friend and biographer, Arnold Jacoby, describes the preliminary discussions on this plan:

Liv (Heyerdahl's wife) thought the plan was madness, and so did I. Couldn't the same point be proved by setting a bottle adrift? Certainly not. The point to be established was that *men on a balsa raft* (Jacoby's italics) could have surmounted all the obstacles and dangers that a voyage across this precise stretch of sea involved.*

Heyerdahl's reaction to the bottle suggestion was pure Ulysses. What mattered was *to find out at firsthand.*

Heyerdahl made his voyage in 1947. On April 28 1947 a balsa-wood raft named *Kon-Tiki* was towed from Callao into the Humboldt current and cast adrift. Heyerdahl and five companions were on board. On August 3 one of the crew, Knut Haugland, rowed ashore from the raft in a rubber dinghy to land on the Polynesian island of Angatau. The raft could not make Angatau, so Haugland returned on board and the party drifted on. Three days later the raft was cast up on Raroia reef, and Heyerdahl and his crew all scrambled ashore safely. They had been voluntarily adrift in the Pacific for 100 days.

What, if anything, did this voyage achieve? It is a reasonable question, for, on the face of things, the survival of six men on a well-stocked raft for 100 days proves no more than that men with plenty of food can survive the discomforts of a raft. Since men have survived on rafts in far worse conditions, this does not mean much. To Heyerdahl, the voyage added powerful elements of proof, if it did not directly prove, his theory of the colonisation of Polynesia by trans-Pacific migration from the American continent. This is rather special pleading. The *possibility* of a raft's drifting westwards from America can be determined equally well from a chart marked with known ocean currents; for a practical test a bottle would do as well. The capacity of balsa-wood to stay afloat long enough to reach Polynesia from Peru had also to be proved— one of the arguments against Heyerdahl before he made the *Kon-Tiki* voyage was that balsa-wood absorbs water, so that although it is light and floats well when launched, it is unlikely to stay afloat long enough for an ocean crossing. *Kon-*

* Arnold Jacoby, *Senor Kon-Tiki.* Allen & Unwin 1968.

Tiki disposed of this argument; but it could equally have been met by leaving balsa-logs to absorb sea water in a tank, and observing how long they took to become water-logged and sink.

All such reasoning is irrelevant. Heyerdahl's approach required the physical testing of his theory at firsthand: he wanted to *know* what it felt like to be adrift on a raft for an ocean crossing. His companions on the expedition—Herman Watzinger, Erik Hesselberg, Knut Haugland, Torstein Raaby and Bengt Danielsson—all accepted completely the rightness, indeed the necessity, of the voyage. That it was dangerous must have occurred to them, but this neither deterred nor, I think, specially attracted, any of them. It is not a Ulysses characteristic to seek danger for its own sake: the gambler's delight in dicing with death is a known human attribute, but it is alien to the Ulysses factor. Ulysses took risks when he had to, but he calculated them as well as he could, and took such precautions as he could.

In his approach to risk-taking Heyerdahl showed the typical Ulysses characteristics. Seagoing rafts have long been obsolete on the Peruvian coast, but the *conquistadores* met them and described them. Heyerdahl argued that what had once given sea-keeping qualities to a raft would do so again if the old design were properly followed, so he began by finding out everything he could about the big balsa-wood rafts known to have been used in ancient Peru. Having worked out what he believed to be the old design, he went to enormous trouble to reproduce it. He insisted that his logs should be grown trees, and he went into the jungle to see them cut, although this added greatly to the cost in money and time of preparing his expedition, for he had to penetrate the jungle, and get his cut logs out, in the rainy season.

To reproduce as far as possible prehistoric conditions on his raft he proposed to live as far as possible on what he could get from the sea, on fish and, if necessary, plankton. In the event, he and his crew succeeded in living quite well from the sea, but they took no chances: the raft was well stocked with preserved food and survival rations. Although he could not hope for much assistance if he got into difficulties far from shipping routes in mid-Pacific, again he did what he could, equipping his raft with a good radio, a rubber dinghy and survival equipment. He chose his crew to make up for his own technical deficiencies, recruiting a skilled navigator, an engineer capable of dealing with the scientific measurement of wind forces and suchlike, two competent radio operators, trained to work with the Norwegian resistance during the war and to keep their sets on the air without having to rely on workshop help. On the voyage itself sensible precautions were adopted as ship's (or, rather, raft's) rules: the man on watch was tied on, no one went over the side for a swim without a look-out for sharks, and (after one narrow squeak when a wind sprang up unexpectedly) no one went off in the dinghy to take photographs without a rope. Heyerdahl and his crew learned from experience quickly—another Ulysses characteristic.

The behaviour of these men during their 100 days adrift in the Pacific was everything that Ulysses himself could have asked of an expedition. They embarked together as free men, each voluntarily accepting Heyerdahl's leadership, they landed as friends still. That alone is a considerable achievement among men who have been cooped together for over three months on a platform roughly 30 ft by 18 ft. Heyerdahl's leadership was never obtrusive, but it was nonetheless real: his decisions were accepted as a matter of course. But no decision was taken in an authoritarian manner; everything was discussed, every opinion listened to. This was Ulysses leadership at its best, making the crew a unity greater than the sum of its individuals.

Analysis of incidents on the voyage reveals many Ulysses characteristics in action. Ingenuity is one of them. About halfway across the Pacific the expedition had trouble when one of the vertically hung logs used as centreboards to give the raft stability came adrift from its lashings and floated awkwardly underneath the raft. It could not be reached from the surface, and the only thing to do was to dive down to try to repair it. Herman Watzinger and Knut Haugland were reckoned to be the best divers, so they went overboard and did what they could. But it was difficult to concentrate on working under water because of the presence of sharks. The divers needed some sort of cage to work in.

A raft in mid-ocean offers little in the way of materials or workshop facilities for constructing a diving cage. The crew was not defeated. Erik Hesselberg reflected that a cage was really no more than a basket, and he decided that they *could* make a basket: they had bamboo canes and rope. So they made a diving basket and it worked well. After using the basket to repair the centreboard they used it as an underwater observation chamber, letting each other down in turn to study the underside of the raft and the wealth of marine life congregated there.

There was a fine example of collective cool-headedness when Herman Watzinger fell overboard. A sudden gust of wind caught up a sleeping bag, and in trying to recover it before it went into the sea Herman fell in. This was an immediate crisis. The raft was carried on by the wind, and a man swimming could not hope to catch it. To go about in a well-designed sailing boat to recover a man from the water is hard enough: the raft was not manoeuvrable at all. They tried to throw out a lifebelt on a line, but the wind was too strong: it simply blew it back.

Heyerdahl had an agonising decision to make. He could go after Herman in the rubber dinghy, but with the dinghy held to the raft by a line the sea-anchor effect of the line in the water made it impossible to row astern. He could cast off the line, and the dinghy could then probably be rowed to the man in the water, but whether in a strong wind it could ever be rowed back to the raft was more than doubtful. Nevertheless, this was what he decided to do. He and Bengt Danielsson would take the dinghy to Herman and trust to their combined strength to row it back. 'Three men in a rubber dinghy had some chance, one man in the sea had none,' he wrote laconically afterwards.

The desperate expedient, however, was not necessary. Every man left on the raft understood the predicament, and before the dinghy was cast off Knut Haugland went overboard to try to swim with a line to Herman. He reached him, and by hauling on the line from the raft the men were recovered. The whole crew's reaction to this emergency shows the Ulysses combination of quick-wittedness and precise calculation of the odds. Heyerdahl was responsible for the lives of all on board: he could not order, or even ask, another man to go into the sea after Herman, for even with a line there was a real risk that it would be impossible to haul him back against the wind. For the same reasons he could not dive in himself—that might have been heroic, but it would have been an abdication of leadership. As Ulysses had done when his boat was breaking up under him, he calculated the odds. To cast off in the dinghy involved risk, but it offered at least some chance of success: it was certainly the best action that he, as leader of the expedition, could take. If they could not get back to the raft there would be three of them in the dinghy to share the physical and moral effort of survival, and although there was not much hope of being picked up in mid-Pacific, the raft had radio, and some ship might be able to get to them in time.

Heyerdahl had to think as leader of the expedition. Knut Haugland, however, without Heyerdahl's personal responsibility, could think differently. He knew that he was a powerful swimmer, and if he chose to risk his own life in trying to swim to Herman with a line, that was a decision for himself. He, too, could calculate the odds, but they were based on different risks from Heyerdahl's. So he acted.

No one analysed his thinking in that emergency on the raft —this sort of analysis is only possible afterwards. In action, the thoughts that prompt a man to act come faster than anything the most elaborate of computers can achieve. That Herman was recovered from a raft moving away from him before a rising gale explains precisely how swiftly these men thought and acted. This later analysis of their actions demonstrates how well the theoretical qualities associated with the Ulysses factor in man can work to practical effect.

On their ninety-seventh day out the expedition and their raft were off the island of Angatau, in the Tuamotus. Polynesians in canoes came out to greet them, and they much wanted to get ashore. But the unmanoeuvrable raft could not make a passage in the reef, and as night fell they drifted past the island. Before giving up hope of making Angatau they tried getting a tow from the canoes to assist paddling on the raft, and Knut Haugland went off in the dinghy to add to towing-power. It was no good. They felt that they might be able to make the island with more manpower, and Knut volunteered to row ashore in the dinghy to try to collect more men. Heyerdahl decided against this, feeling that it would be too much of a risk for Knut to attempt in darkness a passage through the reef that he did not know: instead, Heyerdahl

asked Knut, who was still in the dinghy, to bring the leader of
the Polynesians on board the raft, so that he might be asked if
there were any chance of getting more men. Knut rowed off
in the dinghy, but he did not come back. He had found the
leader of the Polynesians, but instead of bringing him back to
the raft he had taken him in the dinghy as pilot through the
reef. Signals by Morse lamp instructing Knut to return had
no effect.

Knut made the island safely. Heyerdahl, who was much
concerned about the difficulty of navigating a rubber dinghy
—not the easiest of craft to steer at any time—in the wild
water of the reef sent a note after him by a Polynesian in a
canoe, saying:

> Take two natives with you in a canoe, with the dinghy in
> tow. Do *not* (Heyerdahl's italics) come back alone.

This note reached Knut on shore. He was in a situation of
considerable difficulty. He had misunderstood Heyerdahl's
instructions about bringing the Polynesian leader to the raft,
and thought that he had obtained permission to navigate the
reef with the leader as guide. He had seen the Morse signals
calling for his return, but at that time the dinghy was making
the actual passage of the reef and the Polynesian was rowing.
He ignored, or did not understand, Knut's attempts to persuade him to row back to the raft. On shore, Knut received a
great welcome, and the islanders wanted to give him a feast.
He tried to get men to go back with him to the dinghy, but no
one wanted to go. Then a canoe came in with Heyerdahl's
note. Knut did his best in Norwegian and English, but no one
wanted to go back to the raft. Finally, by a mixture of shout-
ing and signs promising presents he got three canoe crews
to put out again, and managed to tow the dinghy back
to the raft. The Polynesians were given hurried presents
of cigarettes and made off back to the island. The raft was
blown on to end the voyage on the Raroia reef three days
later.

The Angatau incident is interesting. Heyerdahl completely
accepted the explanation of misunderstood instructions in the
first place, and in his own record of the incident in his book
on the voyage there is no suspicion of doubt or of resentment

at what he might have regarded, at least partly, as defiance of his orders. The record after Knut's return is of unqualified relief at getting him back. Nevertheless, the whole incident demonstrates Heyerdahl's determination to *be* the expedition's leader. When Knut did not return Heyerdahl signalled instructions by Morse, and when his signals brought no result he sent a clear, terse note ashore. Again he had calculated the odds, and in spite of his own and his crew's eagerness to make land after ninety-seven days on the raft, he decided that the chances of getting effective help from the shore were not worth the risk of sending off the dinghy. And he was right. Knut's trip ashore achieved nothing, and the risks were substantial on two fronts. First, there was the risk of danger to Knut himself and the possible loss of the dinghy, which might have imperilled the rest of the raft's crew, and then there was the risk of Knut's being marooned (with the dinghy) on a remote atoll visited by a copra schooner once a year. The raft could not return to Angatau against the wind, and to recover Knut when they did finally make land would be difficult and probably expensive. All ended well, but things might have turned out very badly. Heyerdahl's own judgment was vindicated, and his persistence in sending his note after Knut was what brought the incident to a happy conclusion.

It is a tribute both to Heyerdahl and to Knut and the other members of the crew that there were no ill-feelings. Three days later when the raft voyage came to a violent end with shipwreck on the Raroia reef the performance of everyone on board was a model of how to meet a crisis.

It was a horrible situation to meet at the end of 100 days of surviving all the perils of the Pacific on a raft, but it was made a little easier by the fact that shipwreck on a reef fringing some atoll had always been in their minds as a possible ending to their voyage—indeed, it was almost a probable ending. Save in the most general way of using a steering oar to keep the raft before the wind, or being able to paddle in completely still water, the raft was unmanoeuvrable. If wind or current took it towards a reef it would break up on that reef, or, with luck, be carried over. Heyerdahl and his companions had discussed the situation over and over again, and they had decided precisely what to do. In spite of the temptation to climb the mast when heavy seas broke over the raft, no one would do so: even if the mast stood with the raft pounding on a reef, it would be next to impossible to hang on. It would be better to stay on deck and to try to cling to the stays. If they could stay on board, the stout logs of the raft would take the first shock of striking a reef, and there was a reasonable chance of being carried with the logs over the reef, or at least of being carried over the worst of the jagged coral. Then it would be a matter of trying to scramble over the rest of the reef and swimming ashore.

To land safely was one thing, but they would have no choice about where they landed, and they were quite likely to fetch up on an uninhabited atoll. Therefore they must try to get some stores on shore with them. No one could hope to carry anything if he were struggling for life in the seas sweeping over a reef, but the rubber dinghy would have a good chance of being washed ashore. So they lashed to the dinghy a portable wireless transmitter in a watertight container, and some containers of food, water and medical equipment. They decided that just before they struck they would leave the dinghy free on the raft, to be picked up and carried in by the sea. To have a chance of hauling in the raft itself if it should survive a reef more or less intact, they also prepared a float on a long line attached to the raft, in the hope that this might be carried ashore somewhere where they could get at it. Heyerdahl's conclusion to his description of their preparations for shipwreck is a complete summary of what tips the balance of human action between disaster and survival. He wrote:

> Every man learned what he had to do when the moment came; each one of us knew where his own limited sphere of responsibility lay, so that we should not fly round treading on each other's toes when the time came and seconds counted.

When shipwreck did finally come they stuck grimly to their plans, clung to the raft and survived to get ashore, battered, but with no bones broken. They could even walk about comfortably. Heyerdahl's Ulysses imagination had reminded him of the effect of coral on bare feet, and he had instructed everyone to prepare for shipwreck by putting on shoes.

H

Ulysses never lacked an audience, and Homer's account of his wanderings in the *Odyssey* has been a best seller for three thousand years. The world likes travellers' tales: the dormant Ulysses factor in man responds to them. Heyerdahl's book on the *Kon-Tiki* expedition has been published in over sixty languages. It has been among the greatest publishing successes since the Second World War, and it has made a great deal of money. For some people this has tarnished Heyerdahl's achievement, illogically and unfairly. But some men are always jealous of other men's successes, and when wealth comes almost incidentally it is the more galling to anyone inclined to such resentment. Ulysses, the type-figure, met the same attitude. When, laden with gifts by the Phaeacians he sailed home to Ithaca, Poseidon, who disliked him, complained to Zeus:

> Now these people have brought him over the sea in their good ship ... after showering gifts upon him, gifts of copper, gold and woven stuffs in such profusion as he could never have won for himself from Troy, even if he had come back unhurt with his fair share of the spoils.

Homer explains by the resentment of a god what we should now call a psychological response. It is understandable. What had Ulysses done to deserve his fortune? He had wandered about the world, getting into a number of scrapes and getting out of them as best he could. What had Heyerdahl done? He had sat on a raft and drifted across the Pacific. Why should the world reward such men when so many other more obviously worthy activities go largely unrecognised and unrewarded?

Common opinion here has a surer instinct. Ulysses pushed back the horizons of the then-known world, giving men new excitement and new understanding. Heyerdahl re-created a remote past and showed men and women concrete-bound in cities that man can still cross an ocean with the most primitive resources and come to terms with the elements. These are rare achievements. Heyerdahl might complain that he has been lauded mostly for the wrong reasons: that the world praises him for his raft voyage as a thing of wonderful courage in itself, whereas it was but an incident in his real achievement of reconstructing a route of prehistoric immigration. Certainly, most of the millions who have been thrilled by his *Kon-Tiki* expedition know little of theories of Polynesian settlement, and perhaps care as little about them.

In spite of the importance that he himself attaches to the scientific value of his voyage, Heyerdahl would be wrong. His *greatest* achievement was to stir imaginations, and it would not really matter whether the scientific basis of his thinking was sound (as it was) or wildly fanciful. President Truman, who was fascinated by the expedition, showed an exact understanding of its achievement when he wrote:

> It is a wonderful thing to have people in the world who can still take hardship and do an exploration job just as the one you young men did on that raft.*

President Truman was a politician, with a politician's instinctive understanding of what people really respond to. His instinct here was sound.

This is not to belittle Heyerdahl's scientific work. He is among the great students of Pacific pre-history, and while some of his theories may remain controversial, he has influenced the study of prehistoric migration profoundly, and introduced almost a new dimension to the study of man's past. In the twenty-two years since his raft voyage he has conducted scientific exploration on Easter Island, in the Galapagos and in many other places, and written much of outstanding scientific value. His theories of primitive ocean migration have led him into the Atlantic, and in 1969, at the age of 55, he led an expedition rather similar to *Kon-Tiki* in an attempt to prove that prehistoric migration from North Africa to Central America was feasible in boats made of the papyrus reed. His thinking and his insistence on physical reconstruction have been consistent. His Atlantic boat *Ra* was less successful than his Pacific raft, because the papyrus became waterlogged and the voyage had to be abandoned some hundreds of miles from the Caribbean, but Heyerdahl had crossed most of his ocean. His failure did not invalidate his thinking—it proved merely that he needed another sort of papyrus. That is not very important: what mattered, and still matters, to him is physical reconstruction of the past.

* Senor Kon-Tiki, p. 184.

Naturally Heyerdahl has met opposition—Ulysses had enemies. The academic world was shaken by his raft expedition, and not at all sure that it approved of raft voyages as a contribution to anthropological studies. He met also much plain jealousy. When the Swedish Society for Anthropology and Geography awarded him its silver Retzius Medal one of his academic opponents observed bitingly:

It seems rather niggardly to hand over a silver coin worth about $9.75 to one who has earned four million by his voyage.*

The money made by the *Kon-Tiki* expedition grated on such nerves, and to some extent it continues to grate.

Yet Heyerdahl did not set out to make money. Like Ulysses, he was glad to take money when it was offered, and, again like Ulysses, who liked giving costly presents when he had anything to give, he has been generous in his use of money. He has financed many archaeological explorations, and the entire profit from his *Kon-Tiki* Museum in Oslo, one of the most popular tourist attractions in Scandinavia, goes to a fund for students. Heyerdahl made his *Kon-Tiki* voyage, as he set out on his more recent Atlantic voyage, because he *had* to find out things for himself. The fortune that has come to him is incidental. The most jealous, however, could hardly say that it has not been earned.

The dividing line between stunt and true manifestation of the Ulysses factor is sometimes thin. To roller-skate from London to Edinburgh, or to attempt to walk backwards round the Mediterranean, may attract attention, but neither is characteristic of Ulysses. It does not wholly follow that the motive for such exploits owes nothing to the Ulysses factor in man, for if some line of thought required firsthand experience of a long journey on roller-skates, or of walking backwards, physical determination to acquire the experience for oneself might be a manifestation of the factor. It can be stated as an axiom that lunatic or utterly irrational action is never a Ulysses characteristic. But this is not quite enough to define the borderline between Ulysses and non-Ulysses, for what may seem lunatic to the rest of the world may be both rational

* *Senor Kon-Tiki*, p. 204.

and necessary to a Ulysses line of thought. The approach to action here is as important as the act itself.

The distinction between stunt and true Ulysses action is well illustrated by Thor Heyerdahl. To set out to cross the Pacific on a raft is, as a detached action, a stunt. It may have a practical purpose—to provide copy for a book, to make a film or perhaps to advertise a brand of soap or cereals. Nevertheless, in all such contexts it remains a stunt, of the same order as standing on one's head on a roof or flying under Westminster Bridge. Such actions may demand skill and courage, even long training and self preparation, but they are essentially stunts, devised to attract attention.

The true Ulysses action must have a primary purpose which requires *that particular act*, and nothing else. The action may, indeed, be part of the purpose, as in climbing a particular mountain in order to reach the summit. It cannot be an action detached from its physical purpose, such as crossing the Thames on a tightrope in order to advertise either oneself or somebody's beer. Heyerdahl's raft voyage was the outcome of his exploratory thinking about the migration of Polynesian peoples: it was the essential physical part of a mental quest, essential to his purpose of *finding out for himself* whether balsa-logs would stay afloat long enough to reach Polynesia from the west coast of South America, and whether the prevailing winds and ocean currents would carry a raft of balsa-logs from South America to Polynesia. To satisfy himself on these matters it was essential *for him* to go with his logs. Others may think that the practicability of his theories could have been determined as well by laboratory experiment and the study of navigational records; for Heyerdahl, no experiment other than a physical voyage made by him would do. His *Kon-Tiki* voyage, therefore, was not a stunt, but the taking of a calculated physical risk in a manner, and for a purpose, typical of the Ulysses spirit in man. His careful planning of the voyage was also typical.

The Ulysses factor in man may prompt action with a hope of personal gain, but it is *with* a hope of gain rather than *in* the hope of gain: it is neither commercial nor uncommercial, but simply a-commercial. Ulysses was quick to take a gift or to sack a city, but the impulse that sent him on his voyages was to find whatever was there to be found, not necessarily material things. Heyerdahl raised every penny he could of his own money in order to finance his raft voyage, and borrowed more. He started heavily in debt, expecting to spend years of lecturing and writing to pay back his debts. He was delighted by the financial success of his book and *Kon-Tiki* film, but he was also surprised. He was not grasping. After his voyage the American magazine *Life* asked how much he wanted for first publication rights of the still photographs he had taken in the Pacific. He suggested $2,000. *Life* paid him $5,000, holding that he had grossly undervalued his own work.

As the ruler of Ithaca, Ulysses could recruit a crew and set off on an expedition without bothering much about how it was going to be financed. Moreover, in his day, piracy—at any rate, successful piracy—was a respectable trade, and he could reasonably expect a voyage to be self-financing. The world has become less simple since. The Ulysses factor drives, but the response requires detailed logistical planning. Few men now can finance an expedition entirely from their own resources: to some extent they must pledge their future, contract to write a book or newspaper articles, or to make a film. Sometimes they must pledge their expedition itself, accepting sponsorship from some commercial organisation in return for publicity. This is not necessarily demeaning—Ulysses would trade a story for gifts when he could. Joshua Slocum, the first man to sail singlehanded round the world, thought it proper to trade when he could. When he was sailing through the Magellan Strait he was delighted to come across some barrels of tallow among wreckage in a cove where he anchored for shelter.

> It was no light work carrying tallow in my arms over the boulders on the beach (he wrote). But I worked on till the *Spray* (his sloop) was loaded with a full cargo. I was happy then in the prospect of doing a good business farther along on the voyage.*

There is nothing demeaning in trade as such, and an honourable man may properly offer services to industry in

* Joshua Slocum, *Sailing Alone Around the World*, p. 114. Collier-Macmillan 1962.

return for money to make an expedition possible, but the intrusion of commerce into adventuring sometimes does mask the purpose of an adventure. I shall have more to say about this later.

IX

The man who found himself—Eric Shipton

ERIC SHIPTON was the architect of man's victory over Everest. He did not climb the mountain, but without him it may be doubted if it would yet have been climbed. His was the inspiration behind the British expedition under Sir John Hunt (Lord Hunt) in 1953 which achieved the summit: his years of exploring in the high Himalaya provided the strategical planning for success; Tensing, the Sherpa who reached the top with Hillary, had been recruited by him. Shipton was originally selected by the Himalayan Committee to lead the 1953 expedition, and he had started work on it when he was replaced by Hunt. Why remains a mystery. Shipton himself, in his autobiography published in 1969, can say only:

> The influences which caused the Committee's *volte face* are still obscure.*

It is as well, perhaps, that they should remain so, for the incident is not a happy one in British mountaineering. But Ulysses was not an administrator. He was content to lead the way. So is Shipton. He is too full a man to be embittered by this piece of curious treatment. His place in mountaineering history will grow with time.

Shipton found more than unmapped routes in mountains by obeying the Ulysses factor in him. He found himself. His whole life has been a manifestation of the factor. He was born in 1907 in Ceylon, where his father was a tea-planter. When he was 2 his father died, and he had a wandering early childhood, his mother travelling restlessly from place to place to Ceylon, India, England and France. In 1914 his mother re-

---

* This and other quotations from Eric Shipton in this chapter, are from his autobiography *That Untravelled World*. Hodder & Stoughton 1969.

married, but the boy scarcely knew his stepfather, as he was killed in action in 1917.

Shipton has all the far-ranging intelligence that is characteristic of the Ulysses factor, but it did not emerge at school. His childhood had been too unsettled for him to adapt readily to a conventional English preparatory school. He was supposed to go on to Harrow, but failed to pass Common Entrance. He read Whymper's books on mountains, and when he went with a schoolfriend for a walking tour in Norway he found absolute contentment. He writes of his boyhood experience:

> As yet my ambitions were not focussed on any one aspect of travel, and I would have been equally enchanted by a desert, a polar ice-cap or a tropical forest. I was very intrigued by volcanic phenomena and had collected a number of books on the subject; the only classical writing which stirred my interest was Pliny's account of the eruption of Vesuvius, and that, naturally, in an English translation and not in the course of my latin studies... I acquired books by some of the early Alpine mountaineers and was thrilled to read in these the expression of so much of my own inarticulate feelings... It was Whymper with his simple approach and exciting narrative, his lively observation and power of description, who most captivated me.*

When he was 21 Shipton went to Kenya with the intention of becoming a farmer. By then he had served his apprenticeship to climbing in the Alps, and in time off from farming he made for the then little-explored highlands of East and Central Africa. With the distinguished Cambridge Mountaineer Wyn Harris, then in the Colonial Service in Kenya, he made the first ascent of Nelion, one of the twin peaks of Mount Kenya. In 1930, after an account of one of his climbs had appeared in the *East African Standard*, he got a letter from another Kenya planter asking for advice on climbing in East Africa. His name was H. W. Tilman. Shipton and Tilman made a number of African climbs together. That was the beginning of a trail of adventure that took both men to Everest and to the exploration of mountain ranges in the farthest parts of the earth.

* Eric Shipton, *That Untravelled World*. Hodder & Stoughton 1969.

A study of Tilman is in the next chapter. He was nearly 33 to Shipton's 23 when they met, but at that time Shipton was the more experienced climber. Each man learned much from the other. They are curiously alike, and sharply dissimilar. Both have the Ulysses factor in them to a high degree, both have been moved by it throughout their lives. Neither can be content with a known horizon: to each a horizon, any horizon, beckons irresistibly—it is a screen of mist that *must* be penetrated, a curtain that *must* be drawn back. Both are magnificent climbers, and both climb to get *beyond* their mountains, not merely to get to the top. They are mountain-explorers rather than mountaineers, pleased with a first ascent if it comes their way, but not particularly competitive in their climbing. If Shipton had been more competitive he would no doubt have led the expedition that finally climbed Everest. He would also have been less interesting as a man.

Both Shipton and Tilman manifest the Ulysses factor in exceptional purity of form, but they are different forms. Shipton's compulson to explore is fundamentally to discover himself; Tilman's is an external curiosity. Tilman is self-sufficient to the point of austerity. Shipton is self-sufficient in action, ready to be responsible for himself, but for him experience is not complete unless he can share it. Writing of his mother, he makes a revealing observation about himself.

> I was very fond of my mother; but though we had a great deal in common we were never very close. This was largely due to her reticence which prevented intimate discussion, an indulgence to which I have always been addicted.

Shipton's eccentric childhood exaggerated tendencies already in him. Impatience with formal schooling is characteristic of the Ulysses factor: he had this impatience, which, added to the inability of a conventional prep-school to understand him, led him to assume that he was no good at learning and incapable of passing examinations. The intellectual power of his later work makes nonsense of both assumptions, but they were facts of his adolescence and intensified his passion for taking to the hills—here was something he *was* good at, a way of life with which he could come to terms.

In 1931, when he was 24, Shipton had to decide between

two opportunities. Some friends of his in Kenya discovered alluvial gold and offered him a partnership in working it; and he was invited to join an expedition to attempt to climb Kamet (25,447 ft) in the Himalaya. He chose Kamet. The expedition, led by Frank Smythe, was successful, achieving what was then the first summit over 25,000 ft to be climbed. In the following year Shipton was invited to join an expedition to Everest led by Hugh Ruttledge. That was the Everest Expedition of 1933, which succeeded in establishing a camp at 27,400 ft but could not reach the summit.

Shipton was now becoming recognised as among the ablest of Himalayan climbers. With Tilman in 1934 he made a remarkable journey to survey the approaches to Nanda Devi, laying the groundwork for Tilman's great ascent of Nanda Devi in 1936. Shipton did not share that climb in 1936 because he was taking part in yet another Everest expedition. From then until the war he travelled extensively in the Himalaya and Karakoram ranges, filling in a number of blank spaces on the map and adding much to geographical knowledge. He travelled light, and kept himself by writing and lecturing on his visits to England.

He was on Everest again in 1938, and in 1939 returned to the Karakoram for another great exploring journey in this wild part of the roof of the world in Central Asia. That journey was interrupted by the war.

Again Shipton had a choice of paths. He was in remote country with a surveying task of obvious value to be done. War had been declared for a month when his party first picked up news of it by radio. Should he carry on as if nothing had happened? There was precedent for this. Shackleton was on his way to the Antarctic when war was declared in 1914: he had held it to be his job to carry on.

Hard as it was to leave his mountains, Shipton went back to India and offered his services to the (then British) Government of India in any capacity that might seem useful. His two companions managed to get back to England. Shipton joined the Indian Army.

His unique knowledge of Central Asia was soon needed. In 1940 he was sent as British Consul-General to Kashgar in Sinkiang. It was an important post. Sinkiang, north of Tibet, was nominally subject to China, but for decades it had been

run by local war-lords and Russian influence was strong. The
Consul-General was the sole British representative in this
strategically important part of Central Asia. Shipton stayed
for two years, and did a remarkable job in a weird political
setting. He was relieved in 1942 and after doing various other
war-time jobs he was sent back to Kashgar in 1946. He stayed
there for another two years and then went as Consul-General
to Kunming, in Yunnan in Southern China. This was a time
of great difficulty as the Communist revolution spread
throughout China. In due course Kunming was taken over,
the British Consulate-General was closed and Shipton had to
go. Two weeks after he got back to England in 1951 he was
invited to lead another expedition to Everest.

Pre-war attempts to climb Everest had been made through
Tibet. The Chinese occupation of Tibet after the war made
this impracticable, so a new approach to the mountain was
sought from Nepal. This southern, or rather, south western
route was the one by which Everest was climbed in 1953. It
was Shipton's reconnaissance in 1951 that found the way. His
removal from the leadership of the triumphant expedition of
1953 was a wry acknowledgment of his immense contribution
to Himalayan climbing.

Shipton refused to be embittered by this shock; but inevitably it was a severe one, both emotionally and in its practical
effect on his affairs. He had given up everything else to lead
the Everest expedition, and now he had no job. He could
have hoped for another consular post, but there was nothing
immediately available. Finally, he got a job as warden of an
Outward Bound school. Then his marriage broke up.

Ulysses shipwrecked does not sit on the beach and wring his
hands. Shipton's whole life was shipwrecked and he reacted in
characteristic fashion. He went to the hills on the Welsh
border and found himself a job as a forestry labourer. He was
close on 50.

Shipton the woodcutter might be content to forget the
world, but the world was less ready to forget Shipton the
explorer. In 1957—the year he reached 50—he was invited by
the Imperial College of Science to return to the Karakoram
with a party of students. He did, and although he went back
to casual labouring after the Karakoram trip 'the enchantment of that untravelled world [as he puts it] had once more

cast its compulsive spell'. The greatest explorer of his generation in Central Asia turned to a wholly new field in the still
more remote ranges of the Southern Andes.

The main outlines of Patagonia and Tierra del Fuego have
long been known, but the interior, guarded by a formidable
coast and the great Patagonian ice-cap, remained largely unexplored before Shipton's first Patagonian journey in 1958–
1959. By that journey, and three subsequent expeditions in
1959–1960, 1960–1961 and 1961–1962, Shipton mapped an
unknown world. He also helped to settle peacefully a boundary dispute between Argentina and Chile. In his sixtieth
year he went to have a look at the mountains of Alaska.

> I cannot rest from travel: I will drink
> Life to the lees...

Shipton has had one objective throughout his life—to find
out. His journeys have had secondary purposes: to collect
botanical specimens, to study the behaviour of glaciers, to
climb a particular mountain, many such things. But always
the real driving force in him has been to climb the ridge to see
beyond it. He has added materially to human knowledge in
many fields; more importantly, by discovering himself
through his own exploring instinct he has inspired, and will
continue to inspire, others to self-fulfilment.

His adventures have needed scale, the immense distances of
Central Asia and the Andes. As the scope for acquiring wholly
new geographical knowledge contracts—as Shipton has himself helped to contract it—can the scale on which the Ulysses
impulse may be satisfied diminish? Can the mastery of mountaineering techniques satisfy the exploring instinct of the
mountaineer? It could not satisfy Shipton. He has written of
himself:

> For a while I was fascinated by the sheer technique of
> moving safely and easily over difficult ground; but even
> then I regarded the art as a means to an end, and neither
> reached nor aspired to more than a modest standard of
> climbing proficiency. After Mount Kenya I became less
> and less concerned with the mastery of technical difficulty,
> or even the ascent of individual peaks, but more and more

absorbed in the problems and delights of movement over wide areas of mountain country. It was not that I lost any of my enjoyment in climbing peaks, but simply that I found the other more rewarding.

Since the war much mountaineering effort has gone into the devising of techniques for climbing difficult rock-faces, often requiring the use of equipment that makes a climb in some sense artificial. But is a horizon less a horizon because it is only inches away? If those inches are a gap demanding every faculty of human courage and ingenuity to cross, the attainment of the far side may bring a satisfaction not less real because its scale is small. To find a way to scale a wall of rock hitherto held to be unclimbable may be a discovery as rewarding as finding an unknown mountain. There is a slight but interesting mutation in the factor here. Shipton has needed mountain ranges, but the Ulysses factor may also manifest itself by sending men to single rock-faces. These two types of manifestations now exist side by side: there are men who climb in order to go somewhere else, and men who climb to get to the top. Shipton is an example of the former, but he respects both. The two British attempts to climb Annapurna in 1970 by routes deliberately selected for their technical difficulty are examples of the latter. Shipton sums up:

> Personally, I welcome wholeheartedly the advance of modern techniques because it has widened the bounds of mountain adventure. There was a time, long ago, when I was oppressed by the thought that soon there would be no new peaks to climb and no new routes to explore. But the more I travelled in the remoter ranges of the world— Karakoram, Kuen Lun, Alaska, Southern Andes—the more I realised how vast is the field of fresh endeavour even for the traditional mountaineer. With the application of these new climbing and survival techniques the horizon is truly **boundless.**

Shipton has always manifested a true Ulysses caution in risk-taking. He has taken risks often enough in his adventurous life, but he has taken them only when he had to, and he has tried to calculate risks carefully. In his view a narrow escape from danger is not a matter for pride, but something to be ashamed of—the escape ought not to have been narrow. He considers the *motive* all important in judging whether a risk is reasonable or not. If some risky course of action is followed out of foolhardiness, to try to win applause or simply to better someone else's performance, then it is to be condemned. If a risk has to be taken in the course of a journey it must be accepted as a reasonable hazard of life. Its possible consequences should be assessed, and the leader of the expedition taking it should be sure of his moral and physical resources for meeting them.

Shipton's clear-headed assessment of risks is well illustrated by his expedition to the Cordillera Darwin, an almost unexplored range of mountains running from Tierra del Fuego through the mass of rocky islands ending with Cape Horn. He was taken to the mouth of an unexplored inlet by a Chilean naval vessel, and here, with three companions and supplies for eight weeks, he cast off in a rubber dinghy. At the head of the unknown inlet the party was fortunate in finding a good rock route up a glacier, and the weather was kindly. Shipton left nothing to luck. He and his companions carried supplies for six weeks to a base camp above the forest line, and on all expeditions from their base camp they buried supplies at intervals against the return journey. Wherever they made a supply dump they took bearings with two compasses, checked against each other. It was as well, for on a ridge of Monte Darwin, the highest peak of the range, they were caught by a storm and a bag containing two days' food was lost. They took no gamble on improvement in the weather, but at once cut their daily ration by one-third. In fact, the weather did improve, and they were able to climb Monte Darwin and set off on the journey back to their base camp sooner than they thought. On the way back, however, the weather worsened and they met severe gales and heavy snow. Again they cut their rations, but did not worry much because of the food they had dumped on the outward journey. When they came to the site of their food dump, however, the whole area was under six feet of snow. Without their carefully checked compass bearings they could never have found the food: as it was it took them two hours of digging in the snow to locate the dump. But they did find it. Without ruthless self-discipline in taking precautions this incident of their journey might easily have become a tragedy.

The Ulysses impulse in Shipton led to the British conquest of Everest and enhanced the prestige of Britain at a time when the greatness of an imperial past seemed to be ebbing away. At a critical time of the war it ensured that a man with firsthand knowledge was available for a diplomatic post of the most delicate importance in Central Asia. Shipton the explorer has served his country well. Shipton the man found himself on the windswept ridges of his mountains to join that small company of individuals who have enriched humanity by living fully as themselves.

X

Insatiable curiosity—H. W. Tilman

THOR HEYERDAHL is a study of one manifestation of the Ulysses factor—the driving force of an intense devotion to one special object. For Heyerdahl this was to reconstruct the pattern of transoceanic migration in primitive times. Although he has since transferred attention from the Pacific to the Atlantic, his object, the object of his whole life's work, remains the same. His curiosity, although it has led him to explore in a number of different fields, is limited. But the curiosity of Ulysses about the physical world can also be limitless. An interesting example of insatiable curiosity to penetrate jungles, traverse mountains, cross the seas is to be found in Harold William Tilman.

Tilman is a man more dedicated and set apart than Heyerdahl, but less obviously dedicated. He was born in 1898, went from school to the Royal Military Academy, then at Woolwich, and at the age of 18 was commissioned into the Royal Artillery. That was in 1915, and he went straight to the western front in the First World War. Having survived the war (with a Military Cross and bar), he went to Africa, to see if he could carve a farm for himself out of the bush in what was then called British East Africa and is now Kenya. He worked at this for ten years, transforming a roadless stretch of virgin bush into a reasonably prosperous coffee plantation. But his heart was not in farming: achievement here brought restlessness rather than fulfilment. He wrote of himself:

> The daily routine of attending to planted coffee was much less congenial to me than the earlier struggle to carve a home out of the forest and to tame the wilderness; to watch the landscape—a waste of bush and jungle, but a familiar one—change daily under one's eyes; to see a new

clearing here, a shed there, paths and roads pushing out in all directions, while seeds, which one had oneself planted, grow into trees big enough to make timber.*

The shade of his own trees was not for Tilman: he was interested in planting them, not in sitting under them. He was fortunate to meet Eric Shipton in Kenya, and with Shipton he explored the mountains of Central Africa, Kilimanjaro, Mt Kenya and the Ruwenzori, or Mountains of the Moon. After some remarkable climbing in time taken off from coffee planting, Tilman gave up coffee farming altogether and went off prospecting (not very profitably) for gold near Lake Victoria. Wanting to return to England, and to see more of Africa on the way, and not having much money, he decided to cross the Congo and what was then the French Cameroons, by bicycle, a journey of some 3,000 miles. His bicycle cost £6.

Tilman's climbs in Africa made him known in the mountaineering world, and he turned to the Himalaya. He puts it thus:

To some the Himalaya may be only a name vaguely associated, perhaps, with a mountain called Everest: to geologists they provide a vast field for the starting and running of new hares; to other learned men, glaciologists, ethnologists or geographers, the Himalaya are a fruitful source of debate in which there is no common ground, not even the pronunciation of the name; while, to the mountaineer they furnish fresh evidence, if such were needed, of the wise dispensation of a bountiful Providence. For, lo, when the Alps are becoming too crowded not only with human beings but with huts, the Himalaya offer themselves to the more fanatical devotee—a range fifteen hundred miles long, containing many hundred of peaks, all of them so much higher than the Alps that a new factor of altitude had to be added to the usual sum of difficulties to be overcome.†

With Shipton he made a reconnaissance to survey the

* H. W. Tilman, *Snow on the Equator*, p. 22. Hart-Davis 1935.
† H. W. Tilman, *The Ascent of Nanda Devi*, 1937, p. 12. Hart-Davis 1937.

approaches to Nanda Devi (25,645 ft) in 1934, and he took part in a reconnaissance expedition to Mount Everest, led by Shipton, in 1935. When the survey which was the prime task of this expedition was completed Shipton and his friends had a kind of high-altitude holiday, climbing twenty-six peaks in some sixty days. Tilman personally went up seventeen of them. In 1936 Tilman led a combined British–American expedition to attempt to climb Nanda Devi and reached the summit with his companion N. E. Odell. This was the highest peak then reached by man.

In 1938 Tilman was invited to lead an attempt on Mount Everest. He was then 40. The weather turned against him and his party, and they did not succeed, but they established a camp at 27,200 ft. The party experimented with oxygen, but Tilman climbed to this camp without oxygen.

In 1939 Tilman rejoined the Army, serving with the artillery in France, the Middle East, the Western Desert and Tunisia, and then with partisan groups in Albania and Italy. After the war, in 1949 and 1950, he went on two more exploring expeditions to Nepal and Central Asia, and then he bought a 14-ft dinghy and turned to the sea. In 1954, at the age of 56, he bought *Mischief*, an elderly Bristol Channel pilot cutter built in 1906 with the intention of sailing to Patagonia to explore the ice-cap at the tip of South America. In 1955 he did so.

Since then he has sailed *Mischief* all over the world, in the north to Greenland and the Arctic coast of Canada, to the Southern Ocean and the south Shetlands in the far south, and on a circumnavigation of Africa. There have been many remarkable small-boat voyages, but Tilman's *cruising* history in *Mischief* is unique for both man and 45-ft boat. *Mischief* was lost in 1968, after an unhappy encounter with ice and bad weather off Jan Mayen island, in the Arctic Ocean east of Greenland. She was then 64, Tilman 70. His efforts to save her were as gallant as a man can make for a friend.

There is a Jack and the Beanstalk quality about the scale of Tilman's life, but just as Jack planted his magic beans with a normal boy's curiosity, so Tilman's manifold achievement is the Ulysses factor in ordinary man carried to the *nth* degree. That is its exceptional interest. The driving force in Heyerdahl is a specialised manifestation of the factor: in Tilman it is general. Heyerdahl set out to prove, or to try to prove, a precisely formulated theory. Tilman set out to find—anything. After climbing Semper Peak (15,843 ft) and Edward Peak (15,986 ft) in the Ruwenzori in 1932, he and his companions had the choice of returning to camp by the way they had come or of going on into an unnamed valley. They decided on the unknown. Tilman wrote:

> It meant a long day and was rather a shot in the dark, but it took us into fresh country, and, in spite of the prudent adage, we preferred the unknown to the known.*

The technical mountaineer achieves his peak, and that is that. To Tilman, a peak has always been a step on towards something else; to what is of no great moment.

His bicycle ride across equatorial Africa in 1933 was a remarkable journey, entirely in keeping with his approach to life. He was no cyclist: he had not ridden a bicycle since boyhood before the First World War. He considered walking in many ways preferable, but decided that it would take too long to cross Africa on foot. The route presented problems. He considered the possibility of cycling to North Africa and riding on overland to England, but concluded that the *sudd*, the vast area of Nile swamp which he would have to negotiate, 'gave little scope for cycling', and that it would not be practicable to cross the Sahara by bicycle. There remained the west coast, and a ship home from some West African port.

He had no detailed maps—he had no maps at all save a general map of Central Africa that he extracted from a magazine. He was not at all sure of what he would come across in the way of roads, but felt that there must be paths of some sort through the bush on which it ought to be possible to ride a bicycle. He travelled light, discarding a tent to keep down weight, and taking only a rucksack and a mosquito net. He sought no publicity, and financed his modest needs from his own (as modest) savings.

His £6 bicycle was an extravagance. He could have had a Japanese machine for £2, but felt that he wanted a *British* one. His sole attempt at commercial exploitation of his trip was to write to the makers of his bicycle when he got home to

* Snow on the Equator, p. 134.

tell them that the machine had behaved well over its 3,000 Central African miles, and that 'no vital part either dropped off, or broke'. In writing this letter he rather hoped that the manufacturers might give him a new bicycle. All he got, however was a polite note expressing the firm's satisfaction that he had had an agreeable journey.

His crossing took fifty-six days. On some days he covered 80 miles or so, and his average was just over 53 miles—good going on a diet mainly of bananas. Tilman has written a charming account of the trip in *Snow on the Equator*. It is such light and pleasant reading that you would think that there were no difficulties. This is not false modesty, but simply part of the man. He recounts a few struggles with punctured tyres in temperatures too hot for rubber to stick, and a few momentary doubts about the route, but having set out to cross Africa by bicycle, such difficulties, in his view, are no more than incidental. It would not occur to him that he merited any credit for overcoming them.

His great ascent of Nanda Devi in 1936 was of the same pattern, a small expedition modestly equipped. This was at a time when the fashion in Himalayan climbing was to march with armies of porters. Tilman took as few as possible, partly for economy, mainly because he believed in travelling light. His account of reaching the summit of Nanda Devi with his companion N. E. Odell could scarcely be more modest.

It was difficult to realise (he wrote) that we were actually standing on top of the same peak which we had viewed two months ago from Ranikhet, and which had then appeared incredibly remote and inaccessible; and it gave us a curious feeling of exaltation to know that we were above every peak within hundreds of miles on either hand. Dhaulagiri, 1,000 ft higher, and two hundred miles away in Nepal, was our nearest rival. I believe we so far forgot ourselves as to shake hands on it.

After the first joy in victory came a feeling of sadness that the mountain had succumbed.*

Achievement? Sadness? If a man can write honestly of his own feelings, the two are inextricable. The type-figure of Ulysses, articulate in Tennyson, felt that

* *The Ascent of Nanda Devi*, p. 134.

... all experience is an arch wherethro'
Gleams that untravelled world, whose margin fades
For ever and for ever when I move.

Tilman had just climbed what was then the highest peak in the world to be reached by man. The planning that had gone into the expedition, the months of travelling, the excitement that had united him and his party in collective effort towards one end—all this was now finished. No one again could ever climb Nanda Devi for the first time: in their very achievement something was gone from the world. There is an element of sadness in Ulysses coming home. This is an essential part in the driving force of the Ulysses factor, an ingredient that separates and distinguishes it from the other motives in man that promote accomplishment. The Ulysses urge is always unfulfilled.

Tilman's reasons for taking to the sea at an age when most men regard a round of golf as about the limit of physical practicability are in part whimsical, in part the reflection of a deep understanding of himself.

The Himalaya (he explained in 1956, when he was 58) are extensive, no less than 1,500 miles in length, but a quiet man might well shrink from going, say, to Katmandu, the starting place for the Nepal Himalaya, if he thought he was likely to meet there eleven other parties with their 5,000 porters...

There is something in common between the arts of sailing and of climbing. Each is intimately concerned with elemental things, which from time to time demand from men who practise those arts whatever self-reliance, prudence and endurance they may have. The sea and the hills offer challenges to those who venture upon them, and in the acceptance of these, and in the meeting of them as best he can, lies the sailor's or mountaineer's reward. An essential difference is, perhaps, that the mountaineer usually accepts the challenge on his own terms, whereas once at sea the sailor has no say in the matter and in consequence may suffer more often the salutary and humbling emotion of fear.*

* H. W. Tilman, *Mischief in Patagonia*, p. 4. Cambridge University Press 1957.

The overcrowded Himalaya is whimsy, though from Tilman's point of view not wholly so: Ulysses would not have gone to Troy if he had needed passports in triplicate for all his crew. It is not so much that the Himalaya are actually crowded as that it is difficult nowadays for a man to go where he wants on his own. The sea is freer. It can meet the same need as mountains, a need that Tilman has tried to express in describing its demand for self-reliance and endurance, and its offer of the 'salutary and humbling emotion of fear'. That, however, is a literary refinement, an attempt to meet the linguistic problem of expressing feeling. No man *wants* to be afraid, no sane man *seeks* fear. Tilman here is not pretending that he does. He is reflecting at leisure, after the event, on the importance of not letting fear inhibit action. Courage is a type-quality in those strongly influenced by the Ulysses factor, but it is not the sort of hot courage that may make a man actually delight in danger. Nor is it the gambler's courage of Russian roulette. It is more an acceptance of the need to face fear, of not being put off from doing something that seems worth while by the possibility that things may go wrong. Tilman's brief explanation of the sea's attraction for him embodies this acceptance of the sea's risks, not as dangers to be sought—indeed, as far as possible to be avoided—but to be met as they come.

Having taken to the sea, Tilman's purchase of *Mischief* was again typical. She was no ocean-racer, or yacht fitted with any refinements of comfort or sail-handling. She was a sturdy old pilot-cutter, essentially a working boat, supremely fitted for her job of going about the sea, but offering none of the more glamorous attractions of sailing. As Tilman himself embodies the *generalised* Ulysses factor dormant in every man, so *Mischief* embodied the tough sea-keeping qualities that have earned the affection and respect of ordinary seamen through the centuries.

His use of *Mischief* reflects the sub-conscious dreams of every man who has looked at the sea. He sailed her hard over fourteen years, and the changing emphasis of purpose in his voyages over those years is a fascinating study. At first he is reluctant to admit to himself that seafaring can be anything but secondary to the exploration of mountain country: *Mischief* is acquired because she offers a means of transport to the

blank spaces marked *inesplorado* on the map of Patagonia. In
his preface to *Mischief in Patagonia* there is a note of apology
—'Some readers may think there is an intolerable deal of sea,
as it were, to but one halfpennyworth of mountain.' As he
continues to live with *Mischief* there is a subtle change: the
mountains do not exactly recede, but the sea takes up more
and more of the foreground. To find a remote mountain to
climb (if one can get ashore to it) remains the *object* of *Mischief's* voyages, but the purpose lies more and more in the
voyage itself, in the taking of a small sailing boat to the uttermost parts of the earth. After Patagonia Tilman took *Mischief*
to the Crozet and Kerguelen Islands in the South India Ocean,
mere dots of land (suitably mountainous) on the lonely edge
of the Antarctic. From the Antarctic he sailed to Greenland
and the Arctic, then back again to the far south. In 1964, between voyages in *Mischief*, he took time off to sail as skipper
and navigator in *Patanela* with Warwick Deacock's expedition to Heard Island, a patch of rock off Antarctica with a
9,000-ft mountain called Big Ben. In 1967 he took *Mischief*
south once more, making the South Shetlands, but failing to
land on Smith Island, whose unclimbed peaks were his objective. This unusual failure was no fault of either Tilman or
Mischief, but was brought about by difficulties with his crew.
It was a miserable voyage. On the passage out to South
America the most experienced member of the crew was lost
overboard. Tilman was ready to abandon the voyage, but the
others wanted to go on. At Montevideo all but one of his remaining crew of four left him, and although one of these later
asked to be taken back, he had to sail on with such chance
volunteers as he could find at Montevideo. He was not fortunate in the provisions of chance, and he had trouble with
fights, drink and the theft of all the ship's money. To have
sailed a 45-ft boat to the South Shetlands at all in such conditions was a performance all but incredible. Perhaps it was
also unwise, but Ulysses did not give up easily. Against difficulties that went on and on Tilman took his boat farther
south than any yacht has ever been, and brought her safely
back to her moorings at Lymington in England.

In 1968 he went north again, intending to climb Beerenberg (7,469 ft) on Jan Mayen Island. Ice conditions in that
year were exceptionally bad. In fog and drifting ice-floes off

Jan Mayen *Mischief* struck a rock. He managed to beach her on the island, but ice drifted into the beach and gave her a further battering where she lay. Still Tilman would not give up. With help from the Norwegians manning a weather station on the island he patched a big hole in her hull, and arranged for a sealing vessel to try to tow her to Norway. While the sealer was on her way to *Mischief*'s beach a gale tore away the patches from her side. The work was done again. With great difficulty *Mischief* was hauled off and attached to the tow. A little petrol-engined pump was installed in *Mischief*'s cockpit, and an electric pump, with power from the towing vessel, was added to assist the petrol-engined pump. The power line broke and the electric pump could not be used. Relying on the little petrol-driven pump to keep down the water, the tow started. After about four hours the pump gave up. There was no more to be done. Tilman and his crew were taken off *Mischief* on board the towing vessel and *Mischief* had to be abandoned.

It was a sickening end to fourteen years of intimate relationship between man and boat. Tilman wrote a brief, dignified account of *Mischief*'s last days, concluding:

> For me it was the loss of much more than a yacht. I felt as one who had deserted a stricken friend, a friend with whom for the past fourteen years I had probably spent more time at sea than on land, and who when not at sea had never been far from my mind.

Tilman's self-reproach in recording the loss of *Mischief* is understandable but unmerited. After she struck he behaved magnificently. No man could have done more, few would have attempted as much.

It may be that the gulfs will wash us down. That is a risk that Ulysses must take.

Tilman's personal achievement is, I think, among the greatest of all manifestations of the Ulysses factor in the twentieth century. The factor is so individual that the actions it engenders are not readily comparable, but Tilman's achievement is so manifold, and has been so sustained, that he must rank high on any short list of men who have done most to extend the frontiers of the physical world. He was born too late to command the international celebrity of the great Polar explorers, Amundsen, Peary, Shackleton and Scott, but he stands with them. In some ways his achievement is even greater than theirs, for it is more varied, and, in a sense, more individually his own. It is hard to assess him. He is one of the greatest mountaineers of all time, and among the greatest seamen. Moreover, he has journeyed without lavish equipment or support, in modest climbing parties, on an old boat with sails much patched. He climbed with boots, axe and rope, without benefit of the oxygen equipment that has given later mountaineers an auxiliary engine, as it were.

Tilman has never attracted the popular *réclame* of Heyerdahl, but he has not sought it; he has sought rather to avoid anything that makes good newspaper headlines. He has written a small shelf of really good books, but they are almost maddeningly impersonal. Under-statement is his habit.

Just what *is* his achievement? I have put him on the short list 'of men who have done most to extend the frontiers of the physical world'. Yet he has added no new continent to the map, crossed no unknown sea. By the time that Tilman was born in 1898 the world was fairly well explored, and the Poles were reached in his boyhood. The direct anthropological importance of the Ulysses factor in man was to stimulate primary discovery, to add to the physical resources of the human community. That direct purpose was largely achieved by the end of the last century. There was vast new wealth yet to be discovered in oilfields, uranium ores and the like, as there remain still sources of wealth as yet unguessed. But the exploitation of these does not depend on primary discovery: oil was not found in Persia until 1908, but men knew well enough how to get to the mountains of Khuzistan, where oil was struck. Purely physical geographical discovery on earth is largely complete. There are deserts, ice-caps and jungles still little known, but if a man sets out to reach them they can be reached.

Yet the driving-force in man, the Ulysses factor that prompts him to seek prime physical discovery *for himself* remains strong. Has it any purpose now? What physical frontiers are there left to extend?

From womb to adult life a developing human being passes through a kind of foreshortened corridor of all human experience. A child who crawls to the far side of a room for the first time is exploring in exactly the same way as those who first launched a tree-trunk on a river to find what lay downstream. The child's world rapidly becomes known, but the instinct to look beyond the garden, beyond the street, remains. In most people it is fairly swiftly dimmed. Parents, conscious of the dangers of the outside world, discourage wandering, and mastery of the mechanics of living demands so much concentration in the child that his known world tends to absorb his energies. So with the world as he grows up: he has enough to do in learning how to make a living, and then in earning a living. But it is not quite enough: he needs a sense of wonder still, and if, as happens sadly often, that sense is overlaid and atrophied he is in danger of feeling frustrated and unhappy. There are checks and balances in life, and the human spirit, like the human body, is remarkably tough. Frustration and unhappiness may not be felt acutely, or for long. Other interests crowd in, adjustments and compromises are made, life goes on.

But for some people the effort of discovery remains acutely necessary, and in all people the instinct of wonder requires *some* nourishment. Physical discovery is personal. It does not lessen a child's sense of discovery in crawling across a room that the other occupants of the house know every stick of furniture. When Tilman set off to ride his bicycle across Africa it did not matter to *him* that the Congo had been discovered. He wanted to see for himself. When he navigated *Mischief* in the Davis Strait between Greenland and Baffin Island it did not matter that those waters bore the name of an Elizabethan seaman.

Physical discovery is personal in another sense. Man knows little enough about himself: there is an infinite field for discovery in his own behaviour in strange physical conditions. The desire to test how one will behave in certain conditions, what it feels like to stand on top of a mountain, may be a powerful driving force making for individual discovery. And this is not discovery of solely individual significance: the record of one's own experience, of the reactions of one's companions, is at least of interest, and may be of real importance, to others.

In the league-table of mountaineering Tilman's obvious achievement is plain. He led the party that climbed Nanda Devi, achieving a notable 'highest' for his period, and he has many lesser 'firsts' to his credit, that is, peaks previously unclimbed first climbed by him. But league-table calculations, though convenient, are a poor measure of accomplishment. Tilman's real achievement in the mountains is not in the (partly fortuitous) incident that his happened to be the first foot to tread the highest peak then climbed by man, but in his *approach* to mountains, in his schooling of himself to go high in the mountains of Central Africa, in his disciplined endurance and care for others on the great peaks of the Himalaya, on the Patagonian ice-cap, and on the remote rocks to which he sailed. His has not been particularly competitive climbing. In mountaineering considered purely as a sport, competition is naturally a driving-force—you 'win' by being first up a peak, you are 'defeated' if you do not make it. Tilman is glad when he secures a 'first' ('I believe we so far forgot ourselves as to shake hands upon it'), but he was just as happy to adventure in the Ruwenzori, although most of its peaks had been scaled before. When he failed to land on Smith Island, in the South Shetlands, to tackle its enticing peaks, he permitted himself the reflection.

> One must hope that this rich prize does not fall to some party that has been landed conveniently adjacent to the mountain by helicopter.*

But there was no tigrish animus in his feeling of disappointment. Tilman is always eager to give credit to others, sometimes, I think, a little unfairly to himself.

His achievement at sea is more elusive, and yet, perhaps, the greater. The world is inclined to applaud long voyages in small boats, but mostly for the wrong reasons: a well-found small boat, with a crew that keeps its head, *ought* to be able to make a long voyage safely. It is not particularly courageous to embark on such a voyage. The challenge is in oneself—to accept discomfort, loneliness or cramped living with com-

* H. W. Tilman, *Mischief Goes South*, p. 103. Hollis & Carter 1968.

panions who cannot be changed, fear sometimes, short rations, maybe; and to accept all these things deliberately, in cold blood. The sea cuts men to size, makes miniscule the scale of human affairs. It is not always pleasant to be cut to size. Self-confidence and self-respect may be drained away. Yet they must not diminish if one is to survive the sea, above all if one is responsible for companions. Tilman has taken *Mischief* on year-long voyages, to seas and ice-girt islets which offer nothing but inhospitality. The notes on Jan Mayen in the Admiralty's *Arctic Pilot* are expressive:

> There is no sheltered harbour on Jan Mayen, and landing is therefore possible only during calms or light off-shore breezes... In misty weather, which is the most common condition, every precaution should be taken and the temperature of the surface water observed hourly. So long as this does no fall below 37°F there need be no fear of encountering the ice barrier. The vicinity of the island may be indicated by the seabirds... The cries of these birds when on land is like the distant roaring of a cascade and may be of assistance by warning vessels of the proximity of the cliffs which they inhabit.

Such waters were Tilman's haunts for years. Why? He was not seeking scientific observation to prove some theory, he was not sealing or hunting, or looking for a fortune. He went to the Arctic and to the even harsher sub-Antarctic because he wanted to go, and he found voluntary companions to go with him. By taking *Mischief* to such places, and bringing her home year after year, he showed that man's life is still unbounded. He extended the frontiers of his own world, and in doing so widened experience for everybody. Those are the physical frontiers he pushed back.

I do not want to make a fuss of age, but action in relation to age is of interest. Ulysses, the type-figure, carried both the desire and the ability for physical exploration into extreme old age, and the persistence of such activity is typical of men strongly influenced by the Ulysses factor. Tilman was nearly 40 when he climbed Nanda Devi, and he made some of his greatest voyages when he was rising 70. Heyerdahl set off to cross the Atlantic in his papyrus boat when he was 55. Chichester was 59 when he made his first singlehanded crossing of the Atlantic, and he celebrated his sixty-fifth birthday during his solitary voyage round the world. This is yet another extension of man's physical frontiers. The human community in the twentieth century is an ageing one, its expectation of life extending and the proportion of the aged to the young increasing. The persistence of the Ulysses factor beyond what is still called the age of retirement may be one of its most valuable attributes influencing the future of the race.

Tilman has not always been fortunate in his companions: indeed, some of his most remarkable voyages have been made with remarkably ill-assorted crews. He was schooled in the Army and on mountains, and both impose a kind of absolute discipline, external to the self-discipline of individuals. If you are roped to another man on a difficult climb your life is bound physically to his, and even if you find yourself hating him personally, you must still act physically together. Discipline at sea must be as absolute, but it is differently obtained: it is not immediately obvious that disagreement means disaster. A mountaineer cannot desert from a climbing party—he has nowhere to go. Once a ship has made port a discontented crew can walk off. Desertion may imperil the rest of the voyage, but it will not do so immediately; it may mean simply that the ship cannot proceed, which may ultimately be disastrous to the owner and other members of the crew in all sorts of ways, but does not put them in immediate physical danger. Tilman started badly when he bought *Mischief* in Malta and recruited a scratch crew to sail her home. Things did not go well, and his crew left him at Gibraltar. There he was joined by a young climber, of whom he wrote:

> He knew nothing about the sea, but being a mountaineer he would stand by me and not desert like the yachtsmen.

Tilman had been unlucky with his yachtsmen, but the remark has a bearing on his later troubles. Leadership is a type-quality of the Ulysses factor, and Tilman can be a magnificent leader. But he is at his best in difficulty or danger: at less trying times his personal austerity has not always seemed easy to live with. If you let it be known that you are planning what

looks like an exciting expedition you will get hundreds of
applicants wishing to join you. All will have private reasons
for wanting to come, which they may not be able to explain to
themselves, let alone to you. It is hard to know whom to
choose. Known friends are safest, but are seldom available.
You make the best choice you can, but must recognise that a
burly young man who looks a tower of strength over a res-
taurant table may show less admirable qualities in a gale. He
may need a lot of nursing. This aspect of leadership is not
Tilman's strong point.

It is because he asks nothing for himself beyond the accomplishment of whatever task he has in hand. Twelve years after
his first voyage in *Mischief*, after sailing tens of thousands of
miles, he set down his thoughts on safety equipment. One of
his crew had left him because *Mischief* did not seem to have
enough safety equipment. Tilman observed:

> His real grievance was that we had no distress signals and
> carried no life-raft. In my view every herring should hang
> by its own tail. Anyone venturing into unfrequented and
> possibly dangerous waters does so with his eyes open, should
> be willing to depend on his own exertions, and should
> neither expect nor ask for help. Nor would equipment of
> this sort be of much use in Drake Passage (between Cape
> Horn and the South Shetlands) where the chances of being
> picked up are so slim as to be hardly worth considering. A
> yacht is supposed to carry distress signals but is not over-
> much reliance placed upon them by owners of small craft?
> Yearly around our coasts so many calls are made upon the
> various rescue organisations that by now the average man
> should be ashamed to think of adding to their number. The
> confidence that is placed, and successfully placed, in being
> rescued fosters carelessness or even foolishness, and con-
> dones ignorance ... The perils of the sea are less apparent
> than the perils of climbing and have to be carefully assessed.
> In climbing the penalty for a mistake is obvious and is
> sometimes exacted instantaneously, so that on the whole
> there are fewer foolish climbers than foolish amateur
> sailors.*

This is hard, clear thinking. Tilman calculates his risks and

* *Mischief Goes South.*

he is not going to curse Fate if the calculations turn out wrong. It is an admirable philosophy for a man himself, but I am less sure how far one should expect others to share it. Many medicines that are more or less useless still give comfort. In unfrequented seas a life-raft may do no more than prolong the miseries of shipwreck, but miracles can happen, and man may be sustained to the last by the adage that while there is life there is hope. It is not weakness to make some concessions to human frailty.

Tilman's dismissal of concessions to frailty may provoke criticism, but his best shipmates have been ready to sail with him again and again. That speaks more for his qualities as a leader than anything else could. The man himself as well as his life has been an inspiration.

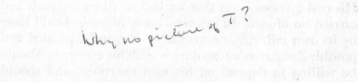

Eric Shipton

Sheila Scott

Thor Heyerdahl

XI

Fortitude—Maurice Herzog

STUDIES of Thor Heyerdahl, Eric Shipton and H. W. Tilman have illustrated various kinds of courage associated with the Ulysses factor; Heyerdahl's readiness to risk an ocean crossing on a type of raft that he believed in against much expert advice, Shipton's courageous adjustment to a bitter personal setback, Tilman's disregard of personal danger in going where he wanted. This chapter is a brief study of what I can describe only as absolute courage.

A French expedition led by Maurice Herzog climbed Annapurna (26,493 ft) in the Nepal Himalaya in 1950. This was the first mountain of over 26,000 ft to be climbed, nearly 1,000 ft higher than Tilman's Nanda Devi. At the time of Herzog's climb some twenty-two previous mountaineering expeditions had attempted to attain a summit of 26,000 ft. All had failed.

Herzog and his party left France with two alternative objectives, to climb either Dhaulagiri (26,795 ft) or Annapurna. Climbing as such was but one of their problems: they had first to find their mountains. Such maps as they had were dubious and turned out to be wrong. They had thus to explore the Himalaya of Central Nepal to find practicable routes for getting to Dhaulagiri or Annapurna, and then to reconnoitre the mountains themselves to devise possible approaches to the summit. All this had to be done, or at least attempted between early April, when spring made Himalayan exploration feasible, and the end of the first week of June, when monsoon weather could be expected to make high climbing out of the question.

By May 14, with perhaps three weeks left before the monsoon, the expedition had spent much time wandering and did not appear to be getting anywhere. Herzog called his whole party together for what he described as a council of war. He began by addressing them thus:

It is now May 14. In spite of all our efforts no real possibility has turned up: we have no route in prospect, we aren't even clear in what direction we ought to set out. We aren't sure of anything. Time's short. The moment has come to take major decisions.*

It had indeed. With the agreement of his companions, Herzog decided to abandon Dhaulagiri, to send a strong reconnaissance party to Annapurna and, if it seemed at all practicable, to convert the reconnaissance into an assault on the summit. His leadership here was outstanding. He had made up his own mind about what ought to be done, but he knew that no attempt at dictatorship would work with fellow mountaineers. So he called his counsel, presented every fact he knew and invited everyone in turn to speak. His own decision emerged from sheer logic.

At first things went fairly well. By May 28 they had established four camps on Annapurna, a base camp at about 16,750 ft and higher camps at 19,350 ft, 21,650 ft and 23,500 ft. Then things began to go wrong. Two of Herzog's companions, whom he had sent high to establish a fifth camp nearer the summit, were overcome by high-altitude sickness and frostbite. With another companion, Louis Lachenal, he took over from them and on June 2 made a camp of sorts—a bivouac tent on an ice-shelf—at 24,600 ft. The monsoon was almost on them and a weather forecast that they had heard on the radio just before coming up was bad. They spent a wretched night in their tent. It snowed heavily. Herzog feared that they would be crushed by snow pressing on the tent, and at one time he had to fold his arms across his chest and force them upwards against the weight of snow in order to breathe at all. After the snow came a gale and they had to grip the tent poles with all their strength to prevent them from being blown out of the ground. 'Why the tent was not blown down I don't know,' Herzog wrote afterwards.

With dawn the weather moderated, and they decided to go for the summit, still nearly 2,000 ft above them. Neither was

* *Annapurna*, p. 92.

using oxygen, both were beginning to suffer from frostbite. After eight hours' climbing they got to the top. Then the weather showed signs of breaking and they had to get down as quickly as they could. On the way down Herzog took off his gloves for a moment to get something out of his haversack— he does not remember what—and he dropped the gloves. They rolled away over a precipice.

The loss was dreadful. To be gloveless at 26,000 ft with bad weather coming on might easily mean the loss of his hands. There was nothing to be done but to go on down.

They reached their bivouac of the night before to find that two more of the party, Lionel Terray and Gaston Rebuffat had come up to help them. Terray and Rebuffat undoubtedly saved their lives. Both Herzog and Lachenal were severely frostbitten, and Herzog's hands were in an appalling state. Rebuffat kept awake all night to massage Herzog, and Terray did the same for Lachenal. And the storm brought more heavy snow.

In the morning the four of them set off on the descent to the next camp, but in snow and thick mist they lost their way. They cast this way and that for the entire day. At nightfall they were still lost. They had no tents and spent the night sheltering from the wind in a crevasse. Towards morning an avalanche swept over the crevasse, deluging them with snow.

During the night Terray and Rebuffat had taken off Herzog's and Lachenal's boots in order to massage their feet. In the avalanche the boots were lost. By sheer effort of willpower Herzog reasoned that they *must* still be somewhere under the snow in the crevasse, and after an agony of digging in the snow they were found. Terray and Rebuffat were both suffering from snow-blindness, but they managed to haul Herzog and Lachenal out of the crevasse.

Still not knowing where they were, they continued the descent. Lachenal could barely walk, Herzog could not stand unless Terray or Rebuffat supported him. But Herzog and Lachenal could see, whereas Terray and Rebuffat were temporarily blind. So the crippled men had to guide the more or less fit as they clung to them.

They could make little progress. Herzog decided that he was simply getting in the way of the others and told them to leave him and try to save their own lives. The others refused to leave him. In this condition they were found by a search party from the camp: they were, in fact, only a few hundred yards away from the camp.

For the rest of the long journey back to the plains, Herzog and Lachenal had to be carried. The expedition's doctor (Jacques Oudot) saved their lives by a series of injections, which had to be given without any anaesthetic. They were excruciatingly painful. After this treatment the doctor was able to give his verdict. He thought that Lachenal would have to lose some toes, but that he would otherwise recover. To Herzog he said:

> I think that the fingers of your left hand will have to be amputated, but I hope to be able to save the end joints of your right hand fingers. If all goes well, you'll have passable hands. As for your feet, I'm afraid that all your toes will have to go, but that won't prevent you from walking. Of course, to begin with it will be difficult, but you will adapt yourself all right.*

Herzog decided that the time had come to open the expedition's one bottle of champagne. He insisted that the Sherpas who had accompanied the party should share in the celebration.

On getting back to France Herzog spent three years in hospital. He was then 35.

The typical Ulysses courage is the cool acceptance of risks, but Ulysses could be dashing, too. Maurice Herzog is a supreme example first of dashing courage and then of continued brave endurance. The question that must be asked, however, is, was it worth it?

Herzog's own reflections are pertinent. In his book, *Annapurna*, written in hospital, he described his approach to the summit:

> An enormous gulf was between us and the world. This was a different universe—withered, desert, lifeless; a fantastic universe, where the presence of man was not foreseen,

* *Annapurna*, p. 237.

perhaps not desired. We were braving an interdict, over-stepping a boundary.*

And on the summit:

> Our mission was accomplished. But at the same time we had accomplished something infinitely greater. How wonderful life would now become! What an inconceivable experience it is to attain one's ideal, and, at the very same moment to fulfil oneself! I was stirred to the depths of my being. Never had I felt happiness like this—so intense, and yet so pure. That brown rock, the highest of them all, that ridge of ice—were these the goals of a lifetime? Or were they, rather, the limits of man's pride?

This is the Ulysses driving force in exceptional purity of form. Herzog thinks of his achievement in terms of 'overstepping a boundary', but not merely a physical boundary; he feels that he has reached, at a particular point in time, perhaps the limits of human pride. For him, the price he had to pay was abundantly worth what it bought.

Yet doubts remain. What of the Ulysses canniness, the careful preparation for action? Herzog's dash for the summit of Annapurna, eight hours' climb away from his highest camp, meant the taking of appalling risks. It would have been sensible to wait in the bivouac at 24,600 ft for the next pair of his party to join him, and then to establish another camp a good deal nearer the summit. Sensible, certainly. But Herzog felt that he could not wait. The weather was breaking, and to wait even one more day might have meant foregoing all chance of getting to the top. To his thinking it was now or never. He chose now.

The loss of his gloves was sheer bad luck. In fact, he was not unprepared for some such emergency, and his hands need not have suffered as they did, for although he had no spare pair of gloves, he did carry a spare pair of socks, which he could have worn as mittens. Why he did not think of the socks he does not know. The precaution of having spare socks in his haversack, good general-purpose protection for either feet or hands, and saving the weight of carrying extra gloves, is good Ulysses

* *Annapurna*, p. 193.

thinking. Why he did not use them when the emergency came is inexplicable. At least, it is inexplicable by rational standards. But at 26,000 ft the mind may not be wholly rational. This is a risk that it is hard to calculate. No one could recommend Herzog's dash for the summit of Annapurna as good mountaineering practice. But it will remain an epic in mountaineering history.

The behaviour of Herzog and his companions in disaster is beyond criticism, as it is beyond praise. I have called it an example of absolute courage, and I can think of no other term for it. As leader of the expedition, Herzog was unquestionably right to tell the others to abandon him in order to have a better chance themselves, but I think that they were equally right to disobey. At the same time, had they left him to die on the mountain, they could scarcely have been criticised: three lives for one is a proper exchange. Herzog's condition *was* jeopardising the others, fatally, for all that he or they could know. Yet the determination of Herzog's companions to die with him rather than abandon him somehow stands out above all the pleadings of sense. They deserved a miracle, and they were granted one: it was miraculous that they were found.

For the rest of the world the French Annapurna expedition was an outstanding example of the Ulysses factor in man that determines him 'to strive, to seek, to find and not to yield'.

XII

Competitiveness—Sir Francis Chichester

COMPETITION is a spur to many men. It is usually present in
the Ulysses factor, but not necessarily strongly so. Heyerdahl
was not much interested in competition when he set out to
cross the Pacific on his raft, Tilman not at all when he bought
his bicycle to ride across Africa. Heyerdahl wanted to prove
that he *could* cross the Pacific on a raft, but he was not driven
by an urge to be the first to do so: indeed, it was essential to
his theory that he was *not* the first, for his object was to show
that prehistoric man had done so. Tilman was influenced by
the climber's wish to be the first to set foot on a particular
peak, and his voyages in *Mischief* were mostly planned to include reaching some remote rock or mountain that had not
been climbed before. But the driving force in Tilman has
been primarily to explore, to see beyond the next ridge,
round the next headland. His joy in mountains has been to
know them, not to 'conquer' them: his sadness in his moment
of triumph on Nanda Devi that the mountain had 'succumbed' is typical of him.

Herzog certainly wanted French climbers to be the first to
achieve a peak of over 26,000 ft, and he had a fierce determination to 'win' on Annapurna. It was, however, almost
chance that he reached the summit himself: he would have
been content for any of the climbers in his party to do so, and
had some of the others not been suffering from high-altitude
sickness the day before, he might well not have gone to the
top himself. The expedition's success on Annapurna was
achieved by his leadership, and he paid personally the highest
price, but he did not regard the final climb as a particularly
personal accomplishment. Competitive climbing, at any rate
in a national sense, was strong among his motives, but it was

only among his motives. The Ulysses factor in him was extremely complex.

Ulysses himself, the type-figure, liked to win, though he could not always do so. He took part in a wrestling match for a prize offered by Achilles during the siege of Troy. The prize was a big cauldron worth (according to Homer) a dozen oxen—far more valuable than the woman 'thoroughly trained in domestic work' offered as a consolation prize for the loser: she was worth only four oxen.

The match is reported in the *Iliad*. Achilles offered his prizes and:

> The great Telamonian Aias rose at once, and so did the resourceful Ulysses (Odysseus), who knew all the tricks. The two put on their shorts, stepped into the middle of the ring, and gripped each other in their powerful arms. They looked like a couple of those sloping rafters that a good builder locks together in the roof of a house to resist the wind. Their backs creaked under the pressure of their mighty hands; the sweat streamed down; and many blood-red weals sprang up along their sides and shoulders. And still they tussled on, each thinking of the fine cauldron that was not yet won. But Ulysses was no more able to bring down his man, and pin him to the ground, than Aias . . .

The result was considered to be a draw. They met again in a race:

> Aias soon shot ahead, but very close behind him came the good Ulysses, close as a girdled woman brings the shuttle to her breast as she carefully draws it along to get the bobbin past the warp. So little was there in it. Ulysses's feet were falling in the tracks of Aias before the dust had settled down again; and he kept up so well that his breath fanned Aias's head. He was straining every nerve to win . . . As they drew near the finish Ulysses offered up a silent prayer to Athene of the Flashing Eyes: 'Hear me, goddess, I need your valuable aid. Come down and speed up my feet.' Pallas Athene heard his prayer, and she lightened all his limbs. They were just about to dash up to the prize when

Aias slipped in full career. This was Athene's doing, and it happened where the ground was littered with dung.

It was bad luck on Aias, but Ulysses won, and took first prize.

Anyone who challenged Ulysses was likely to come off badly, for he was not only good at most things but also had an extremely quick and subtle mind. Athene's aid in his race with Aias would not have been considered unfair by his contemporaries: the gods might aid you or fight against you; that was mortal lot. Aias himself was a bit nettled, and when he picked himself up after slipping on the dung he said disgustedly, 'Damnation take it! I swear it was the goddess tripped me up—the one who always dances attendance like a mother on Ulysses.' But Homer reports that the onlookers 'only laughed at him'. In more modern terms it might be said that Ulysses saw the patch of dung and thought quickly enough to avoid it, whereas Aias did not. That was still bad luck on Aias, but Ulysses won. He took reverses, however, with a good grace, and when he could do no more than draw on his wrestling match with Aias he was not put out.

Competitiveness is a widespread human quality and, as such, may have nothing to do with the Ulysses factor. When a strong competitive spirit is allied to the Ulysses factor in man it can produce extraordinary results. For a case study of this we may consider Sir Francis Chichester.

In Chichester's life there have been two periods of intense personal effort, separated by some thirty years. The first was 1929–1931 during which he flew a small single-engined aeroplane singlehanded round Europe, from London to Australia, made the first east-to-west solo crossing of the Tasman Sea by air and flew alone from Australia to Japan, where his plans for continuing the flight round the world were ended by a serious crash which left him gravely injured. The second peak period was 1960–1967, in which Chichester raced a small sailing boat singlehanded across the Atlantic three times (1960, 1962 and 1964), making another ocean crossing after each race with his wife or wife and son as crew, and sailed alone round the world (1966–1967) to achieve the fastest circumnavigation of any small vessel; a speed record for singlehanded sailing by covering 1,400 miles in eight days; and the longest voyage (15,500 miles) up to that time made by any small vessel without touching port.* Six ocean crossings, three of them single-handed, and a singlehanded circumnavigation of the globe within seven years form a collective undertaking unmatched, as far as can be known, in history, and certainly unmatched by any man aged 59–66.

Chichester's earlier activities in the air are equally unmatched. In the twenties and early thirties of this century flying was still nearer magic than mechanics: for many people in the lands Chichester crossed in his flights in the Far East his little De Havilland Gipsy Moth was the first aircraft they had seen. He had a range of under 1,000 miles fully loaded, and he could not always take off with a full load of fuel; he landed in fields and forest clearings to pick up petrol where he could, pouring it into his tanks from cans through a collapsible funnel. For his sea crossings he converted his Gipsy Moth into a seaplane by replacing the landing-wheels with a pair of secondhand floats. He could not cross the Tasman Sea in one hop because he could not carry enough fuel: the crossing (and his life) depended on his being able to navigate accurately enough to find two minute islands, nearly 600 miles apart, where he could re-fuel on the way. He taught himself astro-navigation and devised a navigational system of his own for finding his pinpoints, entrusting his life to the accuracy of his system. He had, of course, to bring down his seaplane on the sea, adding swell and rocks to his other hazards.

He made his islets, but on his second islet his Gipsy Moth was wrecked at her moorings by a gale, sinking completely. With the help of the islanders he salvaged her, rebuilt her on the island and completed his flight to Sydney.

His flight onwards to Japan was the first solo flight from Australia to Japan, and the first long-distance solo flight by seaplane ever attempted. On taking off from Japan he was wrecked by flying into a line of telephone wires and very severely injured. He recovered, went home to England to visit his family and to write a book and then returned to New Zealand. In 1936 he piloted a friend in another aeroplane from Australia to England, via Pekin.

* In 1969 Robin Knox-Johnston completed a circumnavigation in Suhaili without a port of call.

Chichester was born in 1907, of an old West Country family: his father was a clergyman in North Devon. He had the traditional schooling at preparatory schools and public school (Marlborough), most of which he hated. At 17 he left school (without discussion with his father) because he wanted to emigrate to New Zealand. His father was not pleased. That was just after the First World War, and passages were hard to get. While waiting for a passage he worked as a farm labourer. After nearly a year he managed to get a passage, and went off to New Zealand with £10 given to him by his father. He travelled steerage, and earned a little money on the voyage by working in the stokehold as a fireman.

In New Zealand he tried his hand at various jobs—farm-hand, lumberjack, coalmining, prospecting for gold and selling magazine subscriptions from door to door. He saved a few hundred pounds and set up in business with an acquaintance as an estate agent. The business prospered, and he and his partner went in for land development. At 26 he was making £10,000 a year. At 28 he made a trip to England, bought a Gipsy Moth aeroplane and took some flying lessons. He had already made up his mind to fly back to Sydney by himself. A solo flight from England to Australia had been made only once before, by Bert Hinkler. Chichester wanted to try to beat Hinkler's time of fifteen and a half days. After a trial trip round Europe, taking his Gipsy Moth across France, Italy, Yugoslavia, Rumania, Poland and Germany, he set off for Sydney. He could not beat Hinkler's time, partly because he had under-estimated the delays and paperwork every time he came down for fuel, but mainly because he was held up for ten days at Tripoli with a broken propeller. But he duly made Sydney, becoming the second man to fly from England to Australia singlehanded. This flight left him with a kind of fever to make records in the air. The world slump after 1929 had taken most of his income, and he had few resources. To convert his Gipsy Moth into a seaplane he borrowed a pair of old floats from the New Zealand Air Force. After rebuilding his wrecked aircraft and completing his remarkable flight across the Tasman Sea he set off for Japan with a borrowed £44.

Chichester was 28 when he flew from England to Australia, 30 when he crashed in Japan. He was nearing 60 when he entered his next phase of peak endeavour. There is a curious repetition about these two phases of his life. Each required nearly thirty years of preparation, of self-discipline, self-training and (largely) self-education. As a boy and young man he overcame the handicap of poor eyesight—he had to wear glasses from childhood—by sheer determination, learning to box, to fly and to navigate in spite of his eyesight. In the years between his flying and his sailing he had to overcome first the injuries from his crash and then, in his late fifties, a serious lung-affliction. He learned to sail as he learned to fly, by concentrated effort of will-power. He had been ocean racing for only a few years when the first singlehanded Transatlantic race was mooted, but he decided at once that he wanted to win it. When it appeared doubtful if such a race could ever be organised he offered to race Colonel H. G. Hasler, whose idea it was, singlehanded across the Atlantic for half a crown.* The race, however, *was* organised and sailed for the first time in 1960, by Chichester, Hasler and three other entrants.

Chichester wanted to win, and he did win. His *Gipsy Moth III* was the largest boat in the fleet, which gave him an advantage in waterline length, which determines a boat's maximum speed, but which also put him at a disadvantage by the weight of sails and gear to be handled by one man. An ocean racer the size of *Gipsy Moth III*, 39 ft 7 in overall and 28 ft on the waterline, would normally be sailed by a crew of six.

Chichester's victory in 1960, however, did not satisfy him. He considered that his time of 40 days 11 hours 30 minutes from Plymouth to New York was too long. In 1962, with no one else to race against, he set out to race himself singlehanded across the Atlantic, and made the passage in just over 33 days, knocking the best part of a week off the time for his crossing in 1960. Still he was not satisfied: he believed that he ought to be able to make the crossing in thirty days. The Singlehanded Transatlantic Race is held at intervals of four years, so there was another race in 1964. Chichester, then aged 63, went in for it again, in the same boat, *Gipsy Moth III*. This time he did not win. *Gipsy Moth III* was now seven years old, and in the hard life of ocean racing, that is getting on: moreover, she had been sailed exceptionally hard. On this passage Chichester had serious trouble from a leak, which

* A coin now vanished. It was worth 12½ English New Pence.

demanded constant pumping and held him up badly. This race was won by the Frenchman Eric Tabarly, in a new boat of very light displacement, designed specially for single-handed sailing. Chichester came second, achieving at least the personal satisfaction of completing the passage a few minutes under his estimated time of thirty days.

He was not content. The fever for setting new records burned in him. He wanted a new boat, and he wanted to sail singlehanded not merely across one ocean but round the entire globe. He studied the records of passages by the clipper ships in the great days of sail, and he wanted to see if he could challenge such times sailing alone. He got his new boat and he sailed her singlehanded round the world, with one stop for repairs and a brief rest in Australia. The boat, *Gipsy Moth IV*, was bigger than *Gipsy Moth III* and therefore potentially faster, but she turned out a good deal heavier than he had intended. Her sail plan was divided over two masts to reduce the area of individual sails to be handled, but she was still an immense handful for one man. Moreover, her great length and relatively narrow beam, designed for speed, inevitably made her tender, or inclined to heel easily, thrilling over short races, but wearisome to a man who has to live and work at a steep angle day after day. Chichester had complaints about his boat when she was built. Nevertheless, she carried him safely round the world at a speed that cut by half the time taken for any previous singlehanded circumnavigation. In spite of losing his self-steering gear on the way, he reached Sydney in 107 days, well below the average of about 127 days for the great clippers and not far off the 100 days or so taken by the fastest clippers. In spite of capsizing in a storm in the Tasman Sea after leaving Australia, Chichester and his boat righted themselves physically and psychologically, and went on round Cape Horn to complete their passage home.

The Ulysses factor has been strong in Chichester from boyhood. His restless, rather lonely schooldays, the eager desire to go off by himself, his impatience with formal education, leaving school at the first opportunity to emigrate to New Zealand —all this is typical of the driving force in man that makes him feel that he *must* know what lies over the hill. Other type-qualities are strong in Chichester—courage, endurance, in-

genuity, quick-wittedness and great mental ability. He needs
to navigate, so he teaches himself navigation, and finding no
ready-made system that meets his particular navigational
problem, he devises a brilliant system of his own. His seaplane
is wrecked, so working from first principles with next to no
facilities on a remote island, he rebuilds it to continue his
flight. Time and again this combination of ingenuity and
practical imagination gets him out of difficulties that would
stop almost anybody else. His boat springs a leak in a Transatlantic race, but he has no thought of giving up: he fiddles
with screws and a block of wood in wretchedly cramped conditions, being thrown this way and that in heavy seas, reduces
the leak to proportions that he can keep down by pumping,
and carries on. The self-steering gear on *Gipsy Moth IV* is
fractured beyond hope of repair on the passage to Sydney, the
first half of his voyage round the world. Every argument of
common sense suggests calling off the passage to Sydney and
making for the much nearer port of Fremantle. But Chichester has set out to sail to Sydney, he is out to establish a
record. By taking the tiller himself and heaving-to for sleep he
could amble on for Sydney, but this is no good to him; it
would be nothing like fast enough. He fiddles with the trim of
sails, devises a new system of self-steering and goes on to make
a passage that is a record in most senses, even if it does not
quite meet his private par-time of 100 days. Sailing on from
Sydney, he capsizes in the Tasman Sea—enough, one would
say, for any man, let alone a man of 65. He tidies up, repairs
the damage and carries on to make more records. Greek
mythology could scarcely better this. Chichester might seem to
stand for the modern type-figure of Ulysses.

A deeper analysis shows, however, personal characteristics
in Chichester that are untypical and highly individual. His
personal demon is not simply a compelling need to find out,
though this is strong in him, but an even more compelling
urgency to be *first*, to win, beat all rivals. If there are no rivals
he invents them, or challenges ghosts, as he challenged the
ghosts of the masters of long-vanished clipper ships in his voyage round the world. This is Ulysses-plus. Chichester must
not merely see what lies over the hill but he must get there
faster than anybody else, and if no one has climbed that particular hill before, Chichester must set a time that later comers

will find hard to beat. If Chichester were a mountaineer he would climb against a stop-watch. He would work out what he regarded as par for reaching 25,000 ft, 26,000 ft or 27,000 ft on a particular mountain and remain discontented until he had beaten it.

The desire to beat par is to be found in all competitive sports, and the effort satisfies most sportsmen. Chichester must go farther—he must invent the sport. And to give him complete satisfaction it must be a game a man plays on his own. He will take on competitors: he does not want to be part of a team. When he was preparing for the first Singlehanded Transatlantic Race he wrote in his log:

> Somehow I never seemed to enjoy so much doing things with other people. I know now I don't do a thing nearly as well when with someone. It makes me think I was cut out for solo jobs, and any attempt to diverge from that lot only makes me a half-person. It looks as if the only way to be happy is to do fully what you are destined for.*

That is a revealing bit of self-knowledge. Yet Chichester is in no sense an anchorite or misanthrope. He is a good companion, loves his home and family. His 'oneness' is related to achievement: it is not in *living* that he wishes to be alone, but in *doing*; and his *doing* must be a peak of human effort, preferably something a bit beyond what has previously been regarded as the limit of human effort.

It can hardly be chance that the two peak-periods of intense singlehanded endeavour in his life have each required something like thirty years of preparation. If he had not been injured when his seaplane crashed in Japan in 1931 he would have gone on to complete his solo flight round the world. What then? It is interesting to speculate, but profitless. He might have taken earlier to sailing, he might have invented some quite unguessed form of new endeavour. I think he would not. I think his years of intense personal effort in the air required a long fallow period to prepare for his next adventuring.

If Chichester had lived earlier, would geographical exploration have satisfied him? Again it is interesting to speculate.

* Francis Chichester (Sir), *Alone Across the Atlantic*. Hodder & Stoughton 1961.

On the face of things an unreached Pole, an undiscovered source of the Nile, would have been a magnet to an earlier Chichester. Yet I think not. Arctic journeys are scarcely undertakings for one man. Central African or desert exploration offer more scope to individualism, but the tempo of such journeying is slow. Chichester seeks an intensity of action. He will spend months and years in study and the preparations for action, but, for him, when the time comes to act the action must be swift and all-demanding. It is significant that although Everest remained a challenge to man until Chichester was in his fifties, he never took to mountaineering. There has been a singlehanded attempt on Everest, by Maurice Wilson in 1933, but it was not of the Chichester type. Wilson's effort, which led to his death on the mountain, was more a spiritual pilgrimage than practical expedition. Mountaineering requires team activity. It was not for Chichester.

Chichester has some affinities with Burton, Doughty and other great travellers of the past, but he is not really much like them. I think he has closer affinities with Leonardo da Vinci: if aircraft had not been invented Chichester might well have spent his life devising wings for man, and perhaps have lost his life in experimenting with them. An earlier Chichester would have been primarily an inventor. He might have invented anything with a practical purpose in extending physical boundaries—the aeroplane, the sextant, the slide rule, logarithms. That all were invented already led him to invent his own field of discovery.

That invention is his real achievement. The exploits which have brought him fame and a knighthood have been little understood and, on the whole, wrongly applauded. People have thought, How wonderful for an elderly man to sail across an ocean by himself! How even more wonderful for such a man to take a little boat round Cape Horn! These things are moderately remarkable, no more. Seventy-five years ago, Joshua Slocum, without benefit of radio or self-steering, and in a boat he built himself, sailed round the world singlehanded at the age of 51. True, Slocum was fourteen years younger than Chichester, but there is not all that in it; at 51 you are getting on and Slocum had none of the advantages of modern synthetic yarn for rope and sails and other lightweight materials that Chichester had. It is a feat to sail round

Sir Francis Chichester

Sir Alec Rose

the world singlehanded at any age, but scarcely an earth-shaking matter.

Chichester's achievement has been to *race* singlehanded across oceans with the intensity of the master of a fully crewed ocean-racing yacht, maintained for twenty or thirty times longer than anything normally regarded as an ocean race, a feat perhaps comparable with setting out to climb Everest running. His apprenticeship to this invented self-challenge was formidable enough. In his first Transatlantic race in 1960 he changed sail 118 times in forty days, this in addition to the endless task of trimming sails to get the best out of his boat. Unless you have handled a flogging sail in rough weather it is hard to understand what it means. Chichester describes one such tussle in his first singlehanded race:

> It was now blowing up pretty hard, and I tried to reef the main. It seemed a desperately tough job. Everything jammed or caught up. If I headed the boat into the wind the mainsail could be reefed easily enough, but would flog itself to bits while the least wind I could keep her in to keep her quiet was too much for reefing because it pressed the sail against the shrouds and jammed the slides in their track. I did get two reefs rolled down but the wind increased faster than I could reef. It was blowing a whole gale by now. Finally I gave up reefing and lowered the whole sail. By now even this had become quite a job. As soon as the sail was down the boom began swinging from side to side and must be hobbled before it caused havoc. At the critical moment the topping lift uncleared itself and let the boom on to the lifeline round the ship. But luck was with me. I caught the flying part of the topping lift before it disappeared in the sky above and I hauled on it to lift the boom off the lifeline while I hauled on the mainsheet at the same time to clamp down the swinging boom. What a murderous weapon that boom can be! *

This was in a race in which he had flesh-and-blood competitors against him. It is hard to go on deck to hand sail in bad weather at any time, but at least it stiffens resolution to have known rivals who are probably doing the same thing, or

* *Alone Across the Atlantic*, p. 89

L

on whom you can perhaps steal a march. In 1962 in the Atlantic and in 1966–1967 round the world Chichester had no rivals: his only challenge came from himself. He met it as fiercely.

Chichester has not sailed his oceans: he has driven himself across the seas with the minimum of rest, grudging every minute during which he might be losing a fraction of a knot because his sails were not trimmed to perfection. No hard-case skipper in the clipper days can have driven a crew as hard as Chichester has driven himself. I have called his first single-handed race in 1960 his apprenticeship to this form of self-driving, but that is true only of his experience at sea. In his solo flights thirty years before his solo voyages his performance was the same. In the early 1930s a solo flight over a wild quarter of the world where no aeroplane had been seen before was a task more daunting than a singlehanded ocean passage in a well-found yacht. Chichester had to find somewhere every few hundred miles to come down for fuel, to make repairs without the facilities of even the smallest wayside garage nowadays, to risk the fear or hostility of savage peoples—in some of the jungles over which he flew a very serious risk. One might think that the accomplishment of such flying was enough. Chichester could have made things far easier for himself by accepting more leisurely flights and resting for longer when he came down. But however tired he was, the moment he came down he was impatient to be away again. He fought sleep as he fought anything else that seemed to threaten a mile of his day's race. He was making history in the air by flying alone from Australia to Japan, but it was not enough to make aviation history: it had to be fast history; fast enough to be hard to follow. He drove himself by air as later he was to drive himself by sea. He has felt the chronometer against him whatever he has been doing, and he has fought time on his own harsh terms. In his race round the world against himself—or in some sense perhaps against ghosts—he was not feeling well for much of the time, and during his voyage his arm was badly hurt. These things made no difference to his determination to drive on.

Such extremity of self-discipline is not easy to understand: it is simpler to see Chichester as a grand old seadog making long passages alone for the hell of it. This is a picture so out of focus that it leads to other false pictures. Chichester has done some harm to his own reputation by his complaints against the boat that carried him round the world. In the sentimental tradition of grand old seadogs a man does not complain of his boat. Nor is this tradition only sentiment. Most seamen feel affection for their ships, often a deep love for them, and even if they sometimes behave as bitches, affection is not destroyed. The relationship between man and boat is peculiarly intimate. Tilman's love for *Mischief* as for an old friend is a true emotion, neither forced nor unusual.

In this sense Chichester is not really a seaman, but rather an expert navigator and aero-dynamicist at sea. *Gipsy Moth IV* was planned as a sailing machine, in Chichester's vision she was to be perfection in transforming wind and water forces into forward movement. His hunger in her was for perfection, and when she fell short of being perfect he felt angry and let down. If he had demanded less, or been less honest about his demands, he would have been (or seemed) more content. But then he would not have been Chichester. His approach to the sea, as to the air, is mainly technical. The air was, the sea became, his vehicle for doing things that had never been attempted before, and in the accomplishment of his self-set tasks his aeroplane, his boat, his own body are mere instruments for carrying out his purpose. He is critical of his instruments, of himself often, because his standards of performance are so high.

I have called the picture of Chichester as a grand old seadog out of focus: I have chosen this term carefully, because a picture may be out of focus but yet there. Chichester, the cold calculating aero-dynamicist, is real and often dominant, but he is not the whole Chichester. The Ulysses factor in man is always touched by romance: for some men in whom the factor is strong the romance of seeking the unknown may be its main driving force. Chichester has much poetry in him. The reflection of a star in a still sea can move him deeply, and on his lonely voyages he delights in the company of birds. In mid-Atlantic in 1962, for all his passion to establish a record for a singlehanded crossing, he spent a long time in trying to rescue a racing pigeon which had landed exhausted on his boat and which later fell into the sea. He applied every scrap of technique in boat handling to manoeuvre to recover the pigeon

—it is extraordinarily difficult to pick up an object as small as a pigeon from a big yacht with a high freeboard in an ocean swell. He succeeded, and then spent more time in trying to revive the bird with hot-water bottles and artificial respiration. That Chichester is as real as any other.

Ulysses, the type-figure, was always aware of the immanence of power outside man. In Homer's setting this power is personified in gods and goddesses, who sometimes helped, sometimes hindered Ulysses, and to whom he was careful to pay attention. This sense of an external power is allied to the Ulysses factor in man, though obviously it can exist independently. It is religious in the deepest sense, though it is not necessarily expressed by attachment to the forms of any established religion. Heyerdahl's religious upbringing was contorted by discord between his parents, his father teaching him a simple faith in God, his mother dismissing his father's beliefs as nonsense. Yet Heyderdahl retained acceptance of the power of God. At a critical moment of his life his biographer records that he 'prayed—as he had not prayed since he was a child'.*

Chichester is conscious of this power. He has recorded several occasions in his life when he has been moved to an action that turned out later to have been imperative for his safety by some influence that he cannot explain. During the rebuilding of his aeroplane he forgot to lock some bracing wires in the wing-assembly and fabric was being sewn over the assembly with the wires unlocked. He woke suddenly in the night to realise the omission, 'To be told from within, I would say,'† he writes. In the Transatlantic Race of 1960 he was closing the coast of Nova Scotia but reckoned that he had enough sea room to keep his self-steering gear set to the course he wanted for two hours while he had a sleep. No sooner had he dropped off to sleep than his jib began flapping and the rigging whirred in the wind. The noise woke him, but he could see no reason for going off on the other tack, so he tried to get to sleep again. Noise in the rigging would not let him sleep, and at last he gave up, put about and stood away from land on a tack that he did not want to make. After this things

* *Senor Kon-Tiki*, p. 85.
† Francis Chichester (Sir), *Lonely Sea and the Sky*, p. 148. Hodder & Stoughton 1964.

quietened down and he slept for the next five hours. When he woke up and studied the chart he found that he had made a mistake which could easily have meant disaster. He had changed from one chart sheet to another without realising that the scale of the new chart was less than half that of the old, so that when he thought that he was 20 miles offshore in reality he was only 8 miles off. Had he slept and stood on for two hours it would probably have meant shipwreck. Describing this incident, Chichester observes, 'I am recording plain unmistakeable facts. I do not try to explain them.'* He has experienced other such incidents. His recovery from his serious lung affliction could well be called miraculous, and owes much to his own and his wife Sheila's faith. Chichester has slightly revised the prayer in the Litany for deliverance from sudden death to 'From death *before we are ready to die*, Good Lord deliver us'. This seems to me to make a much better prayer. Merely to fear sudden death is a cringing rather than an ennobling fear. To fear death before one has accomplished a purpose in life reflects both the dignity and the humility of man.

Ulysses called on his gods for help from time to time, but he expected to get out of his own scrapes, with divine aid, perhaps, but not by calling for rescue parties. Self-reliance is a Ulysses characteristic, and it is strong in all manifestations of the Ulysses factor. Tilman's attitude to safety appliances at sea seems to me rather too austere, but it is typical of the man, and in fact Tilman has never had to be rescued from anything. When *Mischief* met final disaster in the ice off Jan Mayen, Tilman brought her to shore without assistance. Herzog owes his life to his companions, but theirs was not a rescue effort from outside: they were members of his own party, and the party met and overcame disaster from its own resources. Chichester has never expected rescue on his solo flights and voyages: he has been consistent in this throughout his life. When he planned his seaplane flight to Japan the Dutch authorities were reluctant to let him fly over what was then Dutch territory in the East Indies because of the difficulty and expense of searching for him if he had to make a forced landing. This made Chichester impatient, for he insisted that he wanted to go at his own risk. 'I did not want anybody to go

* *Alone Across the Atlantic.*

searching for me if I got into a mess,'* he wrote. He carried radio on his voyage round the world, and after his capsize in the Tasman Sea he was asked by radio if he required assistance. He replied that he did not. The record of the true Ulysses type in looking after themselves is extraordinarily good.

Self-reliance is formalised in the rules of the Singlehanded Transatlantic Race, which state:

> Yachts must be fully independent and capable of carrying out their own emergency repairs at sea. Crews have no right to expect or demand rescue operations to be launched on their behalf.

There are practical limits to such austerity. The Tilmans, Chichesters and their peers may not want other people to go looking for them if they are overdue on some adventure, but the rest of the world cannot stand by and let a man go to his death if there is any chance of rescue. In the age of the first Ulysses there was not much to be done anyway if a man disappeared into the unknown: there was no radio, there were no aircraft, and nobody could have much idea of where to look. This situation remained much the same over most of the world's history. Even so, people cannot simply do nothing about a man who seems to have disappeared. When Ulysses was some ten years overdue on his return from Troy his son Telemachus went off to try to pick up news of him. Stanley went to Central Africa to find Livingstone. In the modern world, with swift communications and a great machine of organised search capable of being put into action quickly, an adventurer who disappears will have search parties looking for him whether he wants them or not. Such searches are expensive, and unpopular with Governments or other organisations which may have to foot the bill. They could fairly easily bring adventuring into disrepute. In fact, the cost to the world of adventurers of the true Ulysses type has been negligible, and it is likely to remain so. There is no danger here from the Ulysses factor in man. There is danger from pseudo-manifestations of the factor, of which I shall have something to say later.

* *Lonely Sea and the Sky*, p. 172.

Chichester's achievement, like Heyerdahl's, is felt by some to have been demeaned by the fact that he has made money out of it. This is another picture out of focus. Chichester is a man of great ability in many fields. At 26 he was earning £10,000 a year: partly by the luck, perhaps, of being in New Zealand at a time of rapid development after the First World War. But it was not luck that took him to New Zealand, and it was not luck that showed him there was money in property development. Rather, it was applied vision and imagination, both fairly rare qualities which command their price. If Chichester had been concerned primarily with making money he could have found easier and far more profitable ways of doing so than solo adventuring. As things turned out, his youthful fortune vanished in the slump of 1929. But a slump which makes most men poor also offers opportunities to the astute of buying cheaply and laying the foundations of a later fortune. The young Chichester had all the qualities needed for this sort of business had he wanted to use them. He preferred solo flying on a shoestring. He was thirty-eight when the Second World War came. He tried at once to join the Royal Air Force, but was rejected for his poor eyesight. With his inventiveness and peculiar knowledge of navigational devices there is little doubt but that he could have profited by the war had making money been of much concern to him. Instead, he moved heaven and earth to get into the RAF somehow, and having achieved this by sheer ability as a navigational instructor he was content to spend the rest of the war doing a job as an instructor without bothering about promotion. He was rather casually treated by the RAF, which, because he asked for nothing, gave nothing, and made great use of his peculiar gifts with little in the way of acknowledgment. Precisely the same thing happened to that great engineer W. O. Bentley in the First World War.

After the war he went into business on his own as a map publisher, but he was always more interested in the techniques of map-making than in selling. His business prospered because he produced unusually good maps, but he made no great fortune. When he decided to build *Gipsy Moth III* he was ill and beset by money worries. The decision to go ahead and build the yacht that was to bring him fame on the sea was an act of faith by him and his wife.

It is possible to potter about the world singlehanded in a reasonably sound boat without needing much money: the boat provides a home, and modest tastes can be modestly met. Chichester wanted none of this. His boats had to be sailing machines tuned to the highest pitch, capable not only of making fast passages but also of being driven faster, if possible, than anyone else's boat. The Singlehanded Transatlantic Race which brought Chichester back to prominence after his exploits in the air thirty years earlier is sailed across the Atlantic from east to west. That is the uphill passage: the prevailing winds are from ahead, and for most of the time a sailing boat must be beating into the wind. That is hard sailing, hard on boat and gear. It is expensive sailing on any terms. On Chichester's terms it is very expensive indeed.

Chichester takes a considerable personal pride in being one of the relatively few pre-war (Second World War) pilots who bought his own aeroplane and financed record-breaking exploits in the air wholly from his own money. What could be done in 1931 could not be done in 1960. To compete in yacht races for the America's Cup not merely rich men but syndicates of rich men are needed. In spite of a change in the rules repealing the requirement that competing yachts must sail to the rendezvous on their own bottoms, and reducing the size of yachts from the great J-class vessels of before the war to 12 metres, neither a Lipton nor a Sopwith now could hope to compete unaided. Chichester's demands on a boat are harder than in 12-metre racing. This is seldom appreciated. His boats, of course, are smaller, he applies much ingenuity of his own, and his exploits in the Atlantic and round Cape Horn have cost many times less than it costs to build, equip and crew a 12-metre for the America's Cup. Still, it has been very costly.

He has met the cost by writing for newspapers, and by the sponsorship of a few individuals and industrial organisations who have considered his endeavours of value to Britain and the prestige of their own trade. He has made money, as Heyerdahl has, from best-selling books, and by lecturing. None of this is in any sense demeaning. Ulysses could tell a good story, and he expected to be rewarded for it. Why not? Men who make nails or bread or publish newspapers expect to be paid for it, and the world which uses their products expects to pay them. It is, perhaps, a pity that national heroes have families, grocers' bills and demands for income tax. But they do. A knighthood carries no income with it. Chichester (and his fellows) have suffered too from other people's inability to understand fatigue. A yacht club or a local literary society may consider that the greatest honour it can convey is to invite a man to speak to them. So in that small private world it is, and so it ought to be. But if a man has five hundred invitations by the same post, what is he to do? People are not always kindly in their demands, and when they are refused they say, 'This man is getting too big for his boots.' It is easier to sail an ocean singlehanded than to live up to national notoriety.

Chichester is a national hero: it is reasonable to ask why. What has he done? His exploits in the air are barely remembered: when tourists by the ten thousand queue to fly in jet planes at 600 miles an hour, and soon above the speed of sound, what does it matter that a man once flew from England to Australia in 29 days?

His achievement at sea is even more tenuous. He has taken a small sailing boat across the Atlantic—so have many other men, and at least one woman. He has sailed round the world singlehanded—Joshua Slocum did so in 1895–1898, and a number of other lone sailors have followed Slocum. Chichester has sailed faster: true, but speed records are transitory things. His Atlantic record of 33 days 15 hours 7 minutes in 1962 lasted just two years, when Eric Tabarly made the crossing in 27 days 3 hours 56 minutes. Chichester's time in that race was 29 days 23 hours 57 minutes—three minutes inside his private target of 30 days, but three minutes, although they meant a lot to him, are not much of an endorsement on a passport to eternity. Moreover, he came second, and the world remembers winners.

Yet Chichester will be remembered. The world's instinct to applaud him is right, although its reasons for applause may usually be wrong. Others may sail round the world faster and in smaller boats, but the idea of racing under sail singlehanded round the world was Chichester's own, just as the idea of racing himself across the Atlantic was unique. If age is taken into account, Chichester's performance at 65 will not often be bettered. Tilman has made long voyages in harsh seas when some years older than Chichester, and far older men than either have sailed themselves about the world. But Tilman's voyages, all other men's voyages, are quite different from Chichester's. He has not sailed to arrive anywhere, to climb a mountain, reach a new country, to do anything at his far port. He has sailed always against himself, driving himself to the limit of endurance, and then a bit beyond each former limit. The frontiers that Chichester has extended have been the bounds of man's physical frame, he has explored within himself where no one but he could have explored. And he has found something in man to move the rest of the world to wonder.

XIII

Oriental Ulysses—Kenichi Horie

For reasons which are probably not chance (see Chapters 4 and 22) most major manifestations of the Ulysses factor since the Second World War have come from Western Europe. But the factor is common to mankind, and an outstanding example of modern Ulysses man is Japanese. In 1962, the year in which Chichester set out to race himself across the Atlantic, and at about the same time of year, Kenichi Horie left Osaka for a singlehanded passage of the Pacific to San Francisco. Horie was not much, if at all, influenced by Chichester, who at that time was not widely known outside the specialist field of history in the air. Horie's personal heroes were Joshua Slocum and the French doctor Alain Bombard, who had crossed the Atlantic alone in a rubber boat in 1952 to experiment in human survival. Bombard believed that man can survive at sea by living on plankton if he cannot catch fish, and by obtaining drinking water from the sea itself, either by taking sea water neat in minute sips or, better, by mixing it with the juices expressed from fish, when a near-desalinised liquid is produced. To test his theories he sailed in his rubber boat *L'Heretique*, similar to a survival raft, without fresh water or provisions, from Las Palmas to Barbados. His passage took sixty-five days. For fifty-three days he lived as he had planned, and he then had a brief respite on a steamer which came up to him. He rejoined his boat to continue his voyage alone, making Barbados after another twelve days at sea. Bombard suffered severely, but he survived. Slocum's *Sailing Alone Around the World* and Bombard's *Voyage of the Heretique*, with the log books of the Japanese sail-training ships *Nippon-Maru* and *Umitaka-Maru*, were Horie's mentors.

He was 7 when the war ended with the defeat and occupa-

tion of Japan. His schooling in the years immediately following the war was in a period at once one of the most difficult
but also, perhaps, one of the most outward-looking of Japan's
national history. He was quite good at school, particularly at
maths, but he had the typical Ulysses impatience with formal
education. His father, a fairly prosperous businessman dealing in spare parts for motor cars, wanted him to go to a university, but young Horie did not want to. What he did want
to do was to sail across the Pacific in his own boat. He did not
discuss his ideas much with his parents, mainly because he
didn't want to hurt their feelings. His father and his mother,
to whom he must have been a considerable anxiety, showed a
deep, if perhaps unconscious, understanding. They neither
encouraged nor attempted dictatorially to discourage him. It
is an interesting relationship. One is reminded oddly of
Laertes and Anticleia and their boy, half the world away in
space and three thousand years away in time.

Horie began training for his self-set task in boyhood, joining his school's sailing club and learning thoroughly how to
sail a dinghy. He collected maps, charts, magazine articles,
everything that had the remotest bearing on Pacific weather
and sailing conditions. He struggled to learn English, partly
in order to be able to read books in English, partly to be able
to make himself understood by the natives when he got to the
far side of his ocean.

His parents, although prosperous, were not rich, and he
had to acquire a boat and fit out his expedition entirely from
his own resources. On leaving school he worked in his father's
business and was able to put by the equivalent of £3 to £4
sterling a month out of his wages, because he was able to go
on living at home. Later he added to his savings by doing a
part-time job in a travel agency.

By the time he was 23 he had saved nearly £500, which he
reckoned was enough to buy a boat. She would have to be very
small, but he had brought himself up to sail dinghies, and
small size did not worry him. He bought plans for a 19-ft sailing cruiser, designed by the Japanese naval architect A. Yoko-
yama and commissioned a boatyard to build from them. His
finished boat was 19 ft 1½ in long with a beam of 6 ft 7 in. The
only equipment he did not have to pay for was a suit of sails,
which a friend obtained for him as a gift. Horie's boat was

considerably less than half the size of *Gipsy Moth III* in which Chichester sailed the Atlantic.

An awkward problem was that the design of his boat was new, and that his boat was the fourth of her class to be built. In the ordinary way boats of one class are given sail numbers in serial order of building, so that Horie's boat, which he named *Mermaid,* would have been number 4. The number 4 in Japanese, pronounced *shi,* has ominous implications, because it sounds similar to the word meaning death. Horie persuaded the designer to let his boat be numbered 5. It was not, he argued, that he was actually superstitious for himself, but perhaps he might want to sell the boat one day, and a sail number 4 might put off a possible purchaser. Ulysses would have understood entirely and approved.

Early in May 1962 he sailed. He had no publicity because he allowed no one outside his family and close friends to know of his plans. Even with them he was discreet and almost secretive. He had no passport. To apply for a passport in Japan then it was necessary to state one's proposed journey and mode of travel. He doubted if he would be given a passport to sail to San Francisco singlehanded in a 19-ft boat. He was much more worried about officialdom than the sea. It is pleasing to add that when he reached San Francisco ninety-four days after leaving Osaka the US Customs and Immigration authorities behaved generously. They ignored his passportless state and gave him a thirty-day visitor's visa. Back in Japan, he was given a hero's welcome home and an official reprimand for leaving the country without a passport. Modern Ulysses has troubles that the type-figure could not have guessed.

Horie's personality is of peculiar interest and importance, in that he has managed to convey a more precise description of the Ulysses motive than almost anyone else. Hard as it is to translate Japanese idiom into Western terms, Horie's account of his feelings in preparing for his voyage is simple, lucid, and psychologically profound. It is a sharp illustration of the universality of the Ulysses factor: like music, it can provoke emotional understanding and response that transcend language.

On his return to Japan Horie wrote a book on his voyage called *Taiheiyo Hitoribotchi*, which translated literally, means *The Pacific All Alone*. The Japanese title conveys something both of the uniqueness and the singlehandedness of the exploit. In English it does not—it has next to no meaning at all. So Takuichi Ho and Kaoru Ogimi, who translated the Japanese text into English, changed the title to *Kodoku*, which means *solitude*, with the sub-title *Sailing Alone Across the Pacific*. The change is expressive, both of the difficulty of rendering Japanese thought in English and of Horie's approach to the expedition. *Kodoku* helps to convey the *singlemindedness* as well as the self-reliance of the man. It does *not* mean loneliness. In *Kodoku* Horie writes:

> What made you want to cross the Pacific? Why did you do it? What did you expect to get out of it? I must have been asked these questions hundreds of times since my trans-Pacific cruise. Writers, newspaper reporters and all kinds of other people came to see me, always with these same questions. I guess they expected me to say something that would sound nice or startling or convincing or exceptional... I had a rough time trying to think of something that would satisfy them, but I always ended up with, 'Well, I crossed it just because I wanted to'. Honestly, I didn't have any purpose or motive other than that...
>
> Since the Pacific is the only real open sea for us Japanese, anyone who loves to sail and wants to plan a real cruise—I don't mean a yachting trip along the coast—will turn his eyes to the Pacific... He has to sail on the Pacific, and because there is no other open sea available to him, he has to cross it, if he can.
>
> Has any Japanese yachtsman ever before reached the American coast alone? I'm told the answer is no. Others have done it, but it was always a foreigner who did it... Maybe I had a craving for the fame of being the first Japanese yachtsman to cross the Pacific singlehanded, but I don't know.

That is honest writing. At one American press conference Horie's attempted explanation of his feeling that he had to cross the Pacific because he *wanted* to was interpreted as conveying the same meaning as George Mallory's famous reply to a questioner who asked why he wanted to climb Everest— 'Because it is there.' When he understood what had happened, Horie was bothered by it. He did not at all mean to say that he wanted to sail the Pacific 'because the Pacific is there'. The Pacific exists, certainly: that is a fact of geography. Horie sailed it in his 19-ft boat because he wanted to get to the other side. That is quite different from wanting to climb Everest because the mountain exists as a perpetual challenge. Horie had not the slightest wish to *conquer* the Pacific, and no shred of feeling of conquest when he had crossed it. Of fulfilment, yes: he had done what he had set out to do. But not of victory in an ordinary sense. He sailed because he had to, and he had to sail because he wanted to. That simple passion of wanting to know, to experience, to see for yourself is among the hardest things in the world to put into words. It is the driving force of the Ulysses factor, and it was overwhelmingly strong in Horie.

His is an important case-study in yet another way, because he exemplifies, again in almost text-book terms, the calculated risk-taking of the true Ulysses type. This is shown by the forethought and preparation that went into his enterprise. A good example is his planning of fresh water for the passage. For singlehanded passage-making in boats of the size that Chichester has sailed in, fresh water is no great problem: there is ample room for water to meet the needs of one man. For Horrie it was more difficult. His 19-ft boat was very small, and he had to keep down weight. A gallon of water weighs roughly 10 lb.

He began by taking the usually accepted figure that a man needs half a gallon of fresh water a day to survive without discomfort—this is for drinking and cooking only, and allows nothing for washing. A reasonable time for his Pacific passage would be 100 days, but he had to allow for contingencies, so he estimated his requirement as water for 120 days. At half a gallon a day that meant carrying 600 lb of water. He considered this out of the question.

He made further researches, and discovered that certain lifeboat regulations require only just over one quart of water per man per day to be carried. This, of course, is a ration for survival, not comfort, but he was concerned primarily with survival. A quart a day for 120 days meant 30 gallons, weighing about 300 lb. This also he felt to be too much.

He reflected on Bombard's experience of living on sea water and such desalinised water as he could get from the juices of fish, but decided that his and Bombard's purposes were not comparable: Bombard needed only to survive on a rubber lifeboat, but he had to be fit enough to work his boat singlehanded. Nevertheless, Bombard's experiment was relevant to survival if the worst came to the worst, so Horie felt that he could safely reduce some of his lifeboat ration.

Next he calculated alternatives. So far he had been considering water as water, but for drinking purposes he reckoned that he could include the liquid content of his other stores, such as the juice of his tinned fruits. He preferred tea to beer, but tea required fresh water. He decided to take a proportion of his drinking fluid in canned beer, feeling that he would drink less beer than the tea he might otherwise be tempted to make. He calculated the chances of rain to replenish water supplies during his voyage, and reasoned that he could probably get some water from fog if he was careful to have a bucket handy to catch condensation from his sails. In the end he took 18 gallons of fresh water, on the face of things a fearfully slim life-line for a voyage that might last 120 days, but he was right to have confidence in his reasoning. He reached San Francisco with $2\frac{1}{2}$ gallons of water in hand.

His planning in everything else was as detailed. Fearing the possibility of toothache, he concluded that his best precaution would be strict self-discipline in cleaning his teeth after every meal, so he took three tooth brushes. He considered his own morale. To keep up his strength, he reflected, it might often be necessary to eat at times when he would not feel much like eating, and it would therefore be important to avoid things that might put him off food. He had a personal idiosyncrasy in disliking the feel of plastic cups and plates, so in spite of their greater weight and risk of breakage, he took a china cup and saucer, and four china bowls for soup or rice. On passage, he was meticulous in keeping whatever china he was not using for a meal wrapped up and stowed away safely.

Quite early on the voyage, on the eighteenth day of his ninety-four-day passage, he began deliberately to talk to himself. He felt that there were two people in him, one strong and determined to drive the boat to San Francisco, the other rather a weakling, who preferred to lie in his bunk. He wrote:

One fellow was lazy—didn't have any guts. The other one was pretty rough the way he handled people, specially lazy ones, but he was determined and sure. He always knew exactly what had to be done and was all set to go. He was the one that *had* to come out on top—he usually did. I would never have made San Francisco otherwise.*

He records conversations between his two selves:

'Come on, get to work.'
'Don't be in such a hurry, let me rest a little.'
'No. Work comes first.'
'Why are you so mean to me? Lay off, will you?'
'I don't care. Come on, get going. I'll fix you a meal when you are through work.'
'OK, OK. If it's got to be done, I suppose it has to be done.'*

He pretended that his two selves worked together, tackling the job in hand as if they were two people, one giving instructions to the other. At meals they would carry on long conversations.

This is an extract parallel with the type-figure. In Homer's idiom Ulysses conversed with gods and goddesses, in the guise sometimes of other human beings, sometimes of birds that talked, like the sea-nymph who came to him disguised as a seamew just before he was wrecked off the Phaeacian coast. Horie's self-communing is a precise psychological transliteration of a characteristic that was strong in the type-figure.

The temptation to act on impulse and to ignore reason is often felt. It is a Ulysses quality to be able to resist the temptation. Chichester's life depended on the precision of his navigation when to change course to make a landfall on the islet

* Kenichi Horie, *Kodoku*, p. 116. Collins 1965.

M

in the Tasman Sea which he had selected for re-fuelling. He had planned the navigation for months, and on his flight he had checked and rechecked all his calculations. When the moment came for reason to tell him to change course he duly turned. He writes:

> The moment I settled on this course, nearly at right angles to the track from New Zealand, I had a feeling of despair. After flying in one direction for hour after hour over a markless, signless sea, my instinct revolted at suddenly changing direction in mid-ocean. My navigational system seemed only a flimsy brain-fancy: I had been so long on the same heading that the island must lie ahead, not to the right. I was attacked by panic. Part of me urged, for God's sake don't make this crazy turn! My muscles wanted to bring the seaplane back to its old course. 'Steady, steady, steady,' I told myself aloud. I had to trust my system, for I could not try anything else now, even if I wanted to.

Horie had similar experiences. One night he was below and felt sure that his *Mermaid* was sailing well on a good course for San Francisco. She *was* sailing well, but in fact the wind had been shifting gradually, and she was taking him back towards Japan. He was furious with himself when he discovered this in the morning:

> There was nobody I could take it out on but myself, and I simmered down after a while. The lesson had to be learned, however... From here on I set myself two rules: Keep an eye on the compass as often as possible and do not let 'feeling' be your guide under any circumstances.

As a punishment for having trusted to 'feeling' during that night he sentenced himself to one day's hard labour, forcing himself to spend the day in doing a number of arduous and not immediately necessary jobs, such as reversing all his running rigging so that chafe would fall on new sections of it. His tasks were all good seamanlike precautions, so his sentence was a practical one. But it required strong self-discipline to serve it then and there. Ulysses would have been punished by a god. Horie punished himself. The outcome in readiness to learn from a mistake is the same.

Horie was alone for ninety-four days, but he was not lonely. Partly he had too much to do. This is the common experience of those who have done much sailing alone, but there is another element providing a sort of prophylaxis against loneliness at sea in the sense of kinship that develops between man and boat. It is hard not to feel that a boat is alive: it is not mere fancy that calls a boat 'she' and never 'it'. After living with a boat for any length of time the constant little noises of wind and water on rigging and hull almost become speech. But Horie's lack of loneliness was more than any of this: it reflected his sense of purpose and self-fulfilment. He had a job that required the concentration of all his faculties, emotional as well as mental and physical, and this left nothing for him to feel lonely *about*. Loneliness is a symptom of human inadequacy, and in its common forms contains a considerable element of self-pity. Horie did not feel inadequate. He felt humble in relation to the immensity of the sea and the power of the wind, but he knew what he was doing, he had trained himself to do it, and planned everything he could. There is no trace of self-pity in his thoughts or behaviour during the voyage: he was doing what he wanted to do above all else, and he considered himself fortunate to be able to do it. He came as nearly as a man may to being completely happy. He did not enjoy solitude in the way that a world-weary man may go into the wilderness to seek refreshment of spirit in being alone. He simply accepted solitude as a necessary component of his task.

His approach to singlehanded sailing was quite different from Chichester's. Horie sailed alone because he could afford only a very small boat, and it was simpler and cheaper and more practical to provide stores and equipment for a crew of one than it would have been to sail with a companion or companions. Also, I think he was reluctant to invite anyone else to share a voyage that involved considerable risk. But he had nothing against working with others, and if his circumstances had been different and he had had a larger boat he would not have felt his adventure threatened by a crew. He wanted to sail across the Pacific by his own efforts. If the only practical way was to sail alone, that was that. Chichester had an emotional *need* to fly or sail alone—'Somehow I never seemed to enjoy so much doing things with other people.' In his approach to solitude Horie is nearer the type-figure than is Chichester. Ulysses was an efficient singlehander when he had to be, and he made no complaints about loneliness. But he was at ease with companions and would lead a ship's crew or an army as events required.

To assess Kenichi Horie's achievement calls for an understanding of its setting in time, place and history. Directly, he accomplished a remarkable voyage in one of the smallest boats to make an ocean crossing. *Mermaid* was minute in comparison with Chichester's *Gipsy Moth III* or *IV*, less than half the length of the first and a shade over one-third the length of the second. She was smaller even than *Nova Espero* (20 ft) sailed across the Atlantic by Stanley Smith and Charles Violet in 1951 and *Sopranino* (19 ft 8 in) sailed from Casablanca to Barbados by Patrick Ellam and Colin Mudie in 1952. Size is no measure of seaworthiness in a boat, and for a singlehander a very small boat has advantages. But in a boat as small as *Mermaid* the problem of carrying supplies for a long voyage is formidable. The niceness of Horie's calculations about fresh water is an example of this, and similar careful arithmetic is needed for every tin and package that goes on board. The equation is stern: $x = $ life or death, and the margin is slender. As Chichester trusted his life to the reasoning of his navigation, so Horie risked his life on his calculations about food and water. Both believed that they were right—they could easily have been wrong. Neither was wrong. They calculated their risks and won. Part, a large part, of their achievement came before they started, in trusting to their reasoning. That demands high courage.

Horie showed that if a man knows what he is doing he can take a very small boat safely across thousands of miles of open ocean by himself. That is worth showing, but it is not a particularly novel demonstration; many men have taken very small boats on long voyages. Horie's particular achievement here was not in his voyage itself but in the circumstances of his making it, in his singleminded determination to cross with no resources other than his own the ocean that seemed to bound Japanese life. He could have saved up for an air ticket and travelled with a passport like a respectable tourist. True. But that would not have given him what he wanted. The Ulysses factor in him required that he should go himself, find a way across his ocean, so that it would no longer be a boundary but a road to the far side.

Indirectly, Horie's achievement was more than all this. Japan had lost a war, suffered the poisoned agony of Hiroshima, endured the national shame of occupation. Foreigners made long voyages in small boats: if anyone was going to cross the Pacific singlehanded the world would expect it to be an Englishman or a Frenchman or an American. Most of the books he wanted to read were in English or French. They might or might not be translated into Japanese, but there was nothing Japanese about them to start with. The Pacific was in a sense Japan's own ocean, but it was in the Pacific that the Japanese fleet had suffered crushing defeat. One man and a 19-ft boat might do something to redress Japanese defeat, to extend the frontiers of Japanese national pride. They did. Horie has added Japanese to the literature still largely Greek-inspired of a type of man first chronicled by Homer.

XIV

Determination—John Ridgway

CHICHESTER'S great Atlantic voyages were in 1960 and 1962. In 1964 the Singlehanded Transatlantic Race attracted fifteen entrants: sailing the Atlantic in small boats had become an organised international sport. In 1966 John Ridgway and Chay Blyth crossed the ocean from Cape Cod to Inishmore, in the Aran Islands, Eire, in an open rowing boat.

Ridgway was then a captain in the Parachute Regiment, and Blyth a sergeant in the same regiment—he had been Ridgway's platoon sergeant for three years. The two had done a certain amount of canoeing together, and had shared in many tough training exercises. Ridgway, who had been at school at what was then the Nautical College, Pangbourne, and had spent a brief period in the Merchant Service before deciding to go to Sandhurst and join the Army, knew a good deal about boat handling and had some experience of the sea. Apart from canoeing, Blyth knew next to nothing about boats or the sea.

Ridgway did not invent the idea of rowing the Atlantic. In August 1965 he heard a radio programme in which there was an interview with David Johnstone, a journalist, who was making plans to cross the Atlantic in a rowing boat. Ridgway at once felt that this was something that he himself would like to do. He got in touch with Johnstone to ask if he could join him in the attempt. By that time, however, Johnstone had already selected John Hoare, a fellow journalist, for his crew. Ridgway then decided to fit out his own Atlantic rowing expedition, and, if possible, to race Johnstone and Hoare. Another officer in the Parachute Regiment volunteered to go with Ridgway, but had to withdraw on medical advice. Sergeant Blyth volunteered for the expedition barely two months before the start that Ridgway had planned for the beginning of June 1966. They left Cape Cod in an open dory, *English Rose III*, on June 4. Johnstone and Hoare had left Virginia Beach, at the southern end of Chesapeake Bay, a fortnight before them on May 21 1966.

Johnstone and Hoare were lost at sea. Their boat, *Puffin*, was found waterlogged in mid-Atlantic by a Canadian naval ship on October 14 1966. There was no trace of her crew.

Ridgway and Blyth reached Inishmore, in the Aran Islands, on September 3 1966 after a ninety-two-day passage. The tragedy of Johnstone and Hoare is discussed in the next chapter. This study is concerned primarily with John Ridgway.

Although the idea of rowing the Atlantic in 1966 was David Johnstone's, the ocean had been crossed by two men in a rowing boat sixty-nine years previously. On June 6 1897 George Harvo and Frank Samuelson, both Americans of Norwegian stock, left New York in an 18-ft double-ended rowing boat called *Richard K. Fox* bound for Europe. On August 1 1897 they landed at St Mary's, in the Scilly Isles, and after resting there for a few days they rowed on to Havre. Both men were New Jersey oyster fishermen, accustomed to the sea and to open boats. Their passage of fifty-five days was remarkable, and even more remarkable was their survival when their boat capsized in mid-ocean. In a storm on July 10 1897 they were struck by a breaking sea, both were washed overboard and their boat was overturned. Their experience of small boats had led them to have hand grips fitted along the keel. These came to the rescue, for they enabled the men to right the boat, and they were able to clamber back on board, bale her out and continue their voyage. They lost much of their food and water in the capsize, but they were fortunate in getting fresh supplies from a Norwegian barque which they met five days later. Neither thought of giving up the voyage. Their purpose in rowing the Atlantic is not clear. They hoped to make some money by exhibiting their boat in Europe, and she was exhibited in Paris, but the proceeds seem to have been slender. Both men returned to the United States. It is possible though not certain that they won a prize or wager of $2,000 for their exploit. That would have been a considerable sum to New Jersey fishermen in the 1890s, though rowing the Atlantic was a hard way to earn it.

Ridgway displays marked Ulysses characteristics. There is the typical combination of ability and impatience with formal education. There is a typical Ulysses–Laertes relationship with his father, respect for his father's achievements (as a distinguished civil engineer) coupled with determination not to stay at home and follow his father, but to strike out for himself. As a boy Ridgway wanted to go to sea, and in the days of sailing ships a career at sea might have satisfied him. On leaving the Nautical College at Pangbourne he went to sea for a short time, but modern seafaring in big ships on scheduled routes was not what he wanted. The Army seemed to offer him more scope. Again he showed typical Ulysses characteristics in taking every aspect of military training seriously: if he was going to be a soldier, he would be a better soldier than most. He wanted to be sure that his body would serve him well as a physical machine, so he practised endurance. He became Captain of Boxing at Sandhurst. In one tournament he went through two rounds with a broken nose, winning both bouts, and wept with frustration when his third fight with his nose broken was stopped by the referee with still one minute to go. He has the Ulysses type of courage-with-imagination. His imagination foresees danger, his courage accepts them—this is the antithesis of *berserk* courage, which, in some instances, is more akin to madness than to bravery, brave as it may appear. Ulysses-like, he calculates the risks of action as carefully as he can. Having calculated, he acts calmly.

In war, Ridgway would have been an outstanding paratroop leader. In the Army in peacetime, after the stimulus of his initial training, he felt restless. He was profoundly moved by Chichester's autobiography *The Lonely Sea and the Sky*, published in 1964, feeling that what he also wanted was to achieve something *as an individual*. This is quite distinct from singlehanded achievement. Ridgway is not by nature a singlehander. His personality, reinforced here by his Army training, is that of a leader.

He has not Chichester's inventiveness. Chichester invents challenges for himself: his intense competitiveness requires somebody to be challenged, himself if there is no other competitor available. In many ways Chichester's imagination prefers a challenge from himself: he can then play the whole game singlehanded, having invented the game. Ridgway has not that sort of imagination. He needs a spark from outside, but, his imagination having been sparked, he will go on to create something entirely his own. The idea of rowing the Atlantic in 1966 was David Johnstone's, and it instantly sparked Ridgway. But his approach to the idea was markedly different from Johnstone's. Ridgway's first thought was to volunteer to go with Johnstone, and he got in touch with him for that purpose. When the two men met it was clear to both that they were not thinking on similar lines. Ridgway observed of this interview.

> It was apparent that we both viewed the project in a somewhat different light. I pursued the matter with him no further.*

Johnstone was equally clear that he and Ridgway approached life from different angles. Johnstone's feelings about this interview are recorded by Merton Naydler in his book on the Johnstone–Hoare expedition, *The Penance Way*.

> In no time Johnstone was convinced that they could not possibly get along together in a small boat. Ridgway, a lean, tough parachutist, seemed exactly the right man physically for the adventure, but the sensitive Johnstone was instinctively aware of an assertiveness which he feared would bring about a clash of personalities.†

What Johnstone felt as 'assertiveness' in Ridgway was the true Ulysses determination to do what he set out to do—the determination manifest in the type-figure when he ordered his crew to lash him to the mast of his ship so that he should not surrender to the sweet singing of the sirens as he sailed past them. The difference between Johnstone and Ridgway was that they were really setting out to do quite different things.

Having ruled out the possibility of rowing with Johnstone, Ridgway planned his enterprise in his own way. One of the first things he did was to make a military appreciation of the task under the heading:

---

* John Ridgway, *A Fighting Chance*, p. 14. Hamlyn Publishing Group 1966.
† Merton Naydler, *Penance Way*, p. 22. Hutchinson 1968.

Aim: To win a rowing race across the Atlantic Ocean from the United States of America to the United Kingdom during the summer of 1966.*

Because Ridgway and Blyth were serving soldiers it may be thought that the Army provided all sorts of facilities for their adventure. The Army gave them its blessing and unpaid leave of absence, and the RAF gave them two spare places on a flight to Canada to help them across the Atlantic for the start of their voyage. Everything else they did on their own. Ridgway financed the expedition, and he had to be extremely careful about money. His boat, a Yorkshire dory bought from stock, cost £185.

Sergeant Blyth joined him just one month before they flew to Canada with the RAF. This flight landed them at Ottawa, and they made their way to Boston, Massachusetts, by coach. Their dory went by steamer from Glasgow, and they did their final fitting out at the small fishing port of Orleans, near Cape Cod, from which they took their departure not quite three weeks after their arrival in America.

Ridgway wanted to race Johnstone, and to put up a faster time for rowing the Atlantic if he could. But although the idea of a race gave a certain added spice to the adventure, his aim of rowing across an ocean was more important to Ridgway as a thing in itself. The 'race', indeed, was quite informal: the two boats started neither at the same time nor from the same place. Johnstone, who was irritated rather than attracted by the thought of a race, had intended originally to start from Cape Cod, but had gone south to Chesapeake Bay in the belief that the east-going Gulf Stream to help him on his way would be found closer inshore. Ridgway, who was keener on the challenge of a race, would have liked to start from Chesapeake Bay to make conditions more nearly equal, but he did not have enough money to pay for the transport of his boat there. So he started, as planned, from Cape Cod. The only other men known to have rowed the Atlantic, George Harvo and Frank Samuelson in 1897, had started from New York. Passage times would be, therefore, scarcely comparable.

* *A Fighting Chance*, p. 14.

In any case there were no rules, except the self-imposed rule that the Atlantic was to be crossed by rowing only, without the use of sails. Ridgway was not racing in the sense that Chichester raced the ghosts of the old clipper masters on his voyage round the world. Ridgway's object was simply to row a boat across the Atlantic.

His ninety-two days at sea with Sergeant Blyth were a sustained example of Ulysses-type leadership, determination and self-discipline in conditions of extreme discomfort, sometimes of pain and often of danger. The relationship between the two men through three months of cramped living in an open boat was admirable. It was based to some extent on their Army relationship: Blyth accepted Ridgway's leadership with the unbounded loyalty of a good sergeant towards a good officer; Ridgway accepted his responsibility for Blyth and the success of the expedition as over-riding all personal feelings for himself. But Blyth was a volunteer, and when two men are alone in an open boat in mid-ocean differences of military rank become somewhat artificial. That the reality of function in the Army relationship was maintained throughout their voyage speaks volumes for both men. It deepened and strengthened the personal friendship that developed between them, each knowing not only that he could rely utterly on the other but that in moments of crisis the leadership of the officer and the skilled support of the sergeant would help in a hundred ways, unspoken but completely understood between them.

A severe test of their relationship came on the thirty-third day out. In provisioning their dory they had reckoned their need of fresh water on the standard half a gallon a day per man. They had worked on an estimated passage time of sixty days, which called for a supply of 120 gallons. In addition, they took another 18 gallons in 2-gallon containers as a reserve. On the thirty-third day out, when they were still not nearly halfway across, Ridgway decided that they were carrying too much weight and that the boat would row more easily if they reduced their water supplies. So he told Blyth that he thought they could afford to throw overboard about 25 gallons of fresh water, to save some 250 lb. Blyth was disturbed: deliberately to throw overboard precious fresh water looked like an invitation to death by thirst. But Ridgway had calculated the risk. In thirty-two days they had used only 25 gallons, 7 gallons less than their supposed requirement; moreover, this included the use of some fresh water for washing, so that there was room for economy if need be. He considered that the reduced strain of having to move 250 lb less weight would more than counterbalance the risk of running short of water. With all his instincts aghast, Blyth accepted Ridgway's judgment, and 25 gallons of fresh water went over the side. Ridgway was right. The boat did row more easily, and they were never short of water, continuing to enjoy a weekly wash down and shave in fresh water. But Blyth could not know this. And the feelings of a man in an open boat, with no idea of how many more months of sea before him, at seeing his lifeblood of fresh water go overboard may be imagined. Blyth's acceptance of Ridgway's decision here, and Ridgway's calculated taking of a risk that he knew must affect Blyth as well as himself, show a remarkable combination of human trust and courage.

In the first fortnight of their voyage Ridgway and Blyth endured a hurricane, named by the United States meteorologists as Hurricane Alma. They had some warning on their small radio of the hurricane's approach, and did what they could to make ready for it, lashing everything on board in the hope of keeping it in the boat, and preparing their sea-anchor for streaming. When the hurricane struck their boat was tossed about wildly in a ferocious sea, and masses of water poured into her. They saved their boat and their lives by bailing, continuing to fill and lift buckets of water by willpower long after most men would have collapsed from fatigue. It was brutal work, but they kept the inflow of water under control. But they could not go on bailing together, for even willpower must give in to physical exhaustion in the end, and if both were exhausted at the same time the water could not be kept down. They had a good pump, capable of shifting 8 gallons a minute, so they organised themselves to pump in half-hour shifts, the man not pumping getting what rest he could under a tarpaulin. *English Rose III*, being completely open, could not help taking in a great deal of water, but she had the sea-kindliness of her dory ancestors, and rode astonishingly well. She looked after her men, and they looked after her. After hours of battering the wind relaxed a little as the hurricane

moved on, and Blyth, although half-dead with weariness, got
their stove going and cooked a hot meal. They divided the
food with scrupulous fairness, and took turns to eat, for they
could find only one spoon. The hot food did them immense
good, and at the end Blyth produced his *pièce de resistance*—
a bar of rum fudge as a sweet to follow the main course.

Boils and sores they took as all in the day's work, letting
nothing interfere with the physical task of rowing. Neither
sought to be excused a watch; they relieved each other for
watches and rowing stints as faithfully as if they were watch-
keeping on a big ship. Roughly one-third of their food was
ruined by salt water during the hurricane, but they concluded
that they could survive this by cutting down their rations. As
time went on they became exceedingly hungry, but they
calculated their disciplined meals by the spoonful, never
allowing themselves more than the ration for each day. One
or two ships spoke to them, but they asked for nothing, save a
check on their position. After ten weeks, when they were
down to half-rations, with the prospect of having to go on
quarter-rations, Ridgway asked Blyth if he would regard it as
breaking faith with themselves if they were to try to stop a
ship to ask for food. Blyth said that he thought it would be a
sensible thing to do, and Ridgway agreed. There was no
immediate prospect of meeting a ship, but Ridgway observed
in his journal:

> I felt a lot better after that. I knew that, having made the
> decision, there was absolutely nothing more that we could
> do. It was a position in which I could find, strange as it may
> seem, a little satisfaction.*

A day or so later they did meet a ship (the SS *Hanstellum*),
whose master and crew treated them with respect and kindness, and replenished their supplies generously. After another
three weeks at sea, during which they encountered more
severe weather, they made a landfall on the Aran Isles and
completed their ocean crossing.

Consciousness of an external power able to assist man's

* *A Fighting Chance.*

affairs was felt by both, and deepened by their experiences as their voyage progressed. When they were about to go on half-rations and feeling very hungry, Ridgway reflected on the power of God. He wrote afterwards:

> Suddenly I decided to pray, an earnest prayer which I hoped would mean more than the other prayers I had said at difficult times during the voyage. I have never been a regular churchgoer, and prayer has always been regarded by me as an expedient in an emergency. I had never honestly considered that anybody would bother to listen to any prayer that I said. On the night of August 5 I said my prayers at length, forcing my swollen fingers straight by pressing my hands together in the attitude I had been taught as a child. Indeed, I repeated this action every remaining night of the voyage and felt a union with God that I had never before experienced... From that moment I was convinced that we were being looked after and that a ship would come along with provisions before the last of our rations ran out.*

This conviction did not stop him from taking the hard rational decision to go on quarter-rations when that week's food was finished. He wrote in his log at the time:

> Decided to eat this week's rations over fourteen days and then spread the last pack over twenty-eight days... So impressive is the night that it is hard not to believe there is some Almighty presence which orders these things. We both feel that we will finish all right.†

Ulysses was grateful for divine help when it was given to him, but he never neglected self-help. It is a Ulysses characteristic to accept the maxim that God helps those who help themselves. There is nothing sloppy about asking divine help when you have done everything you can.

Reflecting on their meeting with the *Hanstellum*, Blyth wrote:

> Neither of us considered our meeting with the *Hanstel-*

---

* *A Fighting Chance*, p. 154.
† *A Fighting Chance*, p. 160.

lum a lucky one. It was, we believed, a further proof that
God was watching over us.*

In his history of the type-figure, Homer recounts a meeting
between Ulysses and Athene which illustrates the mixture of
humility and self-reliance with which a man, accepting responsibility for himself, may yet hope that God will help him.
Ulysses has landed on his home island of Ithaca, and meets
Athene, who is looking after him. But the goddess is disguised
as a shepherd, and Ulysses is cautious about revealing himself.
Instead of saying who he is, he tells an ingenious story, describing himself as a refugee from a quarrel in Crete. Athene
is not at all displeased by this wariness:

> The bright-eyed goddess smiled... Her appearance
> altered, and now she looked like a woman, tall, beautiful
> and accomplished. And when she replied to him she aban-
> doned her reserve.
> 'What a cunning knave it would take,' she said, 'to beat
> you at your tricks ... And yet you did not know me Pallas
> Athene, daughter of Zeus, who always stand by your side
> and guard you through all your adventures. Why, it was I
> who made all the Phaeacians take to you so kindly. And
> here I am once more to plan your future course with you;
> to hide the treasures that the Phaeacian nobles, prompted
> by me, gave to you when you left for home, and to warn
> you of all the trials you will have to undergo within the
> walls of your palace. Bear these with patience, for bear
> them you must.'

Ulysses responded with dignity:

> 'Goddess,' he said, 'it is hard for a man to recognise you at
> sight however knowledgeable he may be for you have a way
> of donning all kinds of disguises. But this I know well, that
> you were gracious to me in the old days so long as we were
> campaigning at Troy. Yet when we had sacked Priam's
> lofty citadel and gone on towards our ships, and a god had
> scattered the Achaean (Greek) fleet, I did not notice you
> then, Daughter of Zeus, nor see you set foot on my ship to

* *A Fighting Chance*, p. 164.

save me from any of my ordeals. No, I was left to wander
through the world with a stricken heart, till the gods put a
term to my sufferings and the day came, in the rich land of
the Phaeacians, when you comforted me with your talk and
yourself guided me to their city. But now I beseech you in
your Father's name—tell me am I really back in my own
beloved land?'

'How like you to be so wary,' said Athene. 'And that is
why I cannot desert you in your misfortunes ... Be bold,
and dismiss all doubts from your heart. Our immediate task
is to hide your goods... After that we must decide on our
best course for the future.'

This passage from the *Odyssey* is remarkably perceptive.
Ulysses does not cringe, and the goddess respects him for it.
He is conscious of her power, acknowledges her help, but remains alert to act on his own if he has to. The goddess does
not rebuke this self-reliance: rather, she expects it in him—
'and that is why I cannot desert you in your misfortunes'.
This is not a Christian idiom: Homer was writing some eight
centuries before the birth of Christ. But there is nothing in-
compatible with Christianity in a self-reliant approach to life,
nor in Homer's feelings that a man may merit God's help by
his own efforts to help himself. Ulysses is not arrogant. He
knows that the power of the gods far transcends his own. But
he is never going to sit down and wring his hands, moaning
that unless some god comes to the rescue he is lost.

It may be that the gulfs will wash us down.

It may be. If that is God's will it will be so. But that is not a
reason for giving up. It may not be God's will. Invoke God's
help, but go on quarter-rations and leave His help to Him.
Ridgway's and Blyth's feelings at a critical time of their
voyage reflect a true religious sense that has accompanied the
Ulysses factor in man throughout human history.

Analysis of their achievement is both simple and complex.
The world's instant response to their arrival at Inishmore was
instinctively correct—this was an achievement of great cour-

age, justifying respect for the sheer bravery of it. An ocean crossing in an open boat is far more dangerous than a voyage in the smallest of decked yachts. The risk of being swamped is real and ever-present, and to endure ninety-two days at sea with no shelter but a canvas hood is to risk severe suffering from exposure, with no small likelihood of ultimate collapse. All this required courage. By personal self-discipline, and by their Army training, Ridgway and his crew were prepared morally, mentally and physically for the risks they took, but that does not lessen the courage required deliberately to take such risks.

Yet, apart from demonstrating that two young soldiers can be exceedingly brave men, what did they achieve? The Atlantic had been crossed by men in an open rowing boat half a century before they started. There was no need to prove that an open boat can survive a long passage—that has been proved hundreds of times in the history of the sea. Their passage was not particularly fast—they took nearly twice as long from Cape Cod to Ireland as Harvo and Samuelson had taken from New York to the Scillies. As a feat of sheer endurance, Ridgway's voyage was considerable, but he had better protective clothing and equipment than anything available to New Jersey fishermen in 1897. Objective comparison of the open-boat crossings of 1966 and 1897 would suggest that that of 1897 was in many ways the more remarkable.

But like here is not really being compared with like. Harvo and Samuelson were fishermen, brought up to rowing small boats off the eastern seaboard of America. Ridgway and Blyth were not fishermen—Blyth had scarcely been to sea, and although Ridgway had some knowledge of boats, it was not extensive. He knew enough about the sea to realise what he was taking on, and he understood the first principles of seamanship, but to contemplate such an open-boat voyage at all, still more to accept a crew almost wholly without sea experience, required an extraordinary combination of self-confidence and faith. This is to consider the adventure from another angle. Ridgway and Blyth were tough young men, trained to physical endurance and to expect danger. Yet both are products of the industrialised urban society of Britain in the middle twentieth century. For all their experience of hills

N

and open country and personal liking for outdoor activity, both belong to a generation which considers it natural to get water by turning a tap, to make long journeys in a comfortable, pressurised aircraft, and every other sort of journey by car. The Army in which they were trained to serve is highly mechanised. By pushing an open boat into the sea from a beach and rowing it until they came to the far side of an ocean they cut away every comfort, convenience and assurance of the community in which they had been brought up. More, they cut away most of the physical aids to his existence that man has developed over the past few thousand years. Not quite all: they had compasses, dehydrated foods, protective clothing and a few other such contrivances that assist the modern adventurer. Although valuable, these are incidental. In every major aspect of sea travel and of survival they were no better off than the rowers with the first Ulysses. To propel their boat they had nothing but their own arms and back muscles, to meet the hazards of the sea they had nothing but their own willpower and mother wit. So they crossed their ocean. And they showed not that man can cross an ocean in a rowing boat but that man of the middle twentieth century can still row his way across an ocean.

This was a moral as much as a physical achievement. The moral effort required the physical endeavour, but Ridgway's new frontier, reached by physical means, was an extension of the moral boundaries of his generation. He allowed himself nothing of the labour-saving ingenuity of sails, an ancient human skill, but not for him. He allowed himself nothing of the long-discovered seafaring wisdom that it is better to travel in the box of a decked boat than in the bowl of an open one. He went back beyond all this, nearly to prehistoric man with his hollowed log, to prove at least to himself that the supreme self-reliance of which man was once capable is with him still. I have written 'he went back...' So he did in terms of the physical equipment he allowed himself, but in terms of what he achieved with that meagre equipment he pushed a limiting human frontier forward. He wanted to know if he could row a boat across the Atlantic, and the only way of knowing was to try. Most of us can think of a thousand good reasons for not testing ourselves to the limits of endurance. Ridgway, and Blyth who rowed with him, rejected all such arguments because they felt it more important to find out what they could do. They wanted to learn something about themselves, and in doing so they brought a new dimension to a generation's thinking.

XV

Malignancy in the factor—David Johnstone

EVERY normal human attribute may take sometimes an abnormal form. Sexual instinct, for instance, is a normal and healthy human ingredient, but in some individuals it may be perverted or distorted, with consequences ranging from private unhappiness to grave offences against society. The Ulysses factor is similarly capable of imperfect or even malignant development. The qualities that go with the factor are listed in Chapter II as:

> Courage
> Selfishness
> Practical competence
> Physical strength
> Powerful imagination
> Ability to lead
> Self-discipline
> Endurance
> Self-sufficiency
> Cunning
> Unscrupulousness
> Strong sexual attraction.

Some of these qualities are not wholly admirable. All are valuable towards biological survival, but some at least, if developed beyond a certain point, may produce malignant effects. In the whole man these qualities will tend to counterbalance one another. Selfishness, for example, will be countered by self-discipline, so that the value of the individual impulse to do something for oneself is retained, and the malignant development of over-selfishness checked. Courage, which in itself can lead to rashness, will be tempered by imagination and cunning. Unscrupulousness, or the feeling that an object is so important in itself that no consideration for others may be allowed to stand in the way of attaining it will be tempered by leadership, which requires consideration for others. The healthy factor is an amalgam of characteristics and sub-characteristics which together make a powerful human driving force and provide the qualities to sustain it.

All these qualities are present in all human beings, but in proportions that are infinitely variable. The Ulysses complex consists not of uncommon human qualities but of normal qualities combined in a highly individual way. This combination can never be the same, for every ingredient is infinitely variable, but over a broad spectrum of human activity it can produce outstanding individuals, of outstanding importance to the continuity of the race. It is also capable of being self-destructive.

A case of the Ulysses factor gone wrong, as it were, can be studied in the tragedy of David Johnstone, who, with his companion John Hoare, was lost in an attempt to row the Atlantic at about the same time as Ridgway and Blyth.

Johnstone is dead, and his moods, impulses and emotions cannot be questioned. But he left a journal covering 106 days of his Atlantic voyage, a record which survived the wreck of his boat *Puffin*, and was painstakingly deciphered by his family. This journal has been edited—with scrupulous care to alter nothing—by Merton Naydler, and published with Naydler's commentary on the voyage in *The Penance Way*. Naydler, who knew Johnstone personally, is himself a remarkable man. He sailed with Dr David Lewis in 1963 on a voyage to Iceland in the experimental catamaran *Rehu Moana*, and knows much about small-boat expeditions at firsthand. He is a solicitor who was a war-time fighter pilot, and his book on the Johnstone–Hoare expedition is instinct with human understanding. He is not, of course, responsible for any of the views in this case-study, though without his patient reconstruction of events it could not have been made.

From Johnstone's journal, and from what is known about the origins of his expedition, and his preparations for it, a pattern of Ulysses qualities emerges. But it is a distorted pattern, and a tragic example of the factor turned malignant, of good qualities that ended badly because other qualities were lacking.

Johnstone was not quite 35 when he died. He displayed many characteristics of the Ulysses-type, notably a typical combination of ability and impatience with formal schooling. He was restless and tried a variety of jobs all over the world from Australia to the Persian Gulf. He neither married nor attempted to settle down. When he conceived the idea of rowing the Atlantic he was working as a journalist for a local newspaper in Surrey.

The immediate inspiration of his attempt to cross the Atlantic in a rowing boat seems to have been the arrival in England in 1965 of the American journalist Robert Manry in the tiny sailing boat *Tinkerbelle*, after completing a single-handed passage from America in what was then the smallest boat, only $13\frac{1}{2}$ ft overall, to have made the crossing. Johnstone and a group of companions were discussing this in a pub, and at the end of the evening Johnstone said that he thought he would try to cross the Atlantic himself in a rowing boat. He said that he would advertise for would-be rowers in *The Times*, and he accepted a bet of ten cigarettes on whether he would or would not actually insert the advertisement. He put it in next day.

What must have seemed then no more than a saloon-bar prank was in fact a serious decision. It may have been taken on the spur of the moment, but this was in keeping with the man. His original intention was to try to recruit a crew of six rowers (including himself) for the project, but later he decided to attempt the crossing with one companion. He wrote:

I began to think of a two man trip as a desirable purity of idea: Go the penance way.*

This is a revealing, as well as a moving, phrase. It is a clear indication of the emergence of non-Ulysses factors to distort a Ulysses-type idea. Ulysses was neither penitent nor masochist. He would endure discomfort or danger when he had to, but deliberately to seek either *for themselves* was wholly foreign to his nature. Johnstone, I think, was beginning to be attracted by the *ordeal* that rowing the Atlantic would involve, seeing it as a kind of supreme penance or *self-proving*, something quite distinct from the desire for self-knowledge or

* *Penance Way.*

self-discovery which may animate the Ulysses mind. The distinction is important. Inherent in the Ulysses factor is a desire for personal physical experiment, but this is not related to any form of self-inflicted punishment. A Chichester undertakes the formidable physical task of driving a yacht at racing speed round the world singlehanded not because he wants the physical ordeal, but because he wants to race around the world singlehanded: the ordeal is simply an inescapable part of the task. Ridgway undertook the physical strain of rowing the Atlantic as incidental to the achievement, something to train and prepare for, but not an end in itself. Johnstone, at any rate to some extent, saw prolonged physical strain as a kind of self-purification. There was an element of transcendentalism in his approach to the enterprise.

His preliminary planning was practical enough. He financed his expedition by selling the story of it to a Sunday newspaper, a reasonable, indeed a natural, step, since he was himself a journalist. With the money he obtained he commissioned a leading yacht designer to design a boat for two men to row across the North Atlantic, and he had the boat, *Puffin*, built specially for that task. She was smaller than Ridgway's dory, having an overall length of 15 ft 6 in against the dory's 20 ft, but she was slightly broader, with a beam of 5 ft 6 in against 5 ft 4 in. Being designed specially for an ocean crossing, *Puffin* was constructed with a tiny covered cabin aft with bunks extending as quarter berths under the cockpit thwarts, so that her crew could sleep in shelter. Johnstone sought expert advice on nutrition and other technical aspects of his voyage in a systematic fashion, consulting a number of recognised authorities. His planning here was impeccable.

Physically, he was an enormous man, standing 6 ft 3 in and weighing 17 stone. With this great frame he was endowed with great physical strength. To prepare himself for the expedition he worked as a labourer in a variety of hard manual jobs. John Hoare, who joined Johnstone as a result of his advertisement in *The Times*, was also physically fit. He, too, had been a provincial journalist, and was then working as a press officer. He had done national service as a parachutist, and had continued in the Territorial Army reserves. He was a keen rugby player, and combined a love of outdoor life with a love of books, particularly stories of adventure and of courage.

His response to Johnstone was immediate, an instant, almost boyish eagerness to share in a great adventure. He accepted Johnstone's leadership loyally and apparently uncritically. It might have been better for both men had Hoare been more critical. But both are dead, and Hoare's loyalty to Johnstone shines through their tragedy. Johnstone responded with a touching tenderness. One of the most moving passages in his journal was written on their 100th day at sea:

> We have now scored one victory over the pundits who said we would be at each other's throats all day. We find more and more to talk about.*

Johnstone did the navigating. When a sextant observation told him that they were making much less progress than either had thought, he wrote in his log:

> I did not tell John the precise situation, and he continued to sing.†

For all Johnstone's rational approach to the planning of his voyage, the irrational kept breaking in. He was badly upset by the announcement of Ridgway's plans to row the Atlantic in competition with him. That is understandable, particularly as he was genuinely concerned lest Ridgway should in some way kill the value of the story that he had already sold to a newspaper. What is less reasonable is that he allowed his irritation with Ridgway to upset the timing of his own preparations. He was so anxious to start, and thereby hope to complete the crossing before Ridgway, that he had the newly built *Puffin* shipped to the United States without any trials at sea rowing except for one short trip that he and Hoare had made in her at Cowes.

He changed his plans suddenly again on the way across to the United States. The basis of his planning was to row into the east-going Gulf Stream, to have this ocean current with him on his passage from west to east. All his earlier planning had envisaged a departure from Cape Cod. This was a good starting-point, offering about the shortest direct crossing from the mainland of the United States to the British Isles, and also

---

Penance Way, p. 166.   †*Penance Way*, p. 143.

a clean run out to sea, with no risk of being embayed on the American coast. The Gulf Stream, however, does not wash Cape Cod: it is an ocean current, flowing here a considerable distance offshore, and, particularly in adverse winds, it might require two or three weeks' hard rowing from Cape Cod to reach it. Discussing his plans with a navigating officer on the ship taking him to the United States, Johnstone learned that farther south, off Cape Hatteras, the Gulf Stream swings inshore, and can be met near the coast. At once he decided to change his starting-point from Cape Cod to the southern part of Chesapeake Bay. This would lengthen the crossing by at least 500 miles, but in Johnstone's view the extra distance would be more than compensated by an earlier 'lift' from the Gulf Stream.

It is true that the Gulf Stream does come inshore by Chesapeake Bay, but the sea here is also subject to a bewildering variety of local tidal streams. It is an awkward coast, and the decision to change his plans turned out disastrously for Johnstone. Instead of a brisk departure from the coast, they spent a heartbreaking ten days rowing round and round the entrance to Chesapeake Bay before they could break free of the local tidal set. This change of plan was not a rational decision. In part, it may have been prompted by Johnstone's by then unreasoning fear of Ridgway and a desire to upset him by changing the start. But this again was scarcely rational. If there had to be a race with Ridgway, the best thing—the Ulysses-type reaction—would have been a cool determination to try to win it. Johnstone already had a useful start in time; he was a fortnight ahead of Ridgway in any case. If both left Cape Cod, at least they would start on equal terms, and since Johnstone could be sure of starting first he had a reasonable chance of the publicity advantage of reaching the British Isles first. The winner in terms of time taken for the passage would be determined later, and in terms of the value of Johnstone's newspaper story, what happened later did not matter so much. Switching on the spur of the moment from Cape Cod to Chesapeake Bay was a gambler's throw, not the taking of a calculated risk. There was nothing but a hunch to suggest that the greater distance would be offset by the Gulf Stream's lift: it was a hunch based on ignorance of the precise behaviour of the Gulf Stream, and it turned out to be sadly wrong.

Furthermore, Ridgway could easily have followed to Chesa-peake Bay, as, indeed, he nearly did. Instead of borrowing money to meet the extra cost of getting his dory to Chesa-peake Bay, Ridgway calmly went ahead with his own plans to start from Cape Cod. That is one measure of the difference between them.

It was irrational to allow anything to interfere with sea-rowing trials in *Puffin*, and it was irrational to switch the starting-point. Unlike Ridgway's dory, which was a stock boat of a traditional design well proved by generations of seamen, Johnstone's *Puffin* was an original design, with merits and possibly demerits still unknown. Sea-trials, therefore, should have been imperative. When he decided to abandon sea-trials in England Johnstone thought that he and Hoare could make up by practising in her when she was put in the water in the United States. But between their arrival in New York on May 2 and their departure from Virginia Beach, Chesapeake Bay, on May 21 the two men were so caught up by events ashore that the projected trials never took place. They set off to row the Atlantic with much still left to chance. In particular, the external buoyancy designed to assist *Puffin*'s self-righting qualities was not fitted, and part of her designed storage system intended to distribute weight along her sides was not used.

Johnstone's commitments to various financial sponsors con-tributed to this haphazard departure. Naydler comments:

> There were so many people they were required to meet, so much time to be given to publicity outlets, so many parties at which their attendance was desirable. He was perhaps too close to the situation to be able to recognise the extent to which the initiative had passed out of his hands the moment he entered into the financial arrangements necessary to enable the initial vision to become a practical reality.*

This may have been so. A Chichester would have told his sponsors to go to hell. Ulysses was often tempted to stay where he was and to let preparations for departure wait for tomor-

* *Penance Way*, p. 65.

row; he did not yield to temptation; he let *nothing* interfere with what he considered it necessary to do. This combination of selfishness and self-discipline inherent in the healthy Ulysses factor was not strongly developed in Johnstone.

The strongest element in his personal determination seems to have been to endure rather than to achieve. And his determination to endure was tinged with a transcendentalism which believed beyond all reason that mere endurance would see them through. On the fifty-ninth day out, when things were not going well and survival depended on the chance of getting food from a ship, he wrote:

> We just can't catch fish reliably, we have food for about ten days more, yet we laugh at it all and say it will be all right in the end. It is impossible to believe we are going to get into trouble out here, yet the signs are all there.*

Reason told him that the signs of impending trouble—and for pressing action to try to get out of trouble—were 'all there', but emotionally he did not accept them. He and Hoare had courage to a degree nearly incredible, but in a curious way they did not set out to master fate. The Gulf Stream was the 'escalator' (Johnstone's word) which would somehow carry them across the Atlantic. Rowing might help, but it was somehow secondary to the endurance of staying in their tiny boat and letting the ocean itself carry them along. Neither of them much liked rowing *Puffin*, and, ballasted as she was, she was often horrible to row. Quite early in their voyage, on the fifteenth day out, Johnstone observed in his log:

> There is a strange angle to this effort of rowing which we both seem to notice. When things are very discouraging it is hard to find the energy—say when it is important to row against a wind in the first week of the voyage: and when we are swinging along—100 miles a day—why bother to add on one's puny 15 or 20 miles? We both hate rowing, but not to a serious extent. It is bearable as the day's penance of boredom, but less inviting than doing nothing. The temptation is to do nothing because we are whipping along.†

* *Penance Way*, p. 123.   † *Penance Way*, p. 85.

Again 'penance', and again reason's warning that not to row is a 'temptation'. But reason does not win. They row at times because it is a penance to be endured, and for the rest Hoare sings and plays *Shenandoah* on his mouth organ, while Johnstone writes in his journal and reflects on life. His journal or log was a document of some 35,000 words, an extraordinary performance in the conditions of a 15-ft boat in mid-ocean.

Yet half of Johnstone, the true Ulysses half, was not euphoric. He had great mental ability, and he used it. Before setting out from America he knew little of astro-navigation, but he mastered it from a book in the first month of the voyage, and his positions, from sights taken under great difficulty in a tossing small boat, were remarkably accurate. He was able to check his position from time to time on meeting a ship, and whenever he got such a check his own reckoning proved to be not far out. He knew where he was most of the time—more often than many small-boat sailors—and the knowledge was generally disquieting. The Gulf Stream was not taking them safely across the Atlantic: they drifted incomprehensibly, and were blown hither and yon by whatever wind happened to be prevailing. As often it was easterly, blowing them back to America, as a westerly to help them towards Europe. The truth of the matter is that while a bottle thrown into the sea off the eastern seaboard of America will tend to be blown and drift across to Europe, it will take a very long time over it, and wander over much of the North Atlantic on the way. A boat as small as *Puffin*, without sails to use the wind, or without a sustained effort of rowing, is at the mercy of local winds and wind-formed currents. The Gulf Stream, shown by convenient arrows on a chart, is a long-term tendency in ocean movement: it may vary locally all round the compass in its effect on a small boat. Johnstone had some experience of the sea and he had read widely. Rationally, he must have been aware of all this, and yet emotionally he did not accept his own knowledge. He had the mental equipment to calculate his risks, but not the emotional equipment to act on his calculations.

He had fine Ulysses qualities, but they were bedevilled by some other set of qualities which made the worst of them. He had bad luck; his hunches were wrong. This is where he parts

company with the Ulysses-type—not in having bad luck (the
type-figure had some shocking luck), but in accepting it, and
relying on better luck next time. Kenichi Horie punished
himself for relying on instinct one night instead of checking
his boat's course. Johnstone observed, on the fifty-ninth day
out:

> Our lack of luck is stunning—hard to credit the absence
> of lucky breaks that come our way.*

And on the sixty-third day:

> It is difficult to know where to start thinking objectively
> about the treatment we are getting from the powers that
> govern the apportionment of chance and luck.†

Again the contrast. Part of him knew that he ought to start
'thinking objectively' about luck—that is, to reject it wholly
as a basis for action. But another part of him kept feeling that
the luck would change, a ship turn up to provide food, a
westerly wind set in to blow them home. The ordeal, in a
sense, was what mattered: if they endured the ordeal all
would be well.

On the sixty-sixth day they did meet a ship and got some
supplies from her, insisting on paying for them, and on the
sixty-eighth day they met another ship and obtained a little
more food. Ten days later they were again worried about
food, and Johnstone noted, 'now a ship is vital'. They were
still barely halfway across. On the eighty-third day they had a
fortunate meeting with a US coastguard vessel, whose master
and crew were exceptionally hospitable and friendly. They
were invited on board. Hoare accepted the invitation, but
only so that he could explain just what they needed in the
way of supplies; Johnstone refused to leave *Puffin* because of a
bet he had made with someone that he would cross the Atlantic in her, and he felt that to go on board another ship even
for a few minutes would be cheating. The coastguards replenished their supplies, Hoare returned to *Puffin* and they
rowed away.

They made wretchedly slow progress, and on the ninety-

* *Penance Way*, p. 124.   † *Penance Way*, p. 126.

third day (August 21 1966) took stock of their position. They reckoned that they had enough food for thirty breakfasts and twenty-six dinners, which meant that they would have to try to stop another ship. Neither seems even to have thought of giving up. They contemplated trying to make for Portugal if they could not reach Britain, and considered, apparently quite calmly, the prospects of their voyage's lasting into November. On the 102nd day Johnstone wrote:

> What is unthinkable is to give up because of the food or fed-upness.*

On the 105th day:

> We are both trusting in the bad spell to end suddenly and to find ourselves flying along any day.†

On the 106th day the journal ends. That was September 3 1966. On September 4 a hurricane is known to have swept the area of the Atlantic where they then were, and it is presumed that in this hurricane they were swept overboard and lost.

It is a pitiful story, redeemed by the amazing courage of Johnstone and Hoare. That it was wrong-headed courage is their tragedy: nothing can detract from the sheer heroism of their endurance. The Ulysses qualities in Johnstone clearly included a power of leadership, for Hoare, who could easily have decided when they met the coastguard vessel that he had had enough, deliberately rejoined Johnstone to carry on with him. No one can question loyalty so demonstrated, and it speaks as much for Johnstone as for Hoare.

But why? Why did these intelligent, exceedingly brave men continue with an enterprise that by then both must have known rationally to be hopeless? When they met the US coastguard vessel they had been at sea for nearly three months. Their plans were not working out. Their boat was awkward to row in anything of a sea, hard to hold on course and almost at the mercy of the wind. The Gulf Stream on which they had relied for a steady drift towards Europe had been proved conclusively to be far from reliable as an 'escala-

---

Penance Way, p. 167.   † *Penance Way*, p. 169.

tor'. They had exhausted their own supplies of food and could continue only by getting chance supplies from ships. And the chance of meeting other ships was a pure gamble. Even if they tried to make for the recognised shipping lanes marked on their charts, they were by no means sure of being able to stop a ship: they had already found that for them to sight a big ship was one thing, for a ship to see them, another. A 15-ft boat in an ocean swell is hard to spot if you are looking for it; if you have no idea of its existence the odds against noticing it at any distance are high.

So why did they go on? This is a fruitless question unless one can answer another question first. *What* was the enterprise they were bent on seeing through? To row the Atlantic —that was what they had set out to do, and that, apparently, was what they found 'unthinkable' (Day 102) to abandon. But in their hearts both had already abandoned this particular project. They might still hope to cross the Atlantic, but it would be by favour of the wind rather than their own oars. Without the modifications that sea-trials would have suggested, without the precise ballasting for which she was designed, *Puffin* was hard to row on course, and in many conditions of wind and sea hard to row at all. They had had bad luck with the proportion of easterly winds they met. The prevailing winds in the North Atlantic are westerlies, but this is true only over relatively long periods of time: they had had disheartening proof that over weeks and days easterlies to blow them back towards America may be as common. Given time, they would almost certainly be blown across to Europe; but how much time? They could not possibly estimate this, and they could not possibly *rely* on picking up enough food from chance ships to see them through. So *what* were they unwilling to give up?

Since both are dead, one can but guess. I think that Johnstone's approach to the whole venture was as much metaphysical as physical. He was 34, he had not done much with his abilities, he had flitted from job to job. His journal for the ninety-fourth day at sea (August 22 1966) has a strange entry:

A year since I thought of the idea ... And thought back to that previous fateful August in the Bush (a public house) in 1965, and back farther to the August of '64 ... and how it all begins, and why it's the right time and the right thing to do, and the jobs I'd tried for and failed to get.*

The Ulysses factor in Johnstone prompted him to the idea of rowing the Atlantic, but having had the idea, other factors in him took over. The original Ulysses impulse to discover— something about an ocean, or in himself—was overlaid by an impulse to prove that he could endure, that if he couldn't stick to a job as well as most men he could stick to a small boat in the North Atlantic for longer than almost anyone else in the world. It was not really the crossing that mattered, but the ordeal, the penance, the proof. And just as some mystics have been able to endure incredible physical suffering by reason of their faith that from such suffering something infinitely to be desired would come, so I think Johnstone believed that if only he could endure, something would see him through. He does not seem to have had the typical Ulysses consciousness of an external power capable of helping man. He refers in his journal to 'the powers that govern the apportionment of chance and luck', but this is much like reflecting on the spin of a roulette wheel. Towards the end, on the ninety-sixth day, he notes of a squall:

I prayed for it to ease, under the less undignified guise of a prayer for less of the North and more of the W.†

This one reference to prayer suggests that he felt it somehow demeaning to appeal for extra-human aid. Yet, in the form of luck, he was constantly buoyed up by the hope of extra-human aid. That is a non-Ulysses feeling, but it does seem to indicate a man with more of the mystic in him than, perhaps, either he understood or he admitted.

What was 'unthinkable' on the 102nd day was not to fail to complete the voyage but, more simply, to fail. In this light his intense irritation with Ridgway is more clearly explained: if by any chance Ridgway should succeed in getting across while he, Johnstone, had to give up, the sense of failure would be even more sickeningly acute. So failure was unthinkable. That Johnstone's companion John Hoare should have felt the same way after three months of endurance at sea is at once a personal tragedy and a tribute to them both.

* *Penanace Way*, p. 163.   † *Penance Way*, p. 164.

There remains a need to consider whether Johnstone's financial commitments to his newspaper and other sponsors had any direct bearing on the tragedy. Probably they had, but certainly not in the sense that any of those who had given financial support to the expedition would have expected him to continue at the almost certain risk of life. Newspapers have many sins, but on the whole they are philosophical about losses. If a man contracts in good faith to do something, obviously does his best but cannot do all that he undertook, few newspaper managements would show hard feelings. They may be disappointed, they might be reluctant to consider a future proposition from the same man, but they would not normally invoke penalty clauses, even if a contract contained them. Had Johnstone given up in mid-Atlantic he would still have made a gallant effort, and his story of the exploit would have been valuable to any newspaper which had helped to finance it. But this is to consider only one side of things. No honourable man likes to default on a bargain, even if no fault rests with him. Johnstone obviously wanted to give those who backed him the fullest possible value for their money. It was partly his fear of Ridgway's getting in first, and so diminishing the value—or what he felt to be the value—of his own story, that led him to abandon sea-trials with *Puffin*, and to start on the voyage before he was really ready to go. But that was *in him* rather than in his sponsors, a wholly honourable reluctance to risk letting down anyone. He was in command of the expedition: it was for him to decide what to do. Had he insisted on trials, or on anything else that he considered necessary for the safety of the expedition, he would have been entirely within his rights. That he chose to take risks was a fault of circumstance. Those circumstances, however, related to his financial commitments. This subject is discussed more fully in Chapter XXI.

XVI

The family doctor—David Lewis

DAVID LEWIS was born at Plymouth in 1917, but when he was two his parents went to New Zealand (his mother's home), and he spent his childhood and early youth there. He studied medicine at Otago University Medical School, and in 1939 came back to England to complete his training as a doctor. On qualifying he went straight into the Royal Army Medical Corps, trained as a parachutist and served as a medical officer with an airborne ambulance unit of the Sixth Airborne Division. He took part in the airborne landings in Normany in 1944. After the war he worked for a time in the West Indies, and in 1948 returned to England to enter general practice in East Ham. He sailed his 25-ft sloop *Cardinal Vertue* in the first Singlehanded Transatlantic Race in 1960. Fourteen miles out from the start at Plymouth his mast broke. He put back to Plymouth under a makeshift rig, had his mast repaired and within forty-eight hours sailed again, to finish third in the race 3,000 miles later. He then turned his attention to the Arctic. He had an experimental ocean-going catamaran, *Rehu Moana*, designed and built, and in 1963, with a crew of five (including himself), he took her for a proving voyage to Iceland. He had intended going on to the east coast of Greenland and Jan Mayen, but on the passage to Iceland the catamaran was dismasted. Politely declining offers of assistance, he worked her to Iceland for emergency repairs. All this took so much time that three of his crew had to leave him to go back to their jobs, so he sailed the catamaran back to England with one companion, Axel Pedersen, a Dane. Between Iceland and the Hebrides the catamaran was again dismasted. Again he refused offers of help, and he and Pedersen brought her to Stornoway by themselves. There he fitted a secondhand metal mast, and there he was joined by his wife

Fiona, and their two infant daughters, aged 18 months and 3 months.

With Pedersen, he sailed boat and family to Plymouth, whence he sailed again, this time alone, in the second Single-handed Transatlantic Race in 1964, coming seventh out of fifteen starts (one retired). Fiona and the children joined him in the United States. With his wife and daughters as crew, he re-crossed the Atlantic to the Cape Verde islands, and then sailed on to South America and through the Strait of Magellan to Valparaiso. Here the party was joined by Priscilla Cairns, a young English teacher of mathematics and a keen sailor. In 1965 they crossed the Pacific by way of Juan Fernandez, Easter Island, Mangareva, Tahiti and Rarotonga to New Zealand. Lewis was interested in ancient Polynesian navigation, and one object of his Pacific voyage was to experiment in the practicability of what is known of Polynesian methods of navigation without compass, chronometer or sextant. In Tahiti he put away all modern navigational instruments and charts, and sailed *Rehu Moana* to New Zealand by what he believed to have been the Polynesian system of navigating by observation of sun, stars, winds, ocean swell and the flight of birds. His landfall in New Zealand was just 26 miles out from where he had reckoned to be. To enable his 'Polynesian' track to be compared with *Rehu Moana*'s actual track, and as a precaution against emergency, he arranged for Priscilla Cairns to take normal sextant sights, and to have access to compass, watches and charts. Her observations were not disclosed until the end of the experiment. The results of this experiment are of real importance not only to the history of navigation but also in devising practical means of self-help for ship-wrecked sailors and airmen who have to come down in the sea.

From New Zealand he brought his catamaran back to Plymouth, thus completing his circumnavigation of the globe. He has since returned to the Pacific with another boat to continue his researches into Polynesian history and navigation.

A study of David Lewis's exploits offers a number of illustrations of the Ulysses factor at work, and of some interesting variants in the factor. The impulse in Lewis, like that of

Heyerdahl, is a combination of physical and intellectual curiosity. Again like Heyerdahl, he is intensely interested in reconstruction of the past, but he is more concerned than Heyerdahl with man's personal behaviour. He is quite lacking in Chichester's intense competitiveness, and not greatly interested in competition in any sense. Writing of his approach to the first Singlehanded Transatlantic Race he observed:

> The competitive aspect of the race was outweighed, for me at all events, by the struggle between man and natural forces. The adventure itself assumed greater depth and purpose from the clearer understanding we hoped to gain of man's reactions when he stands revealed, stripped of all outside support, in a struggle, and alone with his soul. So the problem of scientific investigation into the mental and physical experience underlying the fight to inch westwards towards the Americas provided its own exciting challenge to the intellect.*

Nevertheless, the race was necessary to him, and if its competitive aspect was secondary he had an absolute determination to finish, regarding his dismasting at the start as no more than an incident on the way. As Colonel Hasler remarked, 'Cardinal Vertue may well be the only racing yacht that has ever appeared on the prize list after having been dismasted three thousand miles short of the finishing line.' With little hope of winning either that race or the next Singlehanded Transatlantic race four years later he drove himself hard throughout each passage, changing sail and trying to get the best out of his boat, however wet and exhausted he might be.

Those races, however, were really excuses to embark on adventure of a most individual sort. The Ulysses impulse was strong in him from childhood—at the age of 5 he embarked in a dinghy with an 11-year-old cousin and set out to sea, an exploit from which his pursuing father was fortunately able to rescue him. His New Zealand boyhood offered many opportunities to climb and to explore, and at 17 he made a journey

* David Lewis, *The Ship Would Not Travel Due West*, p. 4. Temple Publishing 1961.

of over 400 miles alone by canoe. He was untypical in being prepared to stick at academic training, working hard both in New Zealand and in England for his medical degrees. But medicine is not a typical academic study, and the range of climbing and sailing activities open to him in his schooldays and early university life was, perhaps, also untypical.

The war absorbed his early manhood, and then he had to settle down: or at least there were all the normal social pressures on him to make him feel that he ought to settle down. There were also his own convictions as a doctor, which he took seriously, feeling that a doctor's skill is not something entirely his own but belongs a bit to humanity. He was a good general practitioner, understanding his patients, many of them dock-workers, in east London, and getting on well with them.

But general practice was not enough. Nor was weekend sailing in the Thames estuary. He became deeply interested in Viking seamanship and absorbed himself in studies of the Norse sagas. When he heard of the proposed Singlehanded Transatlantic Race it seemed something that he *must* attempt. It was an excuse, as much as anything else, to himself: society accepts great sporting challenges, and it was far easier to explain that he was going in for an ocean race than that he wanted to explore his reactions to stress in solitude. From the outset he had private aims for the race. With the help of the Medical Research Council he drew up a questionnaire for himself and the other competitors for the daily recording of physical and emotional feelings in isolation, prefacing it with this statement:

> The Singlehanded Race is a unique opportunity to learn about the eating habits, the mental and physical feelings of men in isolation. This sort of information, though very valuable, is usually almost impossible to obtain. In turn, it will help us in problems of survival at sea, especially water requirements.

He also intended to sail back from the United States by a northerly route to the Shetlands which, he felt, would give him firsthand knowledge of the conditions experienced by Viking seamen.

All this he did in a 25-ft boat. His passage from Plymouth to New York took fifty-six days elapsed time, or fifty-four days sailing time if the two days spent in returning to Plymouth to get his mast repaired are excluded. Ten days before reaching New York he broke his nose in an accident with the spinnaker boom. He could have put into various New England ports for help, but he carried on, observing a week later in his log:

> From the distribution of the bruising tracking across the orbit three days after I cracked my forehead with the spinnaker pole I apparently broke not only the nasal bone but also the frontal or sphenoid or both. I was easily tired for several days, possibly due to concussion, but the immediate effect, headache, wore off quickly after three aspirins.*

Fiona met him in New York. He sailed with her to St John's, Newfoundland, and from there took his 'Viking' route to the Shetlands alone. By that time it was September, and the risk of autumn gales in the North Atlantic was severe. However, he wanted to take the sea as it came, so he carried on with his original plan. It was not that he *wanted* to experience gales—no man in his senses *wants* to meet gales at sea in a small boat. He *did* want to sail himself in seas through which he believed the Vikings had sailed a thousand years before, and he wanted to observe his own behaviour on the passage. If gales came, they came.

They duly came. Lying a-hull in a Force 10 wind (around 55 mph) he noted:

> *Cardinal Vertue* tends to lie broadside or by the quarter, with a 10–20 degree list; but when hit by a sea she heels to 50 degrees ... I felt that I was getting demoralised down below and had better go out and face it. So I crawled about the deck, lashing down the sails more firmly, and took some photographs, doubting if they would survive the spray. I feel calmer since going on deck, but I am still scared.†

His Viking passage completed, he returned to general practice in London.

---

* *The Ship Would Not Travel Due West*, p. 70.
† *The Ship Would Not Travel Due West*.

The Ulysses impulse in him, however, was now too strong to be resisted. Moreover, he had now satisfied himself that in using his medical training for his own specialised researches he was not wasting it. He returned to his boyhood interest in New Zealand and the Pacific and read everything he could lay hands on about Polynesian canoe voyages. He combined his interest in Polynesia with his Norse studies and decided to build a modern version of the ocean-going Polynesian double-hulled canoe or catamaran with which to make a voyage to the Arctic. If the catamaran turned out as he hoped he would then take his wife and children with him to New Zealand, experimenting with Polynesian navigation on the way.

Finance was an obvious difficulty. He raised the money to carry out the building of the catamaran and the first stage of his plan by selling *Cardinal Vertue*, by writing a book on his Transatlantic voyages and by newspaper sponsorship for his proposed Arctic expedition. He obtained plywood for the hull of his catamaran by interesting a manufacturer in the experimental construction of his boat. His wife Fiona helped by part-time teaching.

The catamaran, 40 ft overall, 35 ft on the waterline and with a beam across the two hulls of 17 ft, was launched in May 1963 by Fiona Lewis. Instead of the Western European tradition of launching a vessel with champagne, Fiona followed the Polynesian tradition of 'making the canoe drink salt water' by pouring seawater from a gourd over the bow. She also spoke the words of the Polynesian launching song:

> If I sail my canoe
> Through the breaking waves,
> Let them pass under,
> Let my canoe pass over,
> O Tane.*

Tane is the Maori god of craftsmen. The catamaran was named *Rehu Moana*, which means *Ocean Spray* in Maori.

The Arctic voyage was only partly successful. *Rehu Moana* was an experimental and novel design, much of her equip-

* Translated by Teuira Henry.

ment had to be made specially, and there were delays in the delivery dates. The boatbuilders did what they could in working against time, but they could not install fittings which were not made. Lewis was badly let down by a firm from which he had ordered a specially designed metal mast shaped like a wishbone. Two months before his sailing date this firm informed him not only that no work on the mast had started but that they had only then begun ordering materials for it which would take three months to procure. Since sails using a form of junk rig had already been made to fit the mast, at a cost of some £500, this was a serious business. The metal mast had to be abandoned, and a replica in wood was undertaken by a joiner at the boatyard. He did beautiful work, but the structure of curved wood that he produced inevitably lacked the strength of metal.

With all these delays there was little time for trials. Lewis had to decide whether to abandon the expedition or to go ahead with an experimental boat whose sailing qualities were virtually unknown. Postponement in such circumstances is scarcely possible: the choice is between abandonment and going on. Members of the expedition have arranged time off from their various jobs, there are commitments of all sorts. Abandonment may mean forfeiting money under newspaper or book contracts, returning equipment lent by manufacturers, severe financial loss. It is a hard decision for the leader of an expedition, but one that may have to be taken. Lewis decided to go ahead. He was criticised for this when *Rehu Moana* was dismasted. This criticism really reflected irritation that a boat which had had a good deal of publicity should prove fallible. It misunderstood Lewis's problem. He was blamed for taking a risk; but the essence of the whole adventure was a risk. He had to decide not whether to take a risk but whether his risks were justified. In the event, since he and his crew got out of trouble unaided, they were justified. He knew what he was doing, his risks were calculated. He himself explained his decision thus:

We accepted as inherent in our undertaking the experimental nature of our craft and much of her gear ... There was no doubting her inherent strength. For the rest, there was only one way of finding out—by practical experience.

The route was carefully chosen to pass near harbours where alterations could be made, the North Sea ports, the Orkneys, Shetland, Faeroes and Iceland. Longer trials before sailing north would have helped to remedy many lesser faults, it is true, but it is doubtful if a whole season afloat in coastal waters would have revealed the major ones. A gale in the open ocean had to be our teacher here.*

The catamaran's experimental rig failed, and her first dismasting caused the abandonment of plans to reach Jan Mayen or the Greenland ice. This wasted a good deal of Lewis's experimental work, at least until such time as he may go back to it, or someone else take on where he left off. He had planned to test the survival of a boat in ice by riding the hull on to an ice-flow: *Rehu Moana*'s underwater shape had been designed rather like a sea-sledge partly for this purpose. He had also planned various experiments in human survival on ice. These could not be carried out.

But the voyage to Iceland amply justified his conception of the catamaran. *Rehu Moana*'s construction proved to be enormously strong, and gave him confidence that she would carry him and his family safely round the world. The failure of his experimental rig was a disappointment, but it was a necessary lesson, for it told him how the catamaran ought to be rigged. His proving voyage did prove what he needed to know to carry out his later plans.

Lewis's South American and Pacific voyages are unique in the history of small boats, partly for his vessel, partly for his decision to sail with the deliberate handicap of two very young children. He was criticised for this, too. His own answer, in a personal conversation with me, was as follows:

> I want to make this voyage, and Fiona wants to make it with me. We both want to make it together. The children are too young to go to school, so I'm not keeping them away from school. I suppose we could find someone to leave them with in England. But they will get a lot out of being with us, and although they won't remember much in detail, they

* David Lewis, *Dreamers of the Day*. Gollancz 1966.

will learn a great deal which will help in their preparation for life. There is some element of danger, I suppose, but no more for them than for us. And suppose that Fiona and I are lost: is it really better for the children to be left as orphans, or to go with us?

It was another calculated risk. Lewis believed that he could protect his children, but he accepted the possibility of disaster and considered it rationally. A different man might have taken a different decision, but he was entitled to the decision he did take. I had to think a lot about this at the time because *The Guardian*, on whose staff I then was, was among the sponsors of his voyage. I had to consider what moral blame might be attached to the newspaper in the event of disaster, for aiding and abetting Lewis, as it were, to expose his young children to danger. I came to the conclusion that his reasoning was valid, and that if he and his wife felt it right to take their children with them, then they were right to do so. Had the family been lost, I should have had to answer the protests that undoubtedly would have been made. I concluded that responsible parents cannot be denied responsibility for their children, that young children cannot be contracted out of the risks of life; and that although to take under-threes by catamaran through the Magellan Strait was an unusual parental decision, fundamentally it was no different from deciding to let a child ride a bicycle.

The Pacific voyage was beautifully performed. Lewis had trouble with a broken rudder when still 680 miles out from Valparaiso, but constructed a jury rudder and made port without assistance. After visiting Robinson Crusoe's island of Juan Fernandez (the island on which Alexander Selkirk, whose story Defoe turned into Robinson Crusoe, was cast away) Lewis carried out everything he had planned to do. His navigation by ancient Polynesian techniques over some 2,000 miles from Tahiti to New Zealand with a final landfall no more than 26 miles out was an extraordinary achievement. There is no doubt but that the Maori inhabitants of New Zealand came from Polynesia, but there is dispute on whether the Maori settlement was the result of chance voyages when canoes were blown off course, or whether Polynesian seamen were able to make repeated voyages to New Zealand by de-

liberate navigation. There are traditions of deliberate navigation, and ancient sailing directions handed down from
generation to generation by word of mouth. The doubt has
been whether such navigation over ocean distances is practicable. Lewis is modest about the outcome of his own voyage.
He does not claim to have 'proved' whether any particular
Polynesian voyage was or was not made, but simply to have
established that it could be done. It may be argued that while
he put away compass, sextant and all other modern navigational aids, he could not divest himself of his own geographical knowledge of the Pacific, thereby employing mental
equipment that the ancient Polynesians did not have. Against
this, Lewis did not have the lore of stars and sun, sea colours
and bird habits that the Polynesians had acquired from
generations of experience. He could learn from the oral traditions of Polynesia and from the records of early European
voyages in the Pacific, but there was no master-navigator of
the ancient school at whose feet he could sit. Modern geographical knowledge and lack of ancient Polynesian knowledge here roughly cancel out each other. Few now doubt that
Lewis has shown the old Polynesian techniques to be work-
able.

Does any of this matter? Would Lewis's life have meant
more to the rest of the world if he had devoted himself to his
practice? These are reasonable questions. The first is really
unanswerable without a dissertation on linguistic philosophy to define the meaning of 'matter', and whatever conclusion is reached here will be disputable. To acquire knowledge to become a good motor mechanic is clearly useful to
oneself and perhaps to one's neighbours: to decipher the
Cretan Linear B script is unlikely to be of much practical use
to anybody. Lewis's experiments in navigation without instruments have some practical value in devising techniques to
assist shipwrecked mariners, although the development of
small radios to send out automatic distress calls makes long
voyages in lifeboats of less life-saving value than they were:
nowadays it may be wiser for a shipwrecked crew to send out
distress signals and await rescue than to try to reach land.
Nevertheless, radios may be damaged and do not always work,

and alternative techniques of self-help may come in handy. In this sense Lewis's Pacific voyage has given man, if not a new tool, at least a modern way of using old tools. It might be said that the decipherment of Linear B suggests an eccentric but possibly useful way of learning to read, applicable at least to some of the problems of cryptography. But it is nonsense to suppose that the main value in knowledge is material or practical. Material value may sometimes come from new knowledge, but the impulse to climb the ridge to see what lies beyond is not material. To know is an absolute human need, not necessarily recognised by all, or even by the majority, of individuals at any given point in time, but inherent in human survival. It is a Ulysses characteristic to need to know physically and personally, to see with one's own eyes, to steer to the left of the sun or towards a zenith star with one's own hand on the tiller.

Lewis's physical reconstruction of Polynesian navigation was necessary *to him*, and its achievement has added a dimension of knowledge to the world. It may be specialised knowledge, even abstruse knowledge, but it is knowledge that modern man did not have before. It may have been commonplace in twelfth-century Polynesia, but medieval canoe navigation in the Pacific has not survived, and although a tradition remained, it has been left to Lewis to restore the techniques that show tradition here to have been no myth. No one knows what new understanding of man's past may come from Lewis's decipherment of this ancient navigational language, and what may or may not come is irrelevant to his achievement. He has turned theory into fact and brought new thinking to Pacific history.

Whether sailing small boats in remote seas is of comparable value to medical practice is another question. Lewis will be remembered when most doctors of his generation have gone into oblivion, but memory is an uncertain standard of judgment on the value of an individual life. The infamous are remembered with the noble. The Ulysses factor in Lewis has impelled him to a form of exploration which, by stirring imaginations, has enriched innumerable lives, vastly more than he could have helped as an individual doctor. His medical training is part of him, it has influenced his approach to exploration, informed all his research. It may be said that much in his exploits has no very obvious medical bearing, but medicine is concerned with man, and it would be hard to maintain that any human action has no medical bearing. Lewis would not claim his studies of his own children over long periods at sea and in the tropics as a major contribution to child welfare, but his observations here certainly do contribute to the understanding of child health. This is incidental, perhaps, but in a true sense nothing is incidental. The Ulysses factor in Lewis contributed to his determination to become a doctor as it contributed to his later determination to take part in the Singlehanded Transatlantic Race and to explore the Pacific by catamaran. He has not wasted his medical training; he has applied it differently. If he practises again— as I write this he is still only 52—his Ulysses wanderings will at least enhance his understanding of his patients.

Lewis himself has asked of his Pacific voyage, 'Has the adventure been worth while?' His answer deals specifically with only one aspect of it, but embodies a wide general philosophy. He wrote:

The children are bound to forget much they have seen, but not all. They have become accustomed to accepting people of all countries as their friends equally; they have learned to respect the great forces of nature, but are entirely unafraid of them. I hope they will grow up to face life in this same spirit; that they will feel the discontent that makes living just for the daily round not enough, so that they, too, will need to sail beyond their own sunsets; even if, for them also, the course be towards goals they do not fully understand.*

Lewis's decision to take his wife and young children with him on his voyaging is unusual, but not untypical of the Ulysses pattern. Men influenced strongly by the Ulysses factor are not purposeless wanderers. They tend to marry young, and to be deeply attached to their families. The type-figure married young or fairly young, and he had a family before he left Ithaca for the Trojan war. Clearly they meant much to

* David Lewis, *Daughters of the Wind*, p. 287. Gollancz 1967.

him. He does not seem to have contemplated taking Penelope or his son with him on his later voyages, but this may be explained by his setting in history. That it is unusual for modern Ulysses-type adventurers to be accompanied by wives and children is adequately explained by the purely practical difficulties. If these can be overcome, as they were by Lewis, it is not at all out of keeping for the family to share adventures. Chichester's great exploits have been by nature singlehanded, but he has made long family voyages with his wife Sheila and his son Giles. Ridgway and Blyth were both married, and thought constantly of their wives as they rowed the Atlantic. When they discussed the possibility of making a later voyage up the Amazon they decided that they would take their wives with them.

In his admirably readable books Lewis gives a slightly false impression of himself as a somewhat happy-go-lucky planner. He writes lightly, often amusingly, of occasions when things go wrong, implying, for instance, that to plug a hole in a boat's side with a potato is the sort of thing one just accepts at sea. In fact, he is a meticulous planner, basing preparations for his voyages on long theoretical study as well as practical forethought. Before he entered for the first Singlehanded Transatlantic Race he sailed alone from the Thames to Norway and then to Rotterdam, to train himself in handling a yacht singlehanded, particularly in busy sea lanes with much other shipping about. Had he succeeded in reaching the Arctic in his voyage of 1963, he might have had to deal with polar bears during his experiments on the ice. He was careful to add a rifle to his equipment, somewhat startling the sergeant at a London police station by giving as his reason for applying for a Firearms Certificate 'to shoot polar bears'. Throughout all his expeditions he has shown the true Ulysses spirit of self-reliance.

XVII

The commuter—Robert Manry

ROBERT MANRY was 46 when he made up his mind to sail the Atlantic in a 13½-ft boat, and he had his 47th birthday on the voyage. He accomplished the passage from Falmouth, Massachusetts, to Falmouth, England, in seventy-eight days in the summer of 1965 in the minute sloop *Tinkerbelle*, then forty years old, but almost wholly rebuilt by him. It was Manry's successful voyage which gave David Johnstone the idea of rowing the Atlantic, and in turn set off John Ridgway.

In a study of the Ulysses factor in modern man there are three points of special interest about Robert Manry. First, although it is typical of the Ulysses impulse that it should last well into old age, Manry does not appear to have acted on it until he was approaching 50. This is unusual. Chichester, Tilman and others who have performed remarkable feats of endurance in their sixties all started to go on expeditions as young men. Secondly, Manry's effort, like Kenichi Horie's, was wholly self-performed, from start to finish: he had no assistance from companions or crew, no sponsorship of any sort from anybody, no initial publicity. Thirdly, he is American. This may seem a curious point to be of any special interest, but almost all major manifestations of the Ulysses factor since the war have been in Western Europe or Japan. In proportion to population, the United States has had in this period far less than its statistical share in the emergence of Ulysses types.

Except for the apparently late activation of the factor in him, Manry exhibits all the characteristics of the type in almost text-book perfection. On looking more deeply into his life, the apparently late manifestation of the Ulysses impulse in him is explained: it was not late. He was born in India, where his parents were missionaries, and the perpetual interest of life in India, never far removed, as life in Europe or the United States so often is, from the physical bases of existence, clearly gave his young imagination enough to feed on. He was always ready for physical experiment, launching with his brother a sailing boat on the Jumna River, although neither had ever attempted to sail a boat before. Travel was inherent in the circumstances of his youth. He spent some time at a university in Canton, visited Japan and on finishing college in the United States he was caught up by the war. He joined the US Army and served with the 66th Infantry Division in France and Germany. On demobilisation he got a job as a newspaper reporter, which for a time satisfied his Ulysses impulse and gave him at least a vicarious sense of adventure. Marriage and children changed the tempo of his life. His Ulysses sense of responsibility, and the typical deep emotional attachment to his family, made it inevitable that he should try to settle down. He changed from being a reporter for the more stable job, and more regular working hours, of a sub-editor on the Cleveland *Plain Dealer*, and apparently he was set for the useful two-dimensional life of the millions of suburban mortgage-payers who keep going what is called civilisation. He was the picture of the family-man commuter.

Manry was not particularly well off and there was seldom much margin between his household expenses and his monthly pay cheque. He had always longed to own a boat—the craft of his early attempt to voyage on the Jumna River had been borrowed—but he was 40 before he and his wife Virginia felt that the family finances might just be stretched to boat ownership. His hopes were modest. The boat he bought cost $160. She was $13\frac{1}{2}$ ft overall, nearly thirty-five years old and had two large holes in her hull. Still, she was, or had been, a boat. Manry set about rebuilding her.

He was equipped for the job. He was good with his hands, had taken classes in woodworking at a technical school and enjoyed using tools. In nine months he restored his little hull to seaworthiness, and then he taught himself to sail on Lake Erie. His thoughts at this stage were almost all for his family. The boat was to be used for days off and family holidays, and he hoped that his wife and two children would get something out of her. They did. After two summers of lake-pottering he wrote:

It was an enchanting blue-sky day on Lake Opeongo that
we came to the realisation, suddenly, that *Tinkerbelle* had
crept deeply into our lives and hearts. She wasn't a boat any
more; she was a friend. She was helping us to grow, individually and as a family, by bringing us, together, into
confrontation with the basic forces of nature and fundamental situations in living. She was giving us a foundation
on which to make wise decisions about what was important
to life and what wasn't. She was providing experience
through which we were acquiring self-reliance, appreciation for the outdoors, respect for others, instincts of mutual
aid and cooperation and all the other qualities, skills and
attitudes that contribute towards the development of mature
personalities ... Don't assume that the children were
the only beneficiaries, or even the principal ones. Virginia
and I gained enormously, too, in our understanding of our
children, of ourselves and of each other, and in innumerable other ways.*

In 1962 he rebuilt *Tinkerbelle* again, adding a cabin,
lengthening her mast by 8 in and replacing her centreboard
with a winch-operated daggerboard-keel, made of iron and
weighing about 1 cwt. He tested his modified boat with a
singlehanded cruise of some 75 miles on Lake Erie. She behaved well.

Early in 1964 a friend invited him to join a proposed
voyage to England in a 25-ft yacht. Manry spent months planning for this voyage, and then the friend changed his mind
about going. Manry was mentally and emotionally so involved
in the voyage that he felt he could not give up. He determined to sail alone in *Tinkerbelle*.

This was a decision taken after the most careful calculation
of risks. He made a 200-mile cruise on Lake Erie with his 10-
year-old-son and decided that his boat was up to the job.
Manry had never sailed at sea, but Lake Erie is a fair test of
boat and man. *Tinkerbelle* was very small indeed, a few
inches shorter than many sailing dinghies. However, she was
decked and watertight. Manry had read widely of small-boat
voyages, and he accepted that size as such has little bearing on
a boat's seaworthiness. He was not particularly keen on sailing

* Robert Manry, *Tinkerbelle*, p. 25. Collins 1965.

P

to England singlehanded, but he could not afford another boat, and *Tinkerbelle* was too small to carry food and water for two men on a Transatlantic crossing. So the voyage had to be singlehanded.

He made *Tinkerbelle* more or less unsinkable by packing synthetic foam inside her planking, analysed the breakage-probability of every piece of her gear and assembled tools and spare parts to repair or replace breakages. He knew nothing of celestial navigation, so he bought a few text-books and a surplus Air Force sextant with an artificial horizon and practised taking sights in his garden. His sextant could also be used with a natural horizon. He made no attempt to tackle the theory of navigation but concentrated his self-training on the simplest form of sun-sights and the use of tables. He felt that if it came to the worst his navigational problem could be reduced to sailing east: as long as he headed east he would be bound to reach Europe at some time. As things turned out, his navigation was remarkably accurate.

Provisioning his 13½-ft boat was a formidable piece of logistics. He estimated the passage at from sixty to seventy-five days (he took seventy-eight days) and decided to provision for ninety days. Water was the usual problem. He found that he could live on rather less water than the accepted ration of half a gallon a day, comfortably so if he had an occasional tin of fruit-juice to supplement his water-ration. So he took 28 gallons of water, divided as a precaution against spillage or contamination among forty ½-gallon containers, three 1-gallon containers and one 5-gallon plastic drum. He had an emergency survival-kit, packed separately, which included eight vacuum-sealed tins of water and a solar still. He worked out a daily ration of food, carefully balanced for dietary sufficiency, and added one or two treats for special occasions—a plum pudding, for instance, to be eaten when he reached halfway. He had no anxiety about food or water at any stage of his voyage. A few ships spoke (to) him in mid-ocean to ask if he required assistance, and he was always able to reply no, though he was glad to accept a gift of some fresh fruit.

The nicety of his planning is brought out by his considered summary after the voyage of what changes he would make if he were to undertake it in the same boat again. He would take, he thought, a second Dacron genoa headsail—he did have two genoas, but one was an old canvas sail which tore out on the voyage, thus preventing the use of boomed-out genoas for downwind sailing. He had one Dacron genoa which he had made himself. He did not make a second, partly because of time, partly to save cost, partly because he thought his old canvas sail had more life in it than it did. The only change he would have liked in *Tinkerbelle* herself would have been roller-reefing gear or an additional set of reef-points on her mainsail.

The only pieces of equipment that he did not take and missed were a hacksaw, a pair of metal-cutters, a tin of machine oil and a spare radar reflector (he took one radar reflector which was blown away in a gale). He felt the lack of hacksaw and metal-cutters when he had to repair his rudder with a piece of brass plate taken from a camera—a rather special need, difficult to foresee. He did have a spare rudder, but both his rudders broke. However, he achieved an entirely satisfactory repair with the tools he had: hacksaw and metal-cutters would have made the job easier. The tin of machine oil, invaluable on a boat as at home, seems an odd omission, but no man, even with Ulysses characteristics developed to a high degree, can think of everything. Ingenuity made up for the lack of oil to keep his tools from rusting: he melted Vaseline.

Like Horie, and for much the same reasons, Manry told no one outside his family of his plans. He was afraid that if it became generally known that he was proposing to sail the Atlantic in a $13\frac{1}{2}$-ft boat all sorts of pressures would be put on him, and, more seriously on his wife, to stop him. He kept nothing from his wife, and her attitude was splendid: she accepted that this was something her husband needed to do, she had confidence and faith, and gave him all the help she could. Manry had no fear that she would herself try to discourage him: he did want to spare her from being told by neighbours that she *must* stop a lunatic husband from throwing away his life. Ulysses-like, he practised some deception with the outside world. The invitation to sail to England in a larger boat was known generally among his friends and colleagues at the office. He obtained leave of absence from his job to make this voyage, and he went ahead with his preparations without saying that the bigger yacht would not be going and

that he was proposing to sail alone in his own 13½-ft boat. He
did not disclose his plans, even to the newspaper for which he
worked, until after he had sailed—he left a letter, explaining
his real intentions, to be delivered when he was safely at sea.
This was interesting forbearance. 'Cleveland Man to Sail
Atlantic In 13½-ft Boat' would have been big news, and he
could have got all sorts of concessions, and probably much
free equipment, by making use of publicity. He did not want
to. His story inevitably became big news. A huge gathering of
reporters and broadcasters assembled at Falmouth to meet
him, and he had a near-royal reception when he landed. This
worried him. Would his own newspaper want to use his voyage as a promotional stunt? He wrote:

> I hoped earnestly, ardently, that was not so; for I had
> dreamed of the voyage for too long, and it meant too much
> to me, to have it spoiled at the end by being transformed
> into a commercial enterprise.*

It is pleasing to record that the *Plain Dealer* behaved both
well and generously. It did not put any pressure on Manry to
allow his story to be used in any way he did not like, and it
brought his wife and children to England to meet him, an
expense that the family itself could not even contemplate.
When Manry got leave of absence to make an Atlantic voyage
both he and his wife thought that it would be without pay,
and their domestic calculations were made accordingly. When
the newspaper learned precisely what Manry was attempting,
it told Mrs Manry that her husband's salary would be paid to
her all the time he was away. She recorded her relief in her
diary:

> P— called to tell me that a cheque for six weeks' pay will
> be here soon, with another one each week until Robert
> comes home. We surely can use it.

Manry's sole complaint against his paper was that while he
was at sea it printed some letters he had written to his wife
and given to the master of a ship which had spoken him in
mid-Atlantic to post for him in New York. The letters were

* *Tinkerbelle.*

duly delivered, to Virginia Manry's delight, and she herself gave them to the *Plain Dealer*. Later she had second thoughts which she set down in her diary:

Three letters from Robert for me and two for the children. Then began a struggle between the newspapers as to who should print them. Of course the *Plain Dealer* is his paper, and they deserved first chance. The family scolded me for permitting even the *Plain Dealer* to use them. As they said, 'Dad won't like it a bit.'

Manry quoted this passage from his wife's diary in his book *Tinkerbelle*, and added in brackets, 'They were right; I didn't like it.'

To anyone who has been exposed, even remotely, to the pressures generated by press interest in a major news story, Manry will be considered fortunate. The ship which brought his letters to New York also reported having met him at sea, and Mrs Manry would have had no peace from telephone calls or visiting reporters, asking if she had heard from her husband, and what he had said. This may be hard on individuals, but is perfectly legitimate press enterprise. Mrs Manry decided afterwards that what she ought to have done was to have typed an extract from her husband's letters and released only that. At the time, however, she was so delighted at hearing from her husband that she thought of nothing else. Who can blame her? In an ideal world a newspaper would no doubt omit from such letters passages of a personal nature, but this is not an ideal world, and the human interest in Manry's letters was so great that tens of thousands of Cleveland citizens wanted to read them in full. The paper was doing what it considered to be its job—after all, Manry was on its staff, and Mrs Manry had handed over his letters herself. Manry understood all these things, and blamed nobody. He was content simply to record his own feelings.

Manry's voyage made him famous. Did it achieve anything else? For himself, it was a transformation of life, not in the material sense of emerging from anonymous suburban living into national prominence but in enabling him to feel that he had made himself more nearly a complete man. He himself summed up:

> The voyage was something I simply *had* [his italics] to do, had wanted to do for a long, long time... The story in the *Falmouth Packet* had referred to me as a hero, but that was absurd. As far as I was concerned, I wasn't taking any great risks, and I was doing something I enjoyed intensely.*

And again:

> What had the voyage achieved besides making dreams a reality? I think probably the most important thing it had done for me was to enable me to stand back, away from human society ashore, and look at life for a little while from a new perspective. The Atlantic ocean had not been a place for trivialities, and I think, perhaps, that fact may have done something to make me a better person inside than I had been before.
>
> Anyway, I hope it did. Although I was lonely and discouraged at times, my primary feeling was of contentment and peace. My boat was my dearest companion, and though the wind and sea were sometimes my adversaries, they were mostly friendly, and they behaved with straightforward honesty according to their inherent natures. To know them was to respect them.
>
> I must confess that, seen from the peace and quiet of mid-ocean, many aspects of life on land seemed grim indeed. Well, we might as well face it; in some basic ways life ashore *is* [his italics] grim, especially for under-privileged or under-equipped persons. I couldn't help thinking of the grey flannel suit brigades in the big cities ashore, living in a kind of lock-step frenzy, battling noisy highway or subway traffic to get to work in the morning and to return home in the evening, existing on pure nervous energy in between, having to be alert to opportunities to get ahead and on guard against the encroachment of rivals.*

This is an interesting statement. Manry explains the

* *Tinkerbelle.*

Ulysses impulse in him by the single observation that he made his voyage because it was 'something I simply *had* to do'. Then he goes on to discuss his feeling that in some way he was contracting out of the urban–suburban environment in which most of his contemporaries were trapped ashore. But he was not escaping—that is the important point. He was not going on holiday to Miami or the Bahamas or Europe to escape from something, knowing the escape can be only temporary, and that the old prison will be awaiting him when he gets back. The point is that after such a deep personal experience no environment can any longer be a prison.

As things turned out, Manry's extraordinary adventure so touched public imagination that he was materially enriched, but that was not his purpose. It may have been somewhat naïve in him to expect that little notice would be taken of his voyage and that, the voyage ended, his main task would be to try to make good the hole in his savings. But that was what he did expect:

I had thought that since England was a maritime nation and had had her full share of adventurous sailors, little attention would be paid to *Tinkerbelle* and me. I had expected to sail into Falmouth harbour almost unnoticed, moor my boat at a quay, and go to a hotel for a nice bath and sleep.*

He had not set out to cross the Atlantic in what was then the smallest boat ever to have made the ocean passage. His boat was small because it was the only boat he could afford. He was totally non-competitive. He did not expect to be put at the top of the league table for anything. What he did seek —and find—was a new dimension of physical experience in himself. It had to be physical; reading about other men's voyages, though instructive, was not enough. He had to go himself to the crest of his waves, to look across ocean distances with his own eyes. In the passage I have quoted he refers to the 'honesty' of wind and sea, and he makes the same observation a number of times in his narrative of the voyage. This is not sentimental; he has no sentimental 'love of the sea'. He knows well enough that the sea is neutral in human affairs,

* *Tinkerbelle.*

benign or savage according to meteorological chance. But, benign or savage, the sea is 'honest'. If a great wave knocks down your boat it is because your boat is in the path of the wave, and it is the function of thousands of tons of moving water to toss aside whatever may be in the way. Such a wave may occasion fear, but one need have no fear of personal animosity; there can be none. Man does not meet the elements on equal terms. He meets them on no terms, but that is fair enough, because the elements have not the slightest desire to meet man. However, by cunning and skill man may come to terms of his own with the elements, using their strength when he can, patiently yielding to them when he can do nothing else. It is not a fight, it is not a system of mutual aid, for wind and sea ask nothing of man. The so-called 'struggle' with the elements is really a pattern of infinitely varying relationships, in which man depends on his own skill and ingenuity to put himself in the best possible relative position at any given moment. But he can rely on 'honesty'. A gale is a strong wind, a rough sea is a rough sea, and nothing else. Having experienced this at firsthand, having lived with wind and sea as exposed to both as the first Ulysses was, you can go back to suburban life and it will not be a prison any more. It may be only two-dimensional living, but that no longer matters. You have found another dimension.

Manry found his third dimension, and that is his achievement. That, though unconsciously, is what the rest of the world recognised in acclaiming him. When he landed at Falmouth some people in the crowd just wanted to touch him— 'as if I had some magical power to impart'. In a sense, he had.

Manry's voyage is yet another illustration of the Ulysses characteristic in calculating risks. All his risks were calculated. He had no need to prove that a very small boat is capable of crossing an ocean. He did prove that by determination, self-discipline and self-instruction a man without much experience is capable of crossing an ocean in a very small boat. He added his own warning, 'I hope no one will assume that *any* small boat is able to cross an ocean, because in that direction lies potential tragedy.'

XVIII

A personal experience—Griffin

SUBJECTIVE analysis has pitfalls. All the preceding studies analyse human exploits from the viewpoint of a detached observer. I deal in this chapter with an expedition in a small sailing boat to Greenland and North America that I myself created and led. The Ulysses factor is common to mankind, and therefore I have my share of it: how great a share, and in what proportion of characteristics, I do not pretend to know. But the factor had certainly some part in the genesis and execution of *Griffin's* voyage in search of Vinland in 1966. Since I know my own feelings, hopes and fears in a way that no man can know anybody else's, this brief attempt at self-analysis may have a place in these studies.

I was older even than Manry when I set out on my first ocean crossing in a small boat. I was 55. Like him, I spent my early childhood in a somewhat romantic part of the world. I was born in the West Indies, where my father's people had been sugar planters since the eighteenth century, and I had crossed the Atlantic (by steamer) three times before I was 9. I had a rather lonely boyhood, being sent to England to go to school while my parents lived abroad. There were no air passages in those days. Over eight years I saw my mother briefly in the summer holidays every other year: my father I met once only in those eight years. I became a newspaper reporter, and enjoyed the ceaseless travelling and the sense of being at least a looker-on near the centre of great events. I joined the Territorial Army, and my unit was embodied about a month before war actually began in 1939. After serving as an anti-aircraft gunner at Biggin Hill and Dover during the Battle of Britain period, I was sent to India. Early in 1944, after six months in hospital with unpleasant complications of amoebic dysentery, I was sent back to England and invalided out of the Army. I became Military Correspondent of the then *Manchester Guardian*, now *The Guardian*, and went back to the war in Europe as a correspondent with General Eisenhower's headquarters. My war ended in Berlin. I had about a year with a wonderful assignment to wander wherever I could get in ex-occupied Europe for the *Manchester Guardian* and then came home to the job of Labour Correspondent. That was exciting during the first years of the post-war Labour Government, but I was glad to be promoted Assistant Editor of the paper in 1951.

Promotion, however, brought disadvantages, of which gradually I became aware. All my life until then I had been travelling and writing at firsthand; now my job was to help to organise other men's travelling and writing. It was a good job, with a great newspaper, and I would be angry with myself for feeling restless. But I was restless. From my West Indian childhood I had loved small boats, and I acquired a 17-ft boat with a minute cabin. But Manchester is not well placed for the sea. I had a mooring off Anglesey in the Menai Straits—delightful cruising waters, but I could not get there often. Then the *Manchester Guardian* became *The Guardian* and I had to work in London. My boat went to Plymouth—even harder to get to.

In the autumn of 1965 Yale University announced the discovery of the Vinland Map, the only (so far) known map showing a recognisable outline of the coast of North America produced before Columbus sailed. I was absorbed by this map. I wrote about it for *The Guardian*, and the whole Vinland story, the attempt by Norse seamen between the eleventh and the fourteenth centuries to found colonies in North America, came to occupy more and more of my thoughts. Vinland, the Norse name for that part of North America which they attempted to colonise, is well authenticated by the Icelandic sagas, by Adam of Bremen's history of 1075 and by the Vinland Map. But North America is a vast continent, and no one knows precisely where Vinland was. I wondered if it might be possible to interpret the navigational clues in the sagas to make a reasonable reconstruction of the early Vinland voyages. Quite suddenly I felt that I *had* to get hold of a sailing boat and try to do this.

The Guardian was good to me. It financed my Vinland expedition in return for daily stories of the adventure sent by radio. This did not mean that I had an unlimited expense account. Because I was trusted, I had to be extremely careful about money, and I made some mistakes because of this—my mistakes, for the decisions were mine, not dictated to me. To save expense I decided that *Griffin's* old mainsail would do. It didn't. Make-do and mend saw us through, but the sail blew out twice on the voyage. Such follies were my own. I could not have asked for a kindlier partnership than I had with my paper.

So we went. I could do the navigational detective work, but the practical navigation and ship-handling required for an ocean voyage in the difficult seas off Greenland, Labrador and Nova Scotia was beyond me. But I found competent and splendid companions prepared to risk going with me, five in all. Our boat was *Griffin*, a 44-ft cutter, built in 1938 and once the club yacht of the Royal Ocean Racing Club. We sailed from Dover on April 27 1966.

This is not an account of our voyage. We had our gales and troubles, called at the Faeroes to repair our gale-torn mainsail, called at Greenland, where the Vinland story begins, called at Halifax, Nova Scotia, to get our mainsail mended once more and eventually reached Martha's Vineyard, Massachusetts, where I believe the Vinland settlements to have been. The events of the voyage are immaterial here. I am trying to assess why at the age of 55 I wanted to leave a comfortable home and a family which apparently like me and to whom I am deeply attached, for a voyage in a small boat through fairly inhospitable parts of the North Atlantic, with considerable danger from ice.

I can say only with Manry that I *had* to. And I think the same goes for my companions. Two were in their twenties, unmarried and perhaps attracted mainly by the adventurous aspects of our voyage. But the rest of us were all over 40, two of us over 50, all with responsibilities for families, sober middle-aged citizens, the world would call us. Why embark on a twenty-eight-year-old boat on a wild-goose chase after Vinland?

Sober (I hope) we were, but on investigating our lives it could be found that none of us was acting quite out of character. One of us was a yachtsman who had sailed in all weathers over a good many of the world's seas, though he had not before adventured into the Greenland ice, another had been a Chindit in Burma, another had a youth of keen Scouting, and much sailing and travelling since, including some enterprising journeys in the Middle East on his own business. And so on. We were prepared to look after ourselves, we wanted to see the other side of our own particular hills. We knew enough about small boats to expect a rough passage.

The others came because I asked them to, and a more loyal, less self-seeking crew no boat can ever have had. For myself, I was about equally driven by the sheer intellectual delight of trying to unravel a kind of navigational detective story and the physical desire to experience the seas and coasts of its setting at firsthand. The one involved the other. The more I studied the sagas, what is known of old Norse navigation and the characters of the principal Vinland navigators, the more I felt compelled to try to follow physically in the wake of the ships they sailed a thousand years ago. Charts, the tracks of ocean currents, recorded knowledge were all fascinating, but not enough. I wanted to go myself, to make, if I could, the landfalls they had made, from the same sea.

I have been asked since why I was content to sail in a boat of this century instead of trying to obtain a replica of a tenth-century Norse ship. The answer is completely clear to me, though I doubt if I have always managed to make it clear to others. It was not necessary. I was concerned with navigation and the sea, not with the vehicles used. I needed a sailing boat to be subject to wind and sea as the old Norse seamen were, but I was attempting to *reconstruct* a voyage, or rather, a sequence of voyages, not to *reproduce* any of them. The Vinland voyagers sailed with cattle and at least some women. They were colonisers and traders: I was not. The *sea* was our common thread of history, not our purpose on it. In any case, the form of vessel used on these long Atlantic voyages of the tenth and eleventh centuries is not wholly known. It was not the traditional longship, the warship of the Viking raiders, but a decked trading vessel. It interested but did not much concern me. I wanted to go *where* men had sailed a thousand years before me, not to discover precisely in *what* they had sailed. For my purpose one sailing boat was as good as another

—not strictly true, for a boat reinforced against ice would have been better. I sailed in *Griffin* because she was the boat I was able to get. She had some disadvantages of age and she was not reinforced, but she served us well.

I wonder sometimes if any boat has ever sailed completely ready for her voyage—Manry's *Tinkerbelle*, perhaps, excepted. I had committed myself in January to a sailing date at the end of April. All sorts of consequential arrangements depended on this date, but there were many times during fitting out when I despaired of being able to meet it. When men should have been painting *Griffin* three inches of snow covered her; the weather that early spring was dreadful. Before I got her *Griffin* had been changed from gaff to Bermudan rig, which involved lengthening the mast and remaking the mainsail. My plans allowed for sailing trials, but there was no time for trials. She sailed with her new crew for the first time when we started on our voyage on April 27. Her deck was a clutter of gear, fitters were working on board as we locked out from Wellington Dock into Dover Harbour. I was advised by men I respect that we could not possibly sail. I had to decide what to do.

I decided to sail. What looked like clutter was superficial, and would soon be tidied up: all the major work of refitting and stowage had been done. Much new gear was untested, and so were we as her crew. But I knew my companions and I had confidence in *Griffin*. Psychologically we were wound up for departure; the damage to morale from postponing our sailing date seemed to me worse than the uncertainties of sailing as we were. In any case, the first leg of our voyage would take us up the east coast of England and Scotland, and we should not be far from port if anything went seriously wrong. The risk seemed reasonably calculable. And I think it was. Given a week of sailing trials, we might have discovered that *Griffin*'s rudder needed attention before we did discover this in heavy weather in the North Sea, and I might have learned that her old recut mainsail was not strong enough for the long voyage ahead. But equally we might not have discovered these things. As David Lewis observed of his own decision in similar circumstances, 'A gale in the open ocean had to be our teacher here.' We learned our lessons, and we profited by them—for one thing, they took us to the Faeroes, which we should not otherwise have seen. But that bitter day in Dover lives in my memory and, I hope, helps me to understand the problems that other men have to face.

One night in *Griffin*'s open cockpit off the coast of Greenland I had a long discussion with one of my companions about the circumstances in which it might be held irresponsible for a married man to take part in an expedition such as ours. This question nagged at me, for not only was I responsible for wife and children myself but three of my companions had similar responsibilities. They were there by my invitation: had I been right to invite them, or they to accept?

I recall the cold sky and the loom of ice on the horizon in the near-Arctic twilight—at that time of year in those latitudes there is little darkness—as we talked. First, we accepted that no man should use marriage as a refuge from any duty that might involve risk: in war, for instance, a man should not try to avoid service because he happens to be married. But there was no duty in our expedition: we were there because we wanted to be. Was that really selfish? Then I wondered, was it wholly true to say that there was no element of duty in our being on *Griffin*? We accepted the duties of the sea, to the ship and to one another. We had come voluntarily, but we had all felt it right to come. Indeed, I had felt compelled to come. I summed up that conversation later that night in my log:

> Peter argued, and I am sure he is right, that the man who is hazard-unconscious does not amount to anything—it is no credit just to ignore risks. But calculated risk taking is all right: you know that there is a risk; you assess it; take what precautions you can against it; and the rest is with God. That is fair enough. Also, we decided that a man mustn't *not* do things that involve risk simply because he may have a wife and children. Clearly there is a real problem here, and risk taking, to be justified or not, is a matter of degree, but the point is that you must not pack up being a *man* because you have a wife and children. There may be things that you can do justifiably if you are a single man that it would be better not to tackle if you have a wife and children, but this is something that you must decide for yourself. I don't want to die in these Greenland seas, but I've

got to die some time, and to wind up on an expedition like this would not leave a bad taste in the children's mouths.*

Reading this some years later, I don't think that I would alter it. Human duty is always complex, but a man would be no good to his family if he failed to be himself. He might have two-dimensionsl virtues, perhaps, paying bills and mending fuses, but he would not have much to hand on to the next generation.

I do not feel with Manry that our voyage in *Griffin* made me in any way a 'better' person, more sympathetic to, or tolerant of, the weaknesses of others. I suppose that if I had not been able to go in search of Vinland, frustration might have made me more querulous and bad-tempered than I am, and in that sense the voyage may have improved me. But if I had not sailed for Vinland I dare say I should have found something else to do. Manry and I were both, I think, animated by the Ulysses factor, but we were looking for different things. Or rather, perhaps we were both looking for a third-dimension in our lives, but we looked in different ways. I accept his view that a period of isolation at sea is a useful corrective to the pettiness of life ashore, but I doubt if there is much lasting *moral* gain to be had from it. The gain is self-fulfilment. In the sense that a man who is more nearly three-dimensional is a *better* human being, functionally better, than a man who is not, the working of the Ulysses factor in man makes for better people. But this is not a matter of moral values as such. The development of some of the characteristics that go with the Ulysses factor, self-discipline, for instance, may have a bearing on moral values, but it is not a simple relationship.

Did our voyage achieve anything? It taught me a good deal about enduring cold, but I cannot claim that as a particularly notable end of human endeavour. I tried to sum up afterwards:

I do not claim to have 'discovered' or 'proved' anything. The objectives of our expedition were limited, and I kept strictly to the brief that I had given myself. This was to make a *navigational investigation* of the Vinland voyages—

* J. R. L. Anderson, *Vinland Voyage*, p. 134. Eyre & Spottiswoode.

we started and finished with the sea. We were not explorers in the ordinary sense, the seas we sailed are known, the coasts charted. We had no goal that could be reached decisively—the North Pole, say, or a northwest passage from the Atlantic to the Pacific. We were making an experiment in time as well as an experiment in geography, sailing into the past as well as crossing a known ocean. All the time we were concerned with what the lawyers call 'circumstantial evidence', that is evidence to explain some human action built up from all the circumstances surrounding that action and not drawn directly from witnesses who can say 'I saw that man do this'...

I hope that our voyage may add a little to knowledge of the reality of the Vinland colonies. They came too early in history to succeed, but they were among the most gallant of human failures. And as we learn more about them we may learn much of importance to the history of both Europe and America and, perhaps, to our knowledge of ourselves... All human history is a jigsaw puzzle: one man may find a small piece that fits here, but the pattern cannot emerge until many men have found and fitted many pieces. If *Griffin*'s voyage has a final place as a footnote to this brave, sad chapter of human history, we who sailed in her will feel that we did our job.*

On this voyage I was conscious several times of an external power, not exactly watching over us—at least, not in the sense of permitting any relaxation of our own efforts—but present, and able to help. I felt this particularly strongly during a horrible week of fog that we endured between Newfoundland and Nova Scotia, a sea area notorious for fog, and not pleasant for a small wooden boat, with a doubtfully effective radar reflector. It is a sea much used by trawlers, and crossed by the tracks of big ships making for the St Lawrence. We could hear the engines of big ships approaching but see nothing, and although our old manual foghorn made a reasonably sonorous bleat, we could not help wondering how far it might carry. In any case, it is hard to position sound accurately in fog. An apparently efficient modern foghorn, worked by compressed gas, was useless, because the gas condensed on meeting the cold

* *Vinland Voyage*, p. 260.

David Lewis

Robin Knox-Johnston

fog, reducing the machine to a pathetic whimper. There was considerable risk that we might be run down, perhaps by a ship that would not even know that it had hit us. I was often afraid, but heartened to feel the immanence of God's power. I did not think that this would necessarily save us, but I did feel that whatever happened to us would be known to God, His will and therefore all right. I cannot put this feeling into words very well; it was a feeling, not a mental calculation. It was indescribably comforting.

XIX

Assurance—Robin Knox-Johnston

IT may seem odd to consider such a virile physical feat as sailing a small boat singlehanded round the world as primarily a spiritual voyage, but there are aspects of Robin Knox-Johnston's achievement in 1968–1969 which put it in a category rather different from other modern manifestations of the Ulysses factor. A sense of spiritual quest is inherent in the Ulysses character: the type-figure was influenced profoundly by his religious beliefs, and again and again in studying the men and women in whom the factor has been apparent one is struck by their acceptance of a power outside themselves, a power whose aid sometimes they seek, which sometimes comes unsought into their consciousness. The Ulysses factor is a physical impulse, but it is a constituent of an individual's whole being, and in its influence on action the material and non-material are inseparable. Sheila Scott, in trying to explain the reasons for her compulsion to fly, makes an interesting observation:

> Then suddenly my thoughts are crystal clear and I seem able to receive some outside energy from which I receive help when I need it, and also catch a fleeting glimpse of things we do not yet understand.*

It does not follow that Sheila Scott has undertaken her remarkable flights *in order to* enjoy this mystical experience. But the experience is an important part of the fulfilment that flying has brought to her.

Robin Knox-Johnston is a tough, well-adjusted man, with

* Sheila Scott, *I Must Fly*. Hodder & Stoughton 1968.

nothing much of the mystic about him. If you get a glimpse of his eyes when he is looking at something that interests him you may sense a vision that goes far beyond the range of ordinary eyesight—but this is not uncommon among seamen who have thought much for themselves during their hours of watch-keeping. Knox-Johnston is a professional seaman, an officer in the Merchant Navy, no amateur of the sea. He has that slight air of belonging only partly to the land that the sea gives to the more dedicated of those who follow it. There is nothing necessarily in the least mystical about this. It may be simply that the routine of life on land becomes slightly unfamiliar after years at sea. Conrad has written somewhere, 'The peace of God begins a thousand miles offshore.' But that may reflect distrust of landlubbers as much as any search for spiritual comfort. Knox-Johnston has the qualities of any ordinary man who has served his apprenticeship to the sea. There is nothing apparently extraordinary about him; yet his decision to sail around the world alone without touching at any port on the way was something quite extraordinary.

Certain things must be put in focus. Knox-Johnston's circumnavigation can be seen as an attempt to win £5,000 offered by the *Sunday Times* for the first man to sail alone non-stop round the world. In fact, the offer of this prize had little to do with his voyage. He had planned it independently before the *Sunday Times* announced its race, and he entered the race almost fortuitously, because he intended to sail round the world anyway. His boat *Suhaili* was not built for speed, and he thought that he had little chance of winning. When he did win, and received the *Sunday Times*'s £5,000, he gave it to a fund for the widow of Donald Crowhurst, lost from the trimaran *Teignmouth Electron* during the race.

Although it was not inspired by the race, Knox-Johnston's voyage can still be seen as a stunt. Chichester and Alec Rose had just made singlehanded voyages round the world with intermediate stops in Australia, and both had received knighthoods. A non-stop circumnavigation would be to go one better. There might or might not be a third knighthood (there was not), but the material reward in the shape of money to be made from newspaper, radio and publishers could be substantial. Knox-Johnston already had a 32-ft ketch capable of making the voyage. A relatively modest investment in stores and the endurance of some nine or ten months' solitude might be expected to pay a good dividend—far more than could be earned in the normal way by a year's work at sea. For a fit young seaman—Knox-Johnston was then 29—the task of sailing a well-found ketch around the world was not daunting: it would be a matter of endurance more than anything else.

To regard the voyage in this light would be to see it completely out of focus. It is true that Knox-Johnston had his boat *Suhaili* in which he had sailed from India to England with two companions, but he had borrowed from his family in order to buy her, and he still owed £2,000. To refit and store her for a voyage round the world would cost the best part of another £2,000. Moreover, he did not consider her particularly suitable for the voyage: she was heavily built, and in his view, too small and too slow. There might be money to be made out of a successful solo circumnavigation, but storm damage to the boat or illness or accident to himself would mean putting in somewhere for repairs or treatment, and that would rob the voyage of most of its value as a money-making project. The chances of success were—well, they were impossible to reckon. All you could say was that the odds *against* completing a circumnavigation without touching anywhere were pretty high. No one had yet done so. Chichester, with a big boat specially built for singlehanded sailing, had not even tried. Prudence would suggest that a young Merchant Navy officer, already £2,000 in debt, would do better to stick to his career.

For Knox-Johnston none of these arguments really mattered. The idea of attempting a non-stop circumnavigation had come to him in March 1967, after he had brought *Suhaili* from India to England, with time off in South Africa to earn enough money to complete the passage. He had always loved the sea. His first boat was a raft which he constructed for himself from an orange box at the age of four and launched at Heswall, on the Dee estuary, where his family then lived. The raft was not a success, but its rapid foundering at least taught him what a boat should not be like. It was followed by a more seaworthy canoe and a determination to go to sea as soon as he could. Shortly before his 18th birthday he joined the British India line as a cadet. At 21 he got his Second Mate's Certifi-

cate. He passed for First Mate a year later, and at 25 he held a
Master's Ticket.

At 22 he married. He was serving then in a ship trading
between India and the Persian Gulf, and he set up home in
Bombay. With two partners he had *Suhaili*—the name is
Arabic for the South-east Wind—built in an Indian yard
with the idea of sailing back to England on leave. There were
various delays, however, and his partners could not make the
trip. He borrowed from his family to buy out their shares in
the boat, and set out for England in her a year later, with his
brother and another friend.

By that time his marriage had broken up, which meant,
perhaps, that his emotional self turned more than ever to the
sea. If so, however, it was a complex feeling. A yachtsman may
have a love-affair with the sea to make up for a broken
marriage, but Knox-Johnston was not a yachtsman. He was a
professional seaman, familiar with the sea in all its moods,
inoculated against any romantic illusions about it. Yet the sea
held a deep part of his life and offered a healing process perhaps best described as a man's chance of coming to terms with
himself. I think that this had a bearing on the origins of his
voyage of 1968–1969, but not a direct bearing.

Insofar as the springs of human action can be identified, the
basis of Knox-Johnston's decision in the spring of 1967 to
attempt a non-stop circumnavigation of the globe was a
patriotic feeling of the sort that welled up in the first Ulysses
when he instructed his son:

> Telemachus, when you find yourself in the thick of
> battle, where the best men prove their mettle, I am sure
> you will know how not to shame your father's house. In all
> the world there has been none like ours for valour and for
> manly strength.

Knox-Johnston had been keenly interested in the Singlehanded Transatlantic Race, and French national jubilation
when Eric Tabarly won the race of 1964 made him feel that a
British come-back was necessary. In March 1967 Knox-
Johnston read that Tabarly was building an ocean-going trimaran in preparation for the Singlehanded Race of 1968. He
did not know if Tabarly had any plans for continuing to make

a circumnavigation after crossing the Atlantic, but thought it possible that he might. Discussing his feelings at the time, Knox-Johnston wrote:

> I could picture the headlines if Tabarly became the first person to sail right round the world non-stop. We'd never hear the last of it... In any case, someone was going to attempt it sooner or later. By rights, a Briton should do it first.*

Later, on his voyage, he added:

> Once Chichester and Rose had shown that this trip was possible I could not accept that anyone but a Briton should be the first to do it, and I wanted to be that Briton.

Patriotism as an explosive emotional force of the sort that animated Nelson's Navy and the heroes of Victorian boys' stories seems barely credible to some twentieth-century minds. But it *was* real, is real beneath the overlays of more fashionable political philosophies. The instinct to promote the welfare of family, tribe or nation is a natural constituent of a survival factor. Thus it is characteristic of the Ulysses factor. In Knox-Johnston it is unusually direct. Nevertheless, the impulse to his voyage was more complex than an impulse to wave the Red Ensign. That was certainly an ingredient, but it was part of a deeper need to seek physical fulfilment of a spiritual aim. That need was expressed in a conviction that he *had* to attempt the voyage. All rational reasons for the enterprise, patriotic, practical, financial, were secondary.

There were good rational reasons *against* attempting it. Initially, he decided that *Suhaili* was not a suitable boat, and his planning was based on raising the money to build a new boat that would be larger, faster and more convenient for singlehanded sailing. Months of effort went into this: it did not succeed. The cost of a new boat was beyond anything he could hope to obtain by selling *Suhaili*, and he was unable to find sponsors. He did not think of giving up the project. He changed his mind about *Suhaili* and determined to do the

---

* This and other quotations from Knox-Johnston are from his record of his voyage *A World of my Own*, Cassell 1969.

best he could with her. He still needed to find money, but by using *Suhaili* he could manage on a good deal less. The *Sunday Mirror* was prepared to sponsor him, and with the help of an imaginative literary agent who understood what he was trying to do, he obtained useful contracts with book publishers in Britain and in the United States. Advance payments on their various contracts gave him enough to proceed. To go ahead was an act of considerable faith, both by Knox-Johnston and by those who helped him. So the voyage began, and he sailed from Falmouth on June 14 1968. On April 22 1969 he returned to Falmouth after 313 days of solitude, the first man to circumnavigate the globe by sea calling at no port and depending wholly on his own resources.

That is his achievement. What does it mean? The obvious first: through Knox-Johnston whatever national credit there may be in winning this marine marathon has gone to Britain; that it was secured by a professional seaman adds another medal, as it were, to the honours of a long maritime tradition. Like the first ascent of Everest, Knox-Johnston's feat can be dismissed as of little practical value—of little value, but not quite of no practical value, for the experience of surviving extreme physical conditions, of prolonged sea-keeping, of exposure at high altitudes, contributes knowledge that is useful to industry and to society in a number of ways. But the research value of such exploits is modest. Knox-Johnston discounts it completely in his own case. He wrote on the voyage:

I was doing absolutely nothing to advance scientific knowledge; I would not know how to. Nothing could be learned of human endurance from my experiences that could not be learned more quickly and accurately from tests under controlled conditions. I was sailing round the world simply because I bloody well wanted to.

The rest of the world, however, did not take Knox-Johnston at quite this valuation. The rest of the world was right. A great many people were passionately interested in his voyage, and his homecoming was a hero's reception. Popular hysteria can be generated by the engines of modern publicity, but the old saying about fooling people is relevant here—you can fool all the people some of the time, you can fool some of the people all the time, but you can't fool all the people *all* the time. Enough people have been moved by Knox-Johnston's voyage to make their evidence important. Some of the manifestations of the popular adulation given to him may have been a bit hysterical, but the instinct to applaud Knox-Johnston for having done something remarkable reflects that response to the Ulysses factor that is deep in humanity, healthy and real. It is a response quite different from that given, say, to a pop singer. The age range of those emotionally affected by a pop singer is limited to about one decade; the range of those who find some thrill in a Knox-Johnston covers the span of human life. A crowd reacting to a pop singer manifests more than a hint of latent sexual frenzy; the reaction to a Knox-Johnston is more akin to the excitement of getting a telegram of good news. We may accept as valid his countrymen's instinctive feelings that he *did* do something remarkable. But this does not answer the question, What did he do?

Knox-Johnston's own answer is short. 'I did what I bloody well wanted to.' This is more profound than it seems. In modern society it is actually rather rare for people to do precisely what they want, rarer still if it calls for action extended over 313 days and requiring long planning and preparation. The determination that carries through such action is characteristic of the Ulysses factor, and is one of the things that moves others to admiration. Knox-Johnston did what he wanted. But what did he want?

It is possible only to attempt an analysis of the motives of human behaviour; they are deep in the recesses of personality, as often hidden from an individual himself as from those outside him. Knox-Johnston's own assessment of his reasons, a patriotic desire to ensure British supremacy in a particular maritime feat, the personal challenge to endurance and seamanship, the wish to prove to himself that he could do it, are obviously valid. But in my view these are all explanations that only partially explain. The patriotic motive is the most nearly complete—'a Briton should be the first to do it, and I wanted to be that Briton'. Up to a point this explains *what* he wanted to do, and why he wanted to do it. But as an explanation this is a long way from being wholly complete. Why should a non-

stop circumnavigation of the globe be something that a
Briton *ought* to do? Why should one individual British subject rather than another particularly want to do it?

Given the force of the Ulysses factor in him, both these
questions can be answered. Knox-Johnston looked beyond all
known horizons of human performance in singlehanded sailing and wanted to experience what was to be found there; if
something of value was to be found, and if he could find it,
the age-old instinct to promote the survival of family or tribe
made him want whatever might be of value to go to his own
people. That is understandable. There remains to determine
what it was he found.

I have called this chapter 'Assurance', and I think that what
he found on the voyage was a new assurance of faith—of faith
in man himself as well as in whatever divine power may be
outside men. In a remarkable passage in the book on his voyage he puts his own feelings:

> The rules are there, the physical laws that we have slowly
> learned. If we obey them, we have a chance of survival. It is
> no use knowing that your boat is heading towards the eye
> of a storm and praying to God to see you through it safely.
> That's not his job. It's your task to steer the boat away from
> the eye, and you are asking too much if you expect the boat
> to survive when you deliberately ignore the rules. My own
> philosophy is developed about the phrase 'The Lord helps
> those who help themselves'. It is no good lying in your
> bunk, listening to the rising wind and feeling the boat be-
> ginning to strain, and praying to God to take in a reef. No
> one but a fool would expect anything to happen. One has
> to get up and reef the sail oneself... When everything has
> been done that you know you can do, you put your trust in
> your Superior Being ... Because of this belief, throughout
> the voyage I never really felt I was completely alone...
>
> If you are trying to do a particularly difficult job, and
> failing time and again, the knowledge that the Lord will
> assist you if you help yourself keeps you going at it, and in
> my experience the job usually gets done. A simple example
> of this occurred when we were making for Cape Horn and I
> was bending on the old mainsail. The halliard slipped from
> my grasp and pulled through its sheave about fifteen feet,

well beyond reach. I could not afford to lose it, and if I did not catch it quickly it was likely to run right through, which meant I would have to climb to the top of the mast to retrieve it, next to impossible in the sea conditions prevailing then. Three times I tried to reach the halliard, and failed. It was obvious that if I was going to get it back I was going to have to climb some way up the mast. I told my God the problem and explained how I intended setting about it, and asked him to give me a hand. A minute later I was back on deck with the halliard shackled on to the sail.

Analysing this incident, Knox-Johnston accepts that some might say that his Superior Being was in his own imagination, and that what really helped was that telling God about it helped him to think calmly for himself. He adds his own comment:

The fact remains that the job was done, and because I thought there was someone there I was encouraged to keep trying—and surely that is what God is all about.

Time and again on his voyage his combination of faith and practical ingenuity got him out of trouble. He needed to reset the gap on the sparking plug of the charging motor for his radio batteries—and found that he had forgotten to bring a feeler-gauge. He needed a gap of between twelve- and fifteen-thousandths of an inch: how was he to measure in thousands of an inch with nothing better on board than an ordinary ruler? He measured an inch on a pad of writing paper, and counted the pages to the inch. There were 200, so this gave him a thickness of five-thousandths of an inch to one sheet of paper. The job was done. He devised an external patch for a leaking seam below the waterline that he could not caulk. In nearly a year at sea, and in some of the harshest seas of the world, he was constantly faced with damage to gear or equipment that would normally call for shipyard repairs: in every case he managed to rig up something that worked. Was all this solely one man's personal skill? Again his own comment:

I think a man would have to be inhumanly confident and self-reliant if he were to make this sort of voyage without faith in God.

I do not want to press this too far. Robin Knox-Johnston is no visionary seeking some metaphysical explanation of the universe. He is a practical seaman, with an ordinary man's interests, hopes and fears. Since his voyage would offer an unusual study of solitude, he was examined by a psychiatrist before he sailed and again on his return: on both occasions he was found to be completely normal in his reactions. He sums up for himself:

> My mental approach to problems appears to have under-gone a fairly marked change. I now like to consider things a big longer, and I think more deeply, before coming to a decision. Obviously this comes about as one grows older, but I think the voyage has accelerated the process.

This is an interesting piece of self-discovery. It is not exactly the finding of wisdom, but it is certainly to come upon the ingredients of wisdom. Above all, Knox-Johnston brought back assurance, the best sort of self-assurance in the know-ledge that he could sail alone as far as man can sail on earth and meet hazards as they came from his own resources; and the assurance of faith, not a denominational faith, but faith in the conviction that those who use their own powers honour-ably and to the uttermost can confidently leave the event to God. In this kind of faith there is no trace of the arrogance that expects a private loan from God when you have spent your own money: it is a conviction at once deeper and of more humility, that you may expect God's help if you work for it, but that the form or timing of such help as you may be given is not a matter for you.

In an age of uncertainty and lack of confidence this assur-ance that there is still something to be worked for is about as valuable a cargo as any ship has ever brought to Britain. *Suhaili* here may be ranked fitly with Drake's *Golden Hind*.

X X

Women

THE Ulysses factor is not sex-linked. From man's remote past it has been important to the survival of race or tribe, and Nature's efficiency ensured its presence in both men and women. Its manifestations, however, are much less common in women than in men and show interesting differences.

When tribal or family survival might depend directly on physical exploration or migration it was necessary for women to accompany men, or at least to follow quickly. For the effective transmission of the factor it was necessary that women should respond to the excitement of the Ulysses impulse, directly, in mating readily with men in whom the factor was strongly developed, and indirectly by telling adventure stories to children, and bringing them up to respect, and want to emulate the characteristics of the Ulysses type. There is no reason why the primary impulse for physical exploration should not motivate a woman in herself, but in primitive societies, where physical strength and skill in fighting were of major importance to survival away from the domestic surroundings of a tribal settlement, women obviously were less fitted than men for primary exploration.

Our type-figure, the first Ulysses, is male, and it could not be otherwise: in the society of his time women were neither warriors nor sailors, and those women who accompanied men to war were camp-followers or captured slaves—a woman was one of the prizes, and not the first prize, offered by Achilles for a wrestling match. Nevertheless, the female principle is deeply embodied in the Ulysses story. The god particularly well disposed to him was a goddess, and Athene manifested Ulysses qualities in herself to a high degree. She was subtle, cunning, brave and of endless curiosity. When she revealed herself to Ulysses after his landing on Ithaca she was delighted

by his wariness and attempt to deceive her with a wholly ficti-
tious account of his arrival.

Athene recognised her own qualities in Ulysses, and his in
her. Although enchantingly feminine, she was, however, a
goddess, not burdened with the responsibilities of homemak-
ing and looking after children that affect most mortal women.
She is an idealised type-figure, of a woman who had somehow
to be more than a woman.

She is vitally important in the Ulysses story. Without her
succour, encouragement and advice he could not have done
half the things he did. This was not merely the support that
in a good marriage a man gets from his wife, comforting, loyal
always, unquestioning, or even unthinking. Athene was no
subordinate figure, she was Athene of the flashing eyes, a partner and often the senior partner in the enterprises of Ulysses.
In the idiom of his period Homer makes plain that the
characteristics he is describing in Ulysses are both male and
female.

In men the full development of the Ulysses factor is fairly
rare. In women it is rarer still or, perhaps, it is harder to identify. Celia Fiennes, Lady Hester Stanhope, Gertrude Bell,
Freya Stark and a few other outstanding women have combined intellectual and physical curiosity to make journeys of
discovery that rank with any man's. But for a woman to
embark on such adventures is against the main stream of
society. A man may contract out of society for a time and be
admired for it; manifestation of the same quality in a woman
usually provokes social disapproval. Even women who may
come to be admired for highly individual achievement tend to
be considered successfully eccentric rather than really admirable. Women are subjected to enormous pressure to sublimate
instincts for physical adventure into imagination, a sublima-
tion shown, for example, in the lives of Charlotte and Emily
Brontë. The world, perhaps, does not lose by this. *Jane Eyre* is
worth many great physical journeys. The most acceptable
field of physical adventure for women is in the service of religion: a woman may be a heroic missionary without attracting raised eyebrows. One cannot know how many splendid
manifestations of the Ulysses spirit have sent women to remote and inhospitable parts of the earth in the anonymous
habit of the sisterhood of some religious order.

Times change. For half a century in the Western world women have been socially enfranchised. Allowing for the domestic pressures that still affect many, perhaps most, women, one would expect female manifestations of the Ulysses factor to remain less common than male. Even so, the absolute rarity of significant female manifestation is statistically surprising. There was no swift release of pent-up female ambitions after the First World War. Amy Johnson, the Duchess of Bedford (Mary, wife of the eleventh duke), Amelia Earhart and Jean Batten wrote new chapters in the history of the air and showed that women could be as adventurous in this new element available to mankind as men, but it could not be said that their example was widely followed by their own sex. The Duchess of Bedford was a particularly interesting illustration of the Ulysses factor in women, proving that one special characteristic of the factor—its continuance into old age—is not confined to men. She was 62 when she began to take flying lessons to qualify as a pilot. She died at the age of 71 on a flight to complete 200 hours of solo flying required to qualify for a licence as a commercial pilot.

Since the Second World War one woman, Ann Davison, has sailed the Atlantic singlehanded. One, Sharon Adams, has sailed the Pacific, and another woman, Sheila Scott, has achieved record after record in the air, becoming the most outstanding long-distance solo flier of her generation. They have remained rare among women.

Ann Davison's flying career began in Argentina before the war when she was 21. She was given a trip to Argentina by her father as a 21st birthday present. She stayed with friends on a ranch, and one day she was taken up in a light aeroplane on an air search for a swarm of locusts. When she got back to England she told her father that she wanted to learn to fly, to which he replied, 'I don't see why you shouldn't.'* She was working as a freelance commercial pilot on delivery flights, towing advertising banners and the like when she joined her future husband's fleet in 1937.

She married the owner of a small private fleet of commercial aircraft, put out of business when private flying was prohibited during the war. She and her husband tried various ventures, including farming on an island in a Scottish loch,

* Ann Davison. *Last Voyage*, p. 14. Peter Davie, 1951.

but both were restless and sold up to buy a boat, proposing to
make the boat their home and sail the world. Their boat was a
big ex-fishing ketch, 70 ft overall, and costs of fitting out were
more than they bargained for. They were beset with financial
anxieties, and sailed from Fleetwood in 1949 short of much
that they needed, but intending to make for Cuba. They had
trouble with gear and with their auxiliary engine, twenty-
four years old, and experienced a terrifying fire in their
galley, which they managed to put out. Running short of
fuel, they planned to make for a French port, but were swept
up-Channel by a gale and wrecked off Portland. Ann's
husband was drowned, but she survived a severe battering on
a raft and crawled ashore. She spent the next few years working to pay off debts on the lost boat, and in 1952 determined
to complete the voyage to the West Indies that she and her
husband had planned, by herself. She bought a 23-ft sloop,
Felicity Ann, left Plymouth in May 1952 and after calling at
Douarnenez, Vigo, Gibraltar, Casablanca and Las Palmas
reached Dominica in January 1953. That great sailor Humphrey Barton described her voyage as 'really remarkable', and
added, 'we should all be extremely proud of her'.*

She has written of her love of 'poetry and travel, variety,
excitement, adventure, danger'* and described post-war civilisation as 'the frightful bonds man has imposed upon himself
in the name of progress'.† She and her first husband, thirteen
years older than herself, were both independent, pioneering
people. Frank Davison had gone to Canada after the First
World War and worked as cowboy, lumberjack, gold pros-
pector and in a variety of other jobs before coming back to
England to join his father's broking business. He had been a
racing motorist and held a private pilot's B licence—he was
debarred from an A licence, permitting him to fly commercially, because of defective vision in one eye. He left his
father's firm to set up his own aircraft business. Clearly he had
a great influence on his considerably younger wife, but her
preference for wild places and pioneering jobs was as much
her own as derived from him. He introduced her to sailing.
She wrote of this:

---

* Humphrey Barton, *Atlantic Adventurers*, p. 194. Adlard Coles 1962.
† *Last Voyage*, p. 14.

Frank had a love for ships and the sea which I was aware of and accepted, as I accepted his thinness, his yellow hair, his china-blue eyes and quick temper, as part of his make-up. But the ships were also a part of the life he led before we met; that shadowy past existence of one you grow to know well which always remains slightly unreal and out of focus. I accepted this ship passion but at the time hardly understood it; to me ships were something in which one crossed the sea in order to get to the other side.*

Without knowing much about boats she accepted with complete loyalty her husband's wish to abandon farming in Scotland in order to sail the world. The financial disasters that befell them were not their fault: they were brought about by delays and difficulties in getting hold of equipment and getting work done in the years just after the war, and by rocketing post-war costs. The 70-ft ketch they bought was much too big for two people to handle easily, but in those post-war years they had great difficulty in finding any sort of boat. And for their planned purpose of providing a home as well as world cruising, the old ketch's spaciousness was attractive. But the venture was beyond their resources. It is a tragic story.

Ann Davison's reaction was both exceptionally courageous and exceptionally interesting. She told Humphrey Barton, who helped her to find and equip *Felicity Ann*, that she wanted to sail the Atlantic because she had to earn a living by writing, and that she could not write unless she had something to write about. That no doubt was partly true. But to contemplate a singlehanded ocean crossing after her appalling experience at sea, and with little personal experience of sailing, reflected an extraordinary set of human qualities. There were many easier adventures she could have undertaken, not less likely to provide useful copy for her writing. The Ulysses factor was certainly strong in her—she had shown Ulysses qualities before—but I do not think that her exploit can be regarded solely as a manifestation of the Ulysses factor. Her motives were more complex than the working of even this complex factor. She needed, perhaps, to exorcise a fear from her life, and being a very brave woman did so by deliberately exposing herself to it. She had respect and some affection for

* *Last Voyage*, p. 55.

her boat *Felicity Ann*, but it was a critical affection, unlike
the devotion that a man quite often feels towards a boat. After
her Atlantic crossing Humphrey Barton wrote to ask for her
general views on singlehanded ocean sailing. She replied with
a long and extremely practical letter. Of her boat she wrote:

> As for the ship, *Felicity Ann*, as I have no standards for
> comparison the only criticisms I can level at her are the ones
> inherent to all small ships. That is the discomfort of liv-
> ing without headroom or adequate stowage space ... and
> working out your navigation with the chart bundled up on
> your knee. If I was a real sailor there might be certain sail-
> ing qualities of which I would disapprove, but as it is
> *Felicity Ann* tackles really monstrous stuff like a cheerful
> cork, doesn't come apart, open up, sink or frighten me
> much, so I haven't any complaints.*

Boats are female themselves, and perhaps a critical affection
is inherent in a feminine approach. Ann Davison's reflection
on herself as not being 'a real sailor' is also interesting. She
had just completed a voyage which, by any standards, was remarkable: eight years before the first singlehanded Transatlantic Race, which has made the idea of singlehanded ocean
sailing less awesome, few sailors with a lifetime of experience
would have attempted what she performed. Yet she did not
think of herself as 'a real sailor'. Sailing for her was no more
than a vehicle of achievement. It is hard to assess what she was
trying to achieve, no doubt equally hard for her. Whatever it
was, consciously or half-consciously, she achieved it.

I find a similar difficulty of assessment in Sheila Scott. Her
achievement in the air is almost beyond credibility, and has
been sustained year after year since she learned to fly in 1959.
She was then in her early thirties and turned to flying apparently on impulse after various jobs as an actress and model
and six years of a marriage that, as she has put it, 'should
never have been'.† On one flight of 36 hours over May 19–20
1965 she established fifteen new European records. In 1966
she set up a new record for a solo flight round the world in a
single-engined aircraft, her Piper Comanche *Myth Too*. In
1967 she created new records for singlehanded flights between

* Atlantic Adventurers, p. 194.   † *I Must Fly.*

R

London and Cape Town in both directions and for crossing the North and South Atlantic, from Shannon to Gander, and from Natal (Brazil) to Dakar in West Africa. And she has continued to make records for flying faster or farther without stopping than any man or woman in her class of light aircraft has flown before. She has remained an intensely feminine, extremely attractive woman.

She exhibits many typical Ulysses characteristics, including the sense of compulsion to adventure. In her own words:

> I am never alone up there and am discovering every day a new philosophy and ability to live on the ground as long as there is always another flight... It is the passing through to another plane of thought which I can usually find only when I have been concentrating very hard for weeks on the preparations, the actual flying and overcoming modern-day obstacles, and I have got beyond the stage where every limb aches and my brain begs for sleep. Then suddenly my thoughts are crystal clear and I seem able to receive some outside energy from which I receive help when I need it and also catch a fleeting glimpse of things we do not yet understand. This is the essence that is still challenging me to go on and discover more and this is what it is all about to me. It is not just the crowds and cheers, and I am certainly not trying to outdo any man. I merely want to be able to go on flying and to be able to discover these things firsthand for myself. It is simply that I *must* (her italics) fly.*

This is almost a classical description of Ulysses symptoms, but not quite. There is slightly too much mysticism about it. There is an element of mysticism in the Ulysses character, but not a great deal; a need for spiritual as well as physical fulfilment, certainly, but fulfilment is not primarily mystical. Sheila Scott implies, or half-implies, a desire to enter an ecstatic trance-like state beyond physical fatigue, towards the attainment of which fatigue, at least fatigue directed to an acceptable end, is a necessary step. This is untypical.

Yet there is much that is typical. The compulsion to fly in order to be able to live on the ground expresses very well the Ulysses need to feel a whole or complete individual, to be a

* *I Must Fly*, p. 212.

three-dimensional person although having, perhaps, to spend much of life in two-dimensional existence:

> I am a part of all that I have met;
> Yet all experience is an arch wherethro'
> Gleams that untravelled world whose margin fades
> For ever and for ever when I move.

Her feeling that she wants 'to go on flying to be able to discover these things [whatever they may be] firsthand for myself' is also typical.

She may not be 'trying to outdo any man' in the sense that she, a woman, wants particularly to excel at things that men are supposed to be good at, but she is intensely competitive: she wants to excel. Of all the Ulysses types I have discussed she comes nearest to Chichester in competitiveness: a flight must, if possible, make or break a record. Competitiveness is present in the Ulysses character, but the intensity of competitiveness in Chichester is untypical, and so it is in Sheila Scott. It is not, however, competitiveness in quite the same form. Intense competitiveness is inherent in Chichester, a primary characteristic, and it is this that is untypical of the Ulysses factor. In Sheila Scott it may be secondary, deriving from her desire to fly rather than producing it. She is 'a real flier' in the sense that Ann Davison is not 'a real sailor', or Chichester *primarily* a seaman. An uncompetitive, although perhaps more complex, Sheila Scott comes out in her description of an ascent by balloon on a wholly non-competitive flight:

> This was what I had been striving to find ever since I discovered the joys and frequent heartbreaks of flying. So many times in the past I had taken my old Moth alone high into the sky during the last hour of daylight to try to find tranquillity. Often I had found something up there which I could never repeat on the ground. This was the same feeling, but experienced much more vividly. It gave me a sense of incredible happiness, completely uninterrupted by the necessity of moving controls or looking out for other planes.*

* I Must Fly, p. 84.

Her feelings towards her aircraft, *Myth, Myth Sun Pip, Myth Too,* are identical with those of a man towards his boat, compound of love as for a wife or mistress, dependent love, as for a mother, and solicitude, as for a child. She considers her aircraft female, like boats, but her attitude towards them is more akin to heterosexual love, with a sense of reliance on them that a woman may feel about her husband. A number of women feel about cars in this way: they have male qualities of strength, endurance, speed, both protective and to be loved.

In 1969, seventeen years after Ann Davison became the first woman to sail the Atlantic singlehanded, Sharon Adams, a 39-years-old American woman, sailed the Pacific alone in her ketch *Sea Sharp.* She crossed from Yokohama in Japan to San Diego, California, taking seventy-five days over the passage. This was a considerably faster passage than Kenichi Horie's ninety-four days from Nishinomiya Harbour, near Osaka, to San Francisco in 1962, but her boat (31 ft) was substantially bigger than Horie's (19 ft) and therefore capable of greater speed.

Sharon Adams spent several years in training herself for the voyage. She learned to sail at her husband's sailing school in California, and in 1965 she made a singlehanded voyage from California to Hawaii, making the 2,225-mile passage in thirty-nine days. Her planning and preparations were exemplary. She experimented for months with sail-handling gear until she could do almost all her work from the cockpit, reducing the need to go forward to the exposed foredeck. She is meticulous in wearing safety harness, a good test of self-discipline on a long voyage. Sharon Adams is the mother of two children, and her singlehanded exploits are particularly interesting as an illustration of the fact that children do not necessarily inhibit the Ulysses impulse in women.

The Ulysses factor requires physical expression, personal firsthand experience of physical things, particularly of the elemental forces that condition life. Typically, it requires going somewhere, doing something, by personal human effort, relying on one's own strength and skill to engage the wind in a sail, to row a boat or paddle a canoe, to climb a mountain or cross an ice-cap. Great skill may be required to get the best out of an engine, but as the engine becomes more powerful and more sophisticated the skill needed to control it,

although perhaps requiring longer and longer training, becomes more remote and impersonal. It is still at secondhand,
the more creative, firsthand skill having gone into the design
of the engine and its controlling instruments. The engine is
taking you somewhere; you are not taking the engine. It may
be taking you where you want to go, you may be its master;
but your journey remains the engine taking you. This
applies, of course, to all aircraft other than balloons and
gliders. Flying with powered aircraft, therefore, is a modification of the Ulysses factor, and it is questionable at what point
the motive in flying changes from being a manifestation of
Ulysses characteristics into something quite different—the
need to get from London to New York quickly, for instance,
to conclude a business deal.

This is an over-simplification. The Ulysses factor is not easy
to identify; it is present in some forms of flying, not in others.
It is a matter of degree. Chichester's singlehanded flights in
his first Gipsy Moth required an engine, but their achievement depended far more on personal qualities in him. He had
no large supporting organisation to smooth his passage
wherever he landed, with a petrol-tanker waiting to connect a
hose to his fuel tank. True he planned his flights and tried to
arrange for petrol to be available at his stopping places, but it
was petrol in drums from which he fuelled his tanks himself
with a collapsible funnel. His flying was still near to first
principles—so near that when his aircraft sank off Lord Howe
Island he was able to rebuild it without factory facilities and
fly on. His navigation was wholly at firsthand by sun and sextant; he had no radio aids to guide him, he depended solely on
himself.

Sheila Scott's flying thirty years later was done in machines
infinitely more *mechanical* than Chichester's early Gipsy
Moth, and airports and air-control systems, vestigial or non-
existent in Chichester's flying days, were highly developed.
Nevertheless, her flying was still *personal*, her flights required
skill, endurance, enterprise, self-discipline, all the Ulysses
qualities. And her motive, or at least a large part of her
motive, was a true Ulysses impulse.

It is interesting to observe here how many of the *outstanding* female manifestations of the Ulysses factor have been in
the air, personal adventures but requiring dependence on

machines. I have said that this is a modification of the factor, though the degree of mutation may be slight. Perhaps it is a modification particularly likely to occur in women, for it reduces the need for purely muscular strength. It does not, of course, lessen the requirement for courage, endurance or self-discipline.

It may be significant that this modification of the factor occurs mainly in female manifestations of Ulysses characteristics in *singlehanded* exploits (Ann Davison and Sharon Adams are exceptions here). Fiona Lewis and Priscilla Cairns, who sailed with David Lewis, Susan Hiscock, Beryl Smeeton, Anne Pye, Kwailan La Borde and a number of other women who have made long voyages with their husbands in small boats have shown unmodified Ulysses qualities. Husband-and-wife partnerships, however, are extremely difficult to assess individually. The range of motives is infinite. A man may be the prime mover in an expedition, and his wife may go with him out of loyalty and love, preferring to endure discomfort and danger with him than to be left behind. Had she married another sort of man, she might never have left home. Dormant Ulysses qualities may be brought out by circumstance. Equally, a wife may prod her husband into an adventure: dormant Ulysses qualities in him may then emerge. It is possible that a woman with Ulysses qualities in her may be attracted to a man with similar qualities, so that they will reinforce each other. The number of women who have made adventurous journeys with their husbands is high enough to suggest either that the possession of Ulysses qualities in common influences mating or that a dormant Ulysses factor is sufficiently widespread in both sexes for its strong development in one partner to awake it in the other. Another modification of the factor in women may be that it is more often capable of passive satisfaction than in men. The number of wives who have encouraged their husbands in Ulysses-type enterprises, giving every possible help and support, even when they have not wished or not been able to accompany them, can scarcely be statistical chance. Sometimes a strong Ulysses factor in one partner may lead to the break-up of a marriage. When it does, it is usually a first marriage, and a second marriage is commonly a happier mating.

In husband-and-wife partnerships it is probable that the

initiative in a Ulysses-type enterprise normally comes from the man. Going back to primitive origins, this is what one would expect: the male goes off to seek better land or better hunting grounds, and the female accompanies him, to remake their home wherever they may happen to settle, or to maintain a wandering home if continual migration is necessary. In man, the Ulysses factor may inspire singlehanded expeditions, or small expeditionary groups, at random. Chichester's absolute preference for doing things alone is untypical. The more normal male reaction is to be prepared to act alone if necessary, to lead others if circumstances suggest the group. The expeditionary group is usually all-male, but not necessarily so. The smallest group, the group of two, is commonly husband and wife.

In women the modification *tending* to a preference for the group, or to the use of mechanical power for singlehanded exploits, suggests that the normal development of the factor in a woman requires support, from companions in a group, or from a stronger-than-herself machine. The factor's origins in primitive human society would make this an almost necessary female modification. Ann Davison and Sharon Adams remain exceptional here. Although women do much sailing, and many women are extremely competent, of twenty entrants for the first two singlehanded Transatlantic Races, none was a woman. One German woman entered for the third race in 1968 and sailed accompanied by a dog. She did not succeed in crossing the Atlantic, and was fortunate to be rescued.

When I announced the Vinland expedition in *The Guardian* between twenty and thirty strangers wrote asking to sail with me. Only one woman wrote. She was a young American woman, aged 22, and she was so keen to come that she offered to come to England in order to join us. Our quarters on *Griffin* were unsuitable for a mixed expedition, so I had regretfully to decline her offer. I remain puzzled that the preponderance of men to women among volunteers was so heavy. The time required for the expedition, an estimated two to three months, limited the range of potential volunteers, but I reckoned that this limitation applied more severely to men than to women. More men than women are concerned with long-term careers, and more men than women would consider it out of the question to take three months' uncovenanted leave. In the social conditions in England in 1966 there were more vacancies for women's jobs, particularly for the skilled office jobs that many keen sailing women do, than there were women to fill them. Yet no woman in England wanted to come, and only one woman in America. It seemed odd.

A number of women crew with men regularly in ocean racing as distinct from singlehanded racing, and there have been all-women crews in such races. Women take part in mixed climbing expeditions, and in some all-women mountaineering teams. Ocean sailing and mountaineering as such suggest Ulysses characteristics, but it is doubtful if the factor has much part in the activities of all-women groups. In spite of the Sheila Scotts who prove conclusively enough that sex is no barrier to achievement in the modern Western world at any rate, there are still feminists who feel it necessary to demonstrate 'equality' with men. All-women climbing teams and the like may derive more from this feminist motive than from other factors.

Young children obviously may inhibit the development of the Ulysses factor in women during some phases of their lives. This is not necessarily so: Fiona Lewis sailed with her husband from the Hebrides to Plymouth taking their two children aged 18 months and 3 months, and the children were not much more than a year older when she set off with them to cross the Pacific by catamaran. Plenty of women with young families have emigrated in small boats, or made immense journeys with young families in pioneering days in America, Australia and South Africa. This may be more nearly related to primitive manifestations of the factor than to its occurrence in modern times: nevertheless, it shows that children are not a necessary inhibition. In modern society the schooling of children is more likely to be inhibiting than the fact of their existence in itself. However, childbearing and the care of young children are functional and must modify the factor in women at least to some extent and at certain stages of their lives. Late, or relatively late, emergence of the factor might be expected to be more common in women than in men, but so far this is not so. The Duchess of Bedford's example in learning to fly at 62 and in continuing to fly until her disappearance on a flight at the age of 71 remains rare. Her grandson, the thirteenth Duke of Bedford, has suggested that her impulse late in life to fly derived at least partly from increasing deafness, from which she found relief in the air. It may be so; but this is not to imply that the factor in her was not the main inspiration for her remarkable exploits in the air. Its emergence may be triggered by an infinity of things, different in every individual. Sheila Scott says that she was moved to learn to fly by reading an article in a woman's magazine; Mallory said that he wanted to climb Everest 'because it is there'. The precise starting-point is immaterial. It is the journey that matters.

Although the Ulysses factor is common to men and women and is not, in its broad attributes, sex-linked, it is probable that certain modifications are sex-linked. As the status, and, to some extent, even the function of women in society are themselves modified, further modifications of the Ulysses factor in women may be expected. Women may become less emotionally dependent on support—from a group, from a man, from a machine. Ann Davison and Sharon Adams will remain exceptional just as Chichester remains exceptional, but more women may tend to be wholly self-reliant in their response to the Ulysses impulse. Childbearing and the care of children will continue to be *practical* limitations on the freedom of female response over some years of individual life, but will be less inhibitory as *the habit of feeling inhibited* diminishes. Who knows how many women feel stirrings of Ulysses impulses when children have grown up and are off their hands, but do not act upon them because conventions of habit are too strong? Over the next decade some increase in the emergence of Ulysses characteristics in women relatively late in life may be expected. It may be significant that the outstanding manifestations of Ulysses qualities in a woman at the close of the sixties was the singlehanded voyage of Sharon Adams in 1969, a form of exploit hitherto found almost exclusively in men.

XXI

Effects and Consequences

THE Ulysses factor influences individuals and is expressed in individual action, but every individual is influenced by the society in which he or she lives. This influence may modify action itself, the effects that flow from it and the consequences of both action and effects on the individual. These will be seen mainly in methods of organising action and of putting it to use—use that may be solely, or almost solely, in the self-fulfilment of the individual, or in contriving an external profit. There have always been commercial aspects of the Ulysses factor, as of all other human attributes. Sex may be taken as an example. Sexual instincts in man are at once intensely individual and subject to the customs and moods of thought prevailing in society at any given time. Sexual instincts have been exploited throughout man's history. A diplomatic marriage, allying one tribe or nation with another, is as much the exploitation of sex as a traffic in slave girls. That one may be as much for the benefit of a community as the other is to profit from its degradation is irrelevant; both are 'exploitation' of the sexual instinct. Modern commerce exploits sex in every way from the deeply moving to the disgusting. This has profound effects on individual sexual response, some healthy, some dangerous both to the individual and to society.

The difference between twentieth-century exploitation of sex and its similar exploitation in all the other centuries of human existence is of degree: the scope of modern commerce, the range of its communications, are more extensive than at any time in the past. The general influence of sex instincts, for good or ill, is therefore subject to a number of forces which, not necessarily new in themselves, may have novel effects because they are applied in novel ways.

The Ulysses factor is a more specialised human impulse than sex, but it shares with sex, as with all other of man's instincts, a general significance. The economic consequences of exploring adventure have varied from the world-changing to the minimal. The outcome of Columbus's voyaging was to add the resources of a continent to Western Europe and to deflect the history of the world in ways that still influence directly the daily life of almost everybody on earth. The outcome of Peary's reaching the North Pole was economically negligible, whatever it may have meant in terms of human achievement.

Exploitation of the Ulysses factor, however, must be considered from other viewpoints. Columbus exploited the factor in himself to get the backing of Ferdinand and Isabella of Spain and to obtain various titles and concessions for himself. That he did not make much of them is irrelevant; he wanted them and he got them. Is this in any way to degrade his achievement? I think not. He was a man with a dream which compelled him to act; it made him pester monarchs for help until he was given the resources he needed for his project. That he did what he could for himself and his family at the same time is reasonable enough. He was dishonest, or at least deluded, in persisting with his claim that he had reached the Indies when it became more and more clear that he had not. But he had given Spain a new world. The consequences on his own life tended to be destructive. He was not an efficient administrator, and he became, I think, slightly mad. Was this anyone's fault?

A wiser Government would have rewarded Columbus differently. A wiser man would have behaved differently. The combination of the man and of his period made for some sort of personal tragedy. The visionary is liable to suffer when his vision become a commercial success. Is this more or less likely to happen nowadays? Are there any *particular* dangers, or advantages, in modern forms of exploitation of the Ulysses factor?

The main commercial aspect of the factor nowadays is in the material it can provide for newspaper stories, books and radio programmes, and in the advertisement value to be extracted from the use of particular products in exciting or arduous enterprises. There is nothing shameful, or even suspect, in any of this. Newspapers exist to give news, and if a man who is making news agrees to sell his story to a particular newspaper he is entitled to his payment and the newspaper is entitled to whatever it can make from publishing his narrative. If a piece of gear or equipment stands up well to the demands made on it, why not advertise its virtues? There are seeds for corruption here, no doubt, but they need not be planted. It is a matter of mutual aid. A newspaper needs good stories, a manufacturer needs good publicity, a man planning an expedition needs help in money and material to carry it out. The individual almost always needs to find partners for the most individual of acts. They may be non-commercial partners—a wife who looks after home and children while a man crosses his ocean—but they are not less *essential* partners. A commercial partner or sponsor is often equally essential. There is no difference in kind between looking to a newspaper to finance an enterprise and looking to a monarch or other rich patron of earlier times. There may be differences in degree of dependence on the sponsor, but these are not all in favour of the older world. A monarch dissatisfied with the performance of a protégé might have his head cut off. That is not a risk in signing a contract with a newspaper.

The resources and the imagination of a sponsor may add to an expedition's chances of success, and to the value of what comes out of it. There are dangers in accepting sponsorship as well. I shall look at a number of practical examples of modern sponsorship and assess the human gains and loss as fairly as I can. I shall also consider a question which disquiets many people—the degree of responsibility that a sponsor may have to the person sponsored, and the responsibility of the sponsored to his sponsor.

On June 7 1963 the British Post Office issued this official statement:

> *Rehu Moana* has successfully transmitted a photograph to the *Guardian* offices in London over the ordinary ship-to-shore radio telephone service of the Post Office and using an ordinary telephone system. This is the first occasion on which a photograph has been transmitted from a ship at sea in this way, and the experiment is even more remarkable

in being from such a small ship as a catamaran and using only 75 watts of transmitted power.

On October 14 1966 the rowing boat *Puffin* was found water-logged in mid-Atlantic, with no trace of her occupants, David Johnstone and John Hoare.

On May 28 1967 over 100,000 people gathered at Plymouth to give Sir Francis Chichester a hero's welcome on completing his singlehanded voyage round the world.

On July 10 1969 the trimaran *Teignmouth Electron* was found abandoned in the Atlantic. There was no trace of her singlehanded occupant, Donald Crowhurst.

All these events were brought about by a combination of the Ulysses factor in man and modern commercial exploitation of it. I use the word exploitation deliberately and with care. In this context it has no derogatory sense. It means simply the use of physical and non-physical assets in an attempt to make money. There is nothing wrong in trying to make money: man cannot live without doing so, but it is not so simple as that. There are good, bad and indifferent ways of getting or of trying to get money. Some ways may be praiseworthy or harmless in themselves, yet may have unlooked-for side effects.

Without newspaper sponsorship it is probable that there would have been no Singlehanded Transatlantic Race. That is not quite certain, for Chichester and Hasler did challenge each other to race singlehanded across the Atlantic for that now-vanished coin a half-crown, and both were capable of acting on the challenge. But practical obstacles were formidable. Whether the race would have been sailed if other things had not happened no one can now say. What did happen was that the *Observer* agreed to sponsor the race, put up prize money and starting money, and made the project practicable. A newspaper is not a benevolent institution. Being an institution run by men, a newspaper is capable of acting illogically, and sometimes in a spirit of pure generosity towards the pursuit of knowledge or the fulfilment of a personal ambition with which one man has been able to fire the imagination of another. But that cannot happen often, at least, not with the same newspaper: if it did the paper would soon go out of business. For most of the time newspapers are concerned—

have to be concerned—with trying to attract readers and advertisement revenue. When a newspaper is invited to support a project its management has to ask itself: (*a*) is it sufficiently interesting to help to hold our present readers by encouraging them to feel that we are an enterprising newspaper; (*b*) will it attract new readers; (*c*) will it attract advertisement revenue, either by increasing our circulation or by persuading the suppliers of particular goods and services to advertise with us because of the publicity we are giving to this project? These are perfectly proper questions. If the project is itself primarily commercial, a motor trip across the Sahara, say, to test a new brand of petrol or a new kind of tyre, the interests of all concerned are clear, and a newspaper will decide to give or to withhold support by reckoning probable gains against probable costs. The sponsorship of established sports is also fairly simple. Millions of people are interested in golf, and to promote a competition, locally, nationally or internationally, may be a useful way of holding golfing readers, winning new golfing readers and attracting advertisements of golfing gear.

If the project is a Ulysses-type adventure the interests are less clear. It may go wrong, in which case a newspaper sponsoring the adventure may come in for obloquy rather than praise. It may be spread over such a long time without anything apparently happening that people will forget about it. It may be so unusual that people are not likely to be very interested in it, anyway. In this situation a newspaper's response to a request for sponsorship is likely to be more or less a gamble, based on the editor's or circulation manager's private hunch. 'If this comes off, this man's exclusive story will be worth having. If it doesn't, well, we are not going to put all that much money into it.'

The *Observer*'s sponsorship of the first Singlehanded Transatlantic Race was an act of considerable courage. If anything had gone wrong, if one or more of the competitors had been lost, there would have been a great deal of criticism, questions in Parliament about how to control irresponsible newspapers, an unpleasant fuss. Nothing went wrong, and the *Observer*'s faith was justified.

From a newspaper point of view, however, there was one weakness in the value of adventure stories concerning small boats on long voyages: from departure to landfall weeks or months might go by with no news whatever of what was happening. In 1960 the radio transmitters carried in very small boats were not of much practical use outside coastal waters, save for sending out distress signals. Morse wireless telegraphy was possible over greater distances, but Morse requires skilled operators, seldom available in the crew of a small sailing boat. When Chichester planned his solo voyage in 1962 he wanted to try to provide a daily narrative by radio-telephone.

This was something that had never been done before from a small boat on a long voyage, and it was doubtful if it could be done. Chichester thought that it was worth trying, told me about it (I was then an Assistant Editor of *The Guardian*) and fired me with the idea. The management of *The Guardian* agreed to support the venture, and with the help of the Marconi Company and the marine wireless section of the Post Office we devised a telecommunications system that enabled Chichester on *Gipsy Moth III* to maintain a direct radio-telephone link with London all the way to New York. *The Guardian* used the same radio-telephone system for David Lewis's voyage in *Rehu Moana* in 1963, and went one better —with a small battery-operated Marconi set and Muirhead scanning equipment he transmitted *pictures* by radio from *Rehu Moana* to *The Guardian* offices. That led to the official statement by the Post Office quoted at the beginning of this chapter. It made telecommunications history.

There is not much to quarrel with here. These radio experiments were of lasting importance, for they perfected a technique of keeping track of small boats over long voyages applicable to much more than newspaper enterprises, and the picture transmissions from *Rehu Moana* have been followed by considerable development in the sending of graphic material, weather maps, for example, to and from ships at sea over radio-telephone links. Put at its lowest, newspaper finance helped Chichester and David Lewis to make voyages that they wanted to make, and newspaper publicity helped to make real to the rest of the world what they were trying to do. The demonstration of the hitherto unknown range and versatility of low-powered marine radio that came out of these adventures was a by-product, but a useful one.

Nevertheless, I had misgivings at the time, and they have

deepened since. Our radio system made small-boat adventures
more saleable to newspapers and magazines: would it thereby
encourage adventurers who were more interested in money
than adventure? There were other risks. The radio which
made such voyages more saleable might even add to their
dangers: in bad conditions a man might be so anxious to get
his story to the paper that financed him that he might hazard
his ship. Of course, the high-grade communications at his dis-
posal also made for safety—on his Transatlantic voyage of 1964
Chichester was able to get advice by radio from a boatbuilder
on how to deal with a leak. Radio has been used widely for
small-boat stories since *The Guardian's* experiment in 1962,
and I do not know of a case in which it has been a hazard.
Still, it is possible.

Next, radio and newspaper sponsorship may give, or seem
to give unfair advantages in racing. Special weather reports,
for instance, may be obtained, or information on the position
of other competitors. Apart from whatever advantages there
may be in highly organised radio communications, a competitor with commercial sponsorship may be able to afford
better gear and equipment, or a better boat. But a man who
simply happens to be better off than his neighbour may also
have better gear. In a singlehanded ocean race over 3,000
miles I doubt if there is much in it: the man is going to count
more than his gear. If his gear is not up to it he should not be
in the race. Pre-race inspection, taken very seriously by the
Royal Western Yacht Club at Plymouth, which organises the
Singlehanded Race, is a precaution against unseaworthy boats
and unsuitable gear.

More serious, in expeditions which, by their nature,
scarcely permit realistic preliminary inspection, is the risk
enhanced by sponsorship of starting inadequately prepared. I
faced this problem with David Lewis in 1963. *Rehu Moana*
was untried for an ocean voyage, and if we were to meet our
commitments there was no time for trials. Naturally I wanted
the expedition to go ahead as planned; I also felt at least
partly responsible for its safety. Lewis was the leader, the decision was his. He decided to sail—I have discussed his reasons
in my study of him. In this instance he was right, but he
could easily have been wrong. Johnstone had to make a similar decision at the start of his tragic voyage with Hoare in

Puffin. I am sure that the newspaper sponsoring his attempt to row the Atlantic put no sort of pressure on him to set off unready. The pressure was in himself: he was anxious not to let down anybody, or even to appear to be doing so. Johnstone's decision to start when he did was wrong: his boat needed the trials she had not had, he and Hoare needed experience in her before undertaking so formidable a voyage. Their situation was quite different from David Lewis's. Lewis had a powerful crew, a catamaran with an auxiliary engine, and he was never going to be more than a few hundred miles from some port of refuge. Johnstone and Hoare were setting off to *row* across an ocean. It is easy to be wise after the event. I think that this was a case in which Johnstone's sponsors *might* have acted, to try to make him postpone his start. But again, the decision was his. He had planned the venture, he knew more about the state of his plans than anybody else. He had to weigh the physical disadvantages of starting with boat and gear inadequately tested against the damage to his own and his companion's morale that delay might entail. He reasoned that they could make adjustments on the voyage. He was wrong, but he cannot be blamed for being wrong. Sponsorship was one factor that contributed to his wrong decision, but not because it was sponsorship. Without sponsorship he could not have mounted his expedition at all. I do not say that without sponsorship he could not have attempted to row the Atlantic —Ridgway, with fewer resources, did row the Atlantic. But Ridgway had planned his voyage in an entirely different way. I have tried to analyse Johnstone's misfortune in my study of him. The availability of newspaper sponsorship contributed to his tragedy, but it neither caused nor hastened it. The tragedy was in the man himself.

We have seen a rather similar personal tragedy in Donald Crowhurst, similar at least in some aspects, though the men were markedly different. Crowhurst, aged 37, was slightly older than Johnstone, and more typical of the Ulysses complex. He was married with four children, had a happy home life and was a town councillor. He had his own business in electronic engineering. He was a good sailor, well read in the sea, and with many ideas for making a sailing boat go faster. When the *Sunday Times* offered a prize of £5,000 for the fast singlehanded voyage round the world he set out to try to win it.

s

But Crowhurst was not rich. The boat he wanted to carry out his ideas on fast sailing was a trimaran, and she had to be built specially. He needed sponsorship, which he obtained partly from a friend, partly from the town of Teignmouth from which he sailed (he called his boat *Teignmouth Electron*), partly from the BBC in return for tape-recordings and a film of the voyage. To be eligible for the £5,000 offered by the *Sunday Times* he had to sail before October 31 1968. This was a sensible rule, to deter competitors from risking the conditions they would be likely to meet in the Indian Ocean and the South Atlantic if they sailed from England later in the year.

Crowhurst suffered all the delays that seem inescapable in preparing for an expedition. As the closing date for the race approached he was not nearly ready, his new boat lacked sea-trials, and he had to load against time all the stores for a voyage that might last the best part of a year—the rules of the race forbade putting in anywhere. He sailed from Teignmouth on the last possible day, October 31 itself.

On July 10 1969 *Teignmouth Electron* was found abandoned south of the Azores, with no trace of Crowhurst. It was thought at first that Crowhurst had completed his circumnavigation, in a time which would have won him the *Sunday Times's* £5,000, and was on the last leg of his voyage back to Teignmouth. On July 27 1969 the *Sunday Times* announced that examination of Crowhurst's logs found in *Teignmouth Electron* indicated that he had never left the Atlantic during the 243 days he was thought to be going round the world, and that entries in his logs suggested that he was under considerable mental strain towards the end of his voyage. The logs also indicated that at one point of his voyage he had put into Rio Salada, a small port in Argentina, to obtain wood for urgent repairs to his trimaran. The landing would have disqualified him for the £5,000 prize.

When *Teignmouth Electron* was found without her master and photographs of her showed that she was not fitted with guard rails, the *Sunday Times* was criticised for not having insisted on such things as guard rails as compulsory equipment for competing boats. The mental distress revealed by Crowhurst's logs stilled that particular criticism: whatever happened to Crowhurst, the presence or absence of guard rails probably had little bearing on it. He was equipped with safety harness, but films he took of himself on board by mounting his camera on a bracket showed that he did not always wear it.

What did happen to him? There is evidence in his tortured logs that he was worried about the cost of his voyage, and that he felt that he needed the prize of £5,000. There is evidence that he was worried by breakages of gear and components on the trimaran, and by the fact that spare parts which should have been on board were not. There is presumptive evidence that he considered the possibility of faking a voyage round the world, staying in lonely waters off the coast of South America until it seemed a reasonable time to sail back to England to claim the prize. Certainly he sailed to the Falkland Islands to film a Falklands landfall for the BBC—the pictures might suggest, of course, that he had reached the Falklands after rounding Cape Horn on his voyage round the world. There is presumptive evidence that he considered such things, but no evidence that he actually intended to claim a faked voyage and an unearned prize. Such evidence as there is points rather the other way: he did not destroy his logs with actual positions in them, and he duly recorded his disqualifying call at Rio Salada. His radio appears to have been out of action for a good deal of the voyage, but he had got it working again as he approached the Azores on what was thought to be the last leg of his circumnavigation. He began to receive congratulatory messages—unhappily he did not reply with the news that he had failed to make a voyage round the world. He may have felt that he would prefer to explain things when he got back to England—a misguided feeling perhaps, but not unreasonable. Apart from the loss of £5,000 he had nothing to be ashamed of: to have sailed a trimaran singlehanded from England to South America and the Falkland Islands and then home was a remarkable small-boat voyage by any standards. The last entry in his log is dated July 1. It is not a navigational entry, but a moving if somewhat incoherent reflection on the philosophical beauty of truth. At some time after writing it he disappeared. How he disappeared is unlikely ever to be known. The mute witness of his boat has told all that she can: she was found at peace and in good order, her mainsail and headsails furled, her mizzen set, rather as if she had been

snugged down for a quiet night. Her logs have disclosed some
tortured moments in her master's mind, but more that is
rational and often deeply moving. In those last days Crowhurst may have been physically injured as well as mentally
disturbed: he may have collapsed and fallen overboard. He
was lost—precisely how is not really relevant. Tennyson's
verses from *In Memoriam* are fitting:

> Let Love clasp Grief lest both be drown'd,
> Let darkness keep her raven gloss:
> Ah, sweeter to be drunk with loss,
> To dance with death, to beat the ground
>
> Than that the victor Hours should scorn
> The long result of love, and boast
> 'Behold the man that loved and lost,
> But all he was is overworn'.

Crowhurst was a fine sailor who made a notable voyage.
The Ulysses factor in him was not, as in Johnstone, distorted
by other qualities. Crowhurst had all the Ulysses qualities,
but some external pressure of anxiety on him hurt his mind,
as he might have been hurt physically by a falling spar. What
was that external pressure? Was it in any way related to newspaper or other sponsorship?

Initially, at any rate, the decision to exploit the voyage in a
commercial sense—again the word exploit is used with no
derogatory implication—was Crowhurst's own. He was
attracted by the £5,000 prize: he liked boats, he wanted to
sail round the world, and the race offered an exciting way of
making £5,000. It was also a very expensive way. Crowhurst
did not want merely to sail round the world; he wanted to
race round the world, to beat all other comers. That, in his
mind, required an unconventional boat, a trimaran, and she
would have to be built for the job. It would also require a lot
of special equipment, some of which he could make, but it
would all cost money. And he would need stores for nearly a
year. So much for the voyage. But that was only half, or less
than half, his problem. He had a wife and four children, his
home to be maintained, his business—it is not easy for a man
in the middle of his working life to take time off for the best

part of a year. Even if he did not want commercial commitments on his voyage, he could not avoid them. To start at all he had to have finance: the voyage *had* to be a commercial venture, at least to a point at which he could hope to recover as much as possible of its cost.

The trouble that immediately arises here is that one is dealing in futures: the planner of an expedition has nothing to sell but hopes. He can offer rights in his story, his film, his broadcasts; but what if there is no story? The world is hard on hopes unfulfilled. A good adventure story may be a best seller, but it is more likely to be profitable if the adventure is a success. Failure takes the edge off public interest. Moreover, books make money after they are written, contracts of most sorts after they have been carried out. The planner of an expedition needs money *now*.

There is a market, of course, in futures: there has to be, or life could scarcely go on. A publisher who can be interested in an idea for a book may be willing to commission it, paying an advance royalty when the contract undertaking to produce the book is signed. A newspaper or a broadcasting organisation may be willing to pay a fairly substantial sum down for exclusive rights in some future story. Even so, there will usually be escape clauses. An expedition, for instance, may have to start, or at least to show physical evidence of being serious—all of which requires preliminary expenditure— before any money is paid. It may be possible to raise funds by other forms of commercial sponsorship—by undertaking, for example, to use some particular equipment, to eat some particular preserved food or to drink some brand of beer, the makers of which then have the right to employ the expedition in their own publicity. Contracts for this sort of thing vary from legal documents to gentlemen's agreements. Often no money is involved: a manufacturer may agree to lend or give equipment or stores in return for whatever publicity he may get. Whatever is sold, in what way it may be sold, it remains the sale of futures, and although potential earnings from an expedition that captures the world's imagination may be substantial, at the start of the expedition they are still potential.

Banks may be willing to advance money against contracts for future payments, but bank advances are not always easy to obtain. Even in a friendly financial climate bank loans cost money—you pledge not only your future earnings but also undertake to pay interest on them.

Chichester has written of the load of financial anxiety he carried during preparations for his voyage round the world. Crowhurst had worries of the same sort.

Once committed to the race, he had to sail. He under-estimated the time it would take to get *Teignmouth Electron* fitted out and ready for sea. It is nearly impossible not to under-estimate time. One never allows enough for the massive inertia of a supposedly efficient industrial society. You order a component that you can reasonably expect to be delivered in a few days, and it takes week to come. This delay holds up something else; there is a dreadful multiplier at work. Delay is an inevitable hazard: the best you can do is to take a calculated risk, concentrate on priorities, and hope that ingenuity may make good deficiencies that you discover after your expedition has started. There *must* be calculated risk-taking, and the degree of serious risk depends on the accuracy of the calculation. It depends still more on the realism with which you are able to accept your own calculations. Crowhurst sailed from Teignmouth on the last possible sailing date to remain eligible for the *Sunday Times*'s £5,000. He was not ready to sail, and he knew that he was not. On one of the tape recordings that he made for the BBC he reflected, 'I have never put to sea in such a completely unprepared state in my life.' But he was not realistic about the implications of his knowledge—perhaps he could not be. By that time so much was at stake, he was so deeply committed financially, that he could not accept the possibility of not sailing. His position was worse than David Johnstone's in having to decide whether to start or to postpone departure. Johnstone might have lost face, or felt that he would lose face, by postponing his attempt to row the Atlantic, but he would not have lost much else, except, perhaps, in morale: he could have started ten days later, and still set off before Ridgway. Crowhurst stood to lose the chance of £5,000 if he sailed after October 31 1968.

Can anyone be blamed? The *Sunday Times* was not sponsoring Crowhurst. It had offered £5,000 for the fastest non-stop single-handed passage round the world, and it had made rules for its race. One of them was that competitors must start by October 31 1968, a reasonable rule, made to safeguard the

competitors themselves. And there had to be some final starting date if a race were to be held at all. I think that the rules
ought to have laid down minimum standards of equipment,
and insisted on inspection of boats before they were regarded
as eligible for the prize. Lifelines round all open deck space,
carried on stanchions through-bolted to the deck, I would regard as compulsory fittings. But the *Sunday Times*'s answer to
criticism on this is not unreasonable: it wanted the race to be
completely open, with competitors free to use craft of any description, provided only that they were propelled by sail.
Once you start making rules about minimum standards it is
hard to know where to stop. Still, it can be done. The rules
drawn up by the Royal Western Yacht Club of Plymouth for
the Singlehanded Transatlantic Race could be a model. That
race is similarly open, and it is specifically stated that no yacht
is to be excluded 'solely on grounds of unconventional type or
design'. But all boats have to be inspected within two months
of the starting date, either by a practising marine surveyor at
any port or at Plymouth before the start of the race by a surveyor appointed by the organisers. Every boat must have a
certificate signed by the surveyor stating that he has inspected
her and found her 'rigged and equipped with all essential sailing equipment (including navigational equipment)' and that
'Insofar as it was possible to inspect them I consider that the
hull, decks, spars, rigging, sails, ground tackle, fittings and
sailing equipment appeared to be in a good and serviceable
condition except for the following items...' The surveyor
lists whatever he thinks should be added or improved, and a
certificate that the deficiencies (if any) have been made good
must be obtained before the boat is permitted to start. Anyone promoting a race of any sort has some responsibility for
the entrants, and if people are to be invited to sail round the
world their boats should surely be inspected for seaworthiness
and safety. But it is possible to make too much of this. A
singlehanded race round the world is not for children. Those
who take part in it can be assumed to know what they are
doing.

Crowhurst's tragedy was not that he did not know what he
was doing but that the responsibilities he felt to the outside
world clouded his responsibility for himself. His trimaran was
not unseaworthy: she carried him some 14,000 miles to the

Falklands and back nearly to the Azores, and she was afloat and serviceable when she was found abandoned. Clearly she was not in what he regarded as *racing* trim: his log shows that he had doubts about her ability to stand up to hard driving in rough seas. More serious still, some of the spares he needed were not on board. His meditations in his log show endless anxiety over money and fear of the financial ruin that he felt might come to him and his family if he gave up the race. His fears may have been exaggerated: he was alone with his thoughts; there was no one to tell him that things seldom turn out quite so badly as one fears in life's darker moments. So far as his actions can be pieced together from his logs—and this is an important qualification, for the entries are not all dated— he left open the possibility of claiming £5,000 for a pretended circumnavigation. *But he did not do this.* He did not destroy any of the actual navigational evidence which would have ruled out a fraudulent claim, and in any case there were witnesses to his putting in at Rio Salada, which disqualified him for the prize. There may have been shame in some of his thoughts—which of us has not had shameful thoughts? One or two of his radio messages, sent in Morse, were misleading, but whether they were intentionally so, or fantasies from a dream world in which he was living when he sent them, cannot be known. Nor can the facts of his presumed loss be known. The incoherence of the last entries in his log suggest a mental strain which may have prompted suicide—perhaps not deliberate self-destruction, but an atonement process in the all-cleansing sea. Radio messages describing the triumphant welcome that awaited him may have turned his tortured sense of failure into an agony to be borne no longer. One cannot know.

As with David Johnstone, a sense of obligation towards his financial sponsors can be blamed to some extent for the tragedy of Donald Crowhurst, but that is not to blame the sponsors. In both cases sponsorship made it possible for them to attempt what they wanted to do. Both would have been wiser had they acted differently—Johnstone if he had postponed his start for sea-trials of his boat and practice in rowing techniques, Crowhurst if he had cut his losses as far as the *Sunday Times* race was concerned and perhaps substituted an individual circumnavigation by trimaran in 1969. There might have been no £5,000 prize, but it would have been a venture attracting considerable publicity in its own right, which might have been turned to financial advantage. But did either do worse than take a reasonable chance—and lose? Both gambled on their luck, certainly, and the Ulysses factor compels risk-taking. The true Ulysses characteristic, however, is *calculated* risk-taking, the calculation being precise, cool and level-headed. For both Johnstone and Crowhurst the calculation should have shown odds weighted heavily against them, too heavily to be a reasonable risk. I think Johnstone ignored the odds; there were factors in his make-up which made this almost inevitable in him. Crowhurst ignored the calculations; he could reckon the odds coolly, he understood, far more clearly than Johnstone, what he was up against. But when the time came to take notice of arithmetic he was beyond caring for arithmetic. What he felt to be his commitments to other people outweighed everything else. He knew that he was unprepared, but he still had to sail.

The *existence* of sponsorship, the undertaking of commitments to other people which limit a man's own freedom of action, or decision, can be held to have contributed to such personal tragedies as those of Johnstone and Crowhurst, but it does not follow that the obligations each undertook *necessarily* contributed to tragedy. I think that in the case of Johnstone a tragic outcome to his venture was nearly inevitable: nothing in life is wholly inevitable, but given Johnstone's complex psychological make-up and Hoare's uncritical loyalty to him the elements of tragedy in their approach to their voyage were present from the start. They had bad luck; and they had not sufficiently discounted luck. Their tragedy was in some sense inevitable, but it was still not *necessary*. A different decision at many points before the voyage, and at some points on the voyage, could have brought about a happier outcome: tragedy was in the decisions they did take. Crowhurst's tragedy was much less due to unreadiness to sail. That had a tragic bearing on later events, but had he been more rational about what he felt to be his obligations to others, he might have overcome the difficulties of an unprepared start. He was an outstanding sailor and of great practical ability: whatever the state of his trimaran when he set out, he succeeded in sailing her safely over 14,000 miles. She might have carried him round the world, though not, perhaps, at a speed sufficient to win the race—or that he *thought* required to win the race, for all the faster competitors gave up. Robin Knox-Johnston, the only man to complete the solo non-stop voyage round the world, took 313 days: his boat, *Suhaili* was not fast. Crowhurst would have stood a good chance of winning the £5,000 had he felt able to keep going.

That is the essence of his tragedy: he *need* not have given up. Above all, he *need* not have given up secretly. Had he given up when he put into Rio Salado for repairs no one would have thought the worse of him; he had made a notable voyage, he might have written a remarkable book. But these are rational reflections in a comfortable study on land: they cannot be transferred to a man sick with worry and alone at sea. Crowhurst's rational mind, his responsibility to himself, was unbalanced by his feeling of responsibility to others. The spring of action from the Ulysses factor in him was not distorted: it was broken.

Money worries helped to break it. But is there anything *specially* disquieting about money worries deriving from sponsorship? If you finance an expedition partly with other people's money, is it any different from building a house partly with other people's money, or from any of the thousand and one actions of normal business life that are carried out with money borrowed from or invested by, other people? If an expedition or adventure is wholly a commercial undertaking—crossing a desert for example, to drill for oil—the risks are accepted as commercial risks. The project will be financed by an oil company, the leader of the expedition can give his whole mind to the achievement of its aims and the welfare of his party. He may have to work within a financial budget, but he will not himself have to find the money for that budget. If he is a good geologist, surveyor or engineer he is bound to be emotionally involved in his job to some extent, but he is unlikely to be emotionally *absorbed* by his job. Having crossed this desert to drill for oil, next year he will be sent somewhere else. His job is a *continuing* part of his life, an important part, but not his whole life. He looks forward to his leaves.

When the Ulysses factor in man moves him to some physical adventure it is a deeply personal thing. The planning of it may dominate his thoughts for months or years; as the time for action approaches, it becomes his whole life. Anything else is an irritation. He does not want to talk to a Public Relations Officer, he wants to pore over maps. No one else can *really* know precisely what he wants to do: to try to explain, over and over again, to seek financial help from other people becomes a torture. Rationally, he understands that he must get financial help, he wants to give value for any help he gets. But his is not a commercial undertaking: it is a dream. The more he is compelled to think in commercial terms, to turn his precious project into a business deal, the more the dream that is the real basis of it may get hurt. This is psychologically dangerous, and may lead to the taking of unreasonable physical risks.

The happiest men, perhaps, are those like Manry and Horie who can act their dreams themselves, telling no one outside their families, keeping everything in their own hands until their adventure becomes public property. But this means accepting limits to your dreams. If you are content with a small cottage, and can save the money to buy it, you will not be worried by a mortgage on your house; but a mortgage may provide a house that brings a deeper sense of fulfilment. The first Ulysses had the revenues of his kingdom, and no one thought the worse of him for adding to them by piracy. The world is less simple now. All personal incomes are taxed, piracy is frowned upon. It is hard to give up time from earning a living. Manry and Horie showed that it can be done. But not all Ulysses-type adventures are possible within the means of those who conceive them. Scientific projects may be able to get money from learned societies; dramatic geographical expeditions, such as climbing Everest or going to the South Pole—the world offers fewer of these than it once did— may obtain support from national funds or public subscription. But if a man wants to sail singlehanded round the world, or to discover Vinland, he must finance himself or obtain some form of private sponsorship.

If you have time, a great deal of money is not necessary: if you have a boat already, and are not going to be competitive about racing, so much the better. Joshua Slocum sailed happily round the world alone in *Spray*, financing himself as he went by giving lectures and selling the abandoned cargo of tallow that he picked up from a wreck in the Strait of Magellan. He took three years over his voyage, accepting hospitality when it was offered on the way. Robin Knox-Johnston had his own boat *Suhaili* for his non-stop voyage round the world. He did not intend a particularly fast passage, and he took 313 days—nearly a year. His requirements for stores were modest, and with some help from writing contracts he financed himself comfortably.

It is a question of time and circumstance. It is possible for a man to go off by himself to climb his mountain or sail his ocean without asking anyone for help if he has more or less unlimited time. If he has time he can do most of his preparatory work for himself, as Manry rebuilt his boat and made sails for her. If he is not a practical carpenter and sailmaker to start with he can learn: a man who wants to do anything badly enough can learn how to do it. But it needs time. And time in twentieth-century life is often harder to find than money. If time can be found, and if time has no particular bearing on what you are trying to do—if it does not matter much if you cross an ocean in fifty or a hundred days—then a singlehanded or a two-man expedition can be carried out at a cost within the means of almost anyone. It will need some money, of course, but it will be money within the scale of what can normally be saved over two or three years by a man in regular work. But here at once is the rub: if a man is in regular work he is not likely to have much time; and if he is not in regular work he is not likely to have much in the way of savings. A few people still have private means or well-to-do parents ready to support them. But not many are in this position. The Ulysses complex makes for independence, for striking out on one's own early in life, usually for fairly early marriage and a family.

It is precisely those who have the Ulysses factor most strongly in them who are least likely to have time or much free money. The young Tilman and the middle-aged Manry may seem untypical here, finding time to cross Africa by bicycle and the Atlantic by *Tinkerbelle* from their own resources. But they really prove the point. Tilman had first to work hard in Kenya to make a living and to earn time for what he wanted to do. Manry worked for years at his newspaper job to provide the money for his voyage and, as he thought, to support his wife and children while he was away. Both Manry and Tilman on his African journey travelled alone, and both chose forms of adventure in which time itself was not of great significance. Tilman wanted to see Africa, and it did not matter much to him whether his bicycle ride took a few weeks more or less. Manry had to cross the Atlantic within the time limit of his stores, but he allowed himself an adequate margin, and within broad limits the time of his passage was not of major concern. It is possible for two people, particularly if they are husband and wife, to practise the same equation in which more time equals less need of money.

As soon as more than two people are required for an expedition—sometimes when even two people are needed—the equation ceases to be valid. Stores and equipment multiply with numbers, and it is not a straightforward arithmetical progression. People have different tastes and different needs, and in this context different means more. A larger expedition needs more elaborate medical equipment than a man alone; not because the risk of injury is any greater—it may be less—but because with help you can do more for an injured man. So costs multiply.

Speed is relatively even more expensive than numbers. If you are content to sail or travel slowly you can hope to keep down costs; the moment you decide on a boat or vehicle to go fast, costs soar. If a boat is to be raced she must be driven hard in conditions which a mariner not pressed for time would heave-to, which means that all her gear must be (or should be) of superlative quality. All this is expensive.

Speed of communications is another thing to be taken into account. The missionary societies that sponsored Livingstone, the newspaper that financed Stanley to search for him, did not expect news every day, or even every month. Before radio an explorer did not fear that if he failed to communicate for a few weeks the outside world would imagine either that he was not trying or that he had met disaster: a lone seaman could disappear for half a year without causing a raised eyebrow. There was a different time scale then, time, if need be, for caution, without feeling that anybody was being let down.

When an expedition has base radio the world knows from day to day what is going on. It knows that an assault party has left for an attempt on the summit, for a dash across the ice-floes. The leader of the assault party, or of the expedition, is liable to feel a compulsion to *go on now*, which he would not feel if nobody could know for weeks precisely what was happening on any one day. This is not an ignoble compulsion: it may come from a desire to relieve anxiety at home as much as anything else. Small boats were spared this tension for some time after it had affected land expeditions. *The Guardian's* experiments with Chichester in 1962, I fear, spread it to the sea.

I have felt it myself. There were black times on *Griffin* off Greenland and Newfoundland when the last thing in the world I wanted to do was to rack my brains to write a message for the paper, and when I dreaded the ordeal of transmitting it. Trying to make radio contact in bad conditions is nervous agony. *Griffin calling GCN 3 ... Griffin calling GCN 3 ... Yacht Griffin calling London GCN 3 ... Yacht Griffin here ... One, two, three, four, five. Can you read me? Over ...*

With *Griffin* standing practically on her head I would be wedged between the radio mounted on a bulkhead and the saloon table, sending words that seemed more and more futile into the ether. Having established contact by what always seemed a miracle, there would come the misery of dictating the message through savage atmospherics. *Sorry, didn't get that. Over ... Sorry, can you repeat? Over ...* and on and on and on. There might be ice in the rigging, it might be so cold below that no one who could help it stirred from his sleeping bag, but I would finish one of these sessions half-blinded with sweat dripping over my glasses. And I had companions, to help with the radio, to take my watch on deck if a radio session ran over the time when I was due to go on watch. I marvelled then and marvel still at what others have accomplished singlehanded.

Yet radio has brought a new dimension of reality to small-boat voyages. Its immediacy is not merely interesting and sometimes exciting: it enables millions of other people to share an adventure *while it happens*. It has quickened response to the Ulysses factor, and given that majority of mankind in whom it is dormant, but who yet need an emotional outlet for it, new opportunity of reaching out in imagination and feeling kinship with adventure.

Economically, the widening of the range of sponsorship by

radio has made possible all sorts of new adventures. But in this, too, is danger. Radio reporting is a commitment that may cloud or diminish your sense of responsibility for yourself. It *need* not do so, but it may. If it does, who is to blame? What of boats without guard rails departing inadequately stored, or expeditions inadequately prepared for the reality of what they attempt? Whenever there is a disaster of any sort people are inclined to say, Why are there no regulations to prevent this happening? Why are people allowed to do this kind of thing at all? *In media vitae mors* ... no one can contract out of the chances and changes of this mortal lot. The world *does* learn (though slowly) from disasters, and many sensible Acts of Parliament have their origin in someone's thoughtlessness or greed that has brought death to others. But much of the clamour that arises at some personal disaster is good-hearted rather than clear-headed: God forbid the day when men are prohibited from climbing mountains without ladders bolted to rock and duly passed by an Inspector of Ladders, or from going to sea in home-made boats.

The situation changes if a man is paid to climb a dangerous mountain or to go to sea in a cockleshell: an employer is rightly held responsible for the safety of his workpeople. But what if a man is not paid to climb a mountain, but given a present to help him climb it? Is the present-giver responsible for his safety? And suppose the gift is not exactly a present, but given on terms something like this, 'Well, if you want to climb that mountain you'll get a pretty good view from the top. Here is £100 to buy a camera, and if you get any photographs from the summit I'll gladly pay for any that I can use in my newspaper—magazine—book.' Is the provider of the £100 *responsible* for safety on the mountain?

I doubt it. But if the climber meets disaster I dare say that some would argue that it was because, or partly because, he was trying to take photographs, and that men ought not to be encouraged to make dangerous climbs by the offer of payment for pictures.

There is something in this argument, but not much. As in most moral judgments, the verdict of guilt or innocence can be only of degree—few of us are ever wholly guilty or completely innocent in anything. A sponsor may be so little guilty of contributing to a disaster that for practical purposes he may be deemed innocent, or he may be sufficiently guilty to be held blameworthy. If a newspaper (or any other sponsor) contributes materially to an expedition, gives it continual publicity and stands to gain materially from it, then it must be held to have considerable responsibility for the adequacy of preparations and planning for the project. The trouble is that few newspapers (or other commercial sponsors) are equipped to inspect the adequacy of planning; nor, as a rule, is anybody other than the planner.

Johnstone's tragedy was not only, or even mainly, that he was physically unprepared for his voyage but that he was emotionally ill-equipped for it, and that his planning was ill-conceived. He did not know this himself; no one else could have known it, although people close to him, such as representatives of his sponsoring newspaper, might have suspected it. But when he said, 'I am going to start today', should he—could he—have been over-ruled? It was his expedition; he was supposed to know what he was doing; his companion was ready to go with him. One may feel now that *someone* should have stopped him or Crowhurst, but it is hard to say who, or how. And if Crowhurst had insisted on sailing, by what authority could he have been held? None. One may feel that this or that unhappy adventurer 'should have been stopped', but if one tries to think clearly, Why? Is there any moral basis for interfering with a man's right to risk his life, if he chooses, for a dream? One may think him misguided, one may wish that he wouldn't, but I do not think that any third party has a right to prevent a man from taking a lawful risk that the third party may consider unjustifiable but that the man himself does not. We are inclined to be obsessed with death as a kind of awful calamity which it ought to be within the power of Parliament, the Welfare State, a sponsor or some paternal authority to prevent. If men are prepared to risk their lives (and you can risk your life playing football) sometimes men will die. Few can really hold that no man should ever take a risk.

This does not solve the problem of what degree of sponsored risk-taking can be considered permissible, but it does put it into rather clearer perspective. Men are risking life for employers all the time, miners at the coalface, fishermen on deep-sea trawlers, newspaper reporters sent out to cover wars or riots. There are Factory Acts and codes of law for the protection of employees, never wholly adequate, because they can never be up to date: the best code in the world cannot guard against an unguessed danger until after an accident has happened. Still, the law can and does give some protection. But this is protection against the risks of organised, long-understood activity. An adventure, by its nature, contains at least an element of something new. The safe reply to Columbus seeking a sponsor for his project of sailing westward to India would have been that he would do better to buy a farm. He found his sponsor and changed the world because of the factor in man which accepts that there are higher values than playing for safety. Had he been lost it could have been argued that Ferdinand and Isabella sent him to his death, but it is not an argument that either the monarchs or Columbus himself would have accepted. He sailed with their money, but at his own risk.

It is still right for men to do things at their own risk. In a litigious age a sponsor might do well to get a man to sign a piece of paper saying that he does whatever he is doing at his own risk, but with or without a piece of paper the relationship is clear: the risk is individual and freely undertaken for reasons that the sponsor may neither ask nor understand; the sponsor provides money in return for a by-product, a story, a film, an advertisement for his beer. What the by-product may be is irrelevant; it remains a by-product of adventure, giving the sponsor neither right nor duty to influence the adventure itself. In practice this clear relationship will be coloured by human personalities. If the sponsor is an ordinarily decent man he will be concerned for the wellbeing of the person he sponsors; as a businessman he will be concerned that the project on which he is spending money should not be a flop. The sponsored individual will want to give value for the money he is getting. From this interplay of interests both will benefit, provided, of course, that both are reasonable people, acting in good faith.

There cannot be hard-and-fast rules for this sort of relationship, but it does call for integrity on both sides. If the representative, say, of a sponsoring newspaper develops doubts about the fitness of an individual to carry out an expedition he has planned, then he should say so. If an indivi-

T

dual has serious doubts about his timetable, or whether he can in fact perform all that he has promised, then he should explain things frankly, ask for his agreement to be modified or, if necessary, to be relieved of his promise. It is easy to write this: it can require great courage to do it. Still, people should nerve themselves to try. Unhappily, considerable sums of money may be involved, and the individual may feel that his bargaining position is weak in relation to that of a big newspaper or commercial organisation. Yet the only proper course is to be frank. Newspapers and large companies may sometimes seem heartless, but they are composed of men and women. Few even of the toughest business executives would hold a man to a bargain that seemed likely to invite his death. The problem is not in the *actual* attitude of commercial sponsors but in what the person sponsored *fears* that their attitude may be. Therein may sometimes lie tragedy, but it is tragedy within men, not external to them.

A successful adventure nowadays can make quite a lot of money. There are not only literary and broadcasting rights: an adventure that sufficiently touches imaginations may fill shops with tea-towels, toys and knick-knacks featuring it, and there are royalties or licence fees to be had from all. It can become big business. But something goes out of adventure when it becomes *primarily* professional. What if the main purpose of an expedition is really a matter of business? It becomes more or less indistinguishable from a film made on location, interesting, perhaps a considerable artistic achievement, but no longer pure adventure. Again, value-judgments are hard to make, and can be made only in degree. There is no such thing as pure adventure. A man has to live; even a man driven by the unworldly missionary fire of Livingstone needs his stipend, and subscriptions to pay for what he does. Manry, among the least worldly of adventurers, hoped that he might make something out of his voyage. In his own words:

No one had given me financial assistance and I wasn't sponsored by anyone, not even by the *Plain Dealer*, my own newspaper. Nor was I actuated by the hope of vast monetary gain, although I did dare to hope that I might, by writing articles or a book, recoup the cost of the voyage and, if I was lucky, make enough more to help my children through college without going deeply into debt.*

Tilman, equally unworldly, financed his voyages in *Mischief* by writing books about them. Slocum made money by his book on *Spray*. Hope of gain, or at least of avoiding loss, cannot be wholly absent from a man's mind when he is pursuing an activity into which he has put time, effort, part of his life: the adventurer must pay bills like other men, and if he has wife and children, he would prefer them not to suffer from the springs of adventure in him. No clear dividing line can be drawn between pure and applied adventure, as it were. The first Ulysses kept a sharp eye open for the main chance; the primitive origins of the Ulysses factor in man were partly economic.

But there is a distinction between motives for adventure which are primarily from a compulsion to see what lies over the hill and those which are primarily commercial. Sponsorship does not invalidate purity of motive—and it may be as non-commercial in the sponsor as in the sponsored. There are exceptions, but newspapers seldom expect to make much money out of sponsored expeditions. They may hope to gain prestige, to demonstrate that they are enterprising, to interest readers, but mostly a newspaper will support an expedition because it seems something worth doing in itself. Costs will probably be high. The financial returns from buying the memoirs of a pop-singer are likely to be much greater than from sponsoring an expedition. Manufacturers who provide money or goods may hope for publicity, but they could usually buy more publicity more certainly by giving the money to their own advertising department. Businessmen in their own offices may respond to the Ulysses factor, sometimes even against their own commercial judgment. When a business firm commissions a painting or a piece of sculpture its motives are not wholly commercial: its directors are quite capable of a genuine wish to encourage art. A similarly genuine wish to help an adventurous man with a bold idea may be present in sponsorship. The writing of books is commercial, but usually only partly so: the writer hopes to make some money, but he also wants to communicate experience.

* *Tinkerbelle.*

If an adventure adds, or seems to add, anything to human experience a man may feel under an obligation to record it. Tea-towels that exploit a successful adventure do not necessarily commercialise its motive: they are a by-product of success.

Nevertheless, the commercialism that latches on to modern adventure can confuse motives and work harm. The rewards of fame *can* be so glittering that they rouse hopes which are not going to be fulfilled. The pretty girl who craves to be a film-star *may* become one, but she is as likely to make a mess of her life. It is one thing to be inspired by Chichester or Heyerdahl to sail one's own oceans. It is another to want to emulate their worldly success. As long as the tea-towels *are* a by-product all will be well. If they become an *aim* the risks taken to achieve them are no longer true Ulysses risks, but more like gambling at long odds. The girl who is going to become a great actress is driven by something in her that makes prostituting herself in the hope of getting parts unthinkable. The man who wants to cross an ocean because it is something he must do for himself will plan everything he can and go ahead, ignoring, sometimes it may seem rudely, demands on him for anything that conflicts with his purpose. If his *purpose* is fame he may take risks that bring disaster, just as the girl whose attraction to the stage is really glamour may take disastrous risks with her own life. The danger in commercial sponsorship is that it may sponsor the wrong impulses. That may not be anybody's fault: it may be someone's tragedy.

The first Ulysses could keep what he got. Modern systems of society compel a treadmill of commercialism because the rewards from a successful venture are so heavily taxed that unless a man can practise an exceptional austerity he feels compelled to become more and more commercial in order to keep anything at all. The barbarian emperor Tamerlane remitted the poet Hafiz's taxes because he was a good poet. Civilised governments reward their best poets and explorers alike with increased tax demands. Most of us like to feel that our heroes are not troubled by the bills of lesser men. When one of them asks money for speaking at our annual dinner or for opening our garden party we tend to resent it, muttering, 'Oh he's gone all commercial.' If we buy a tea-towel with his picture on it we think that he has demeaned himself for trade. We are illogical and unfair. The man who excited our imaginations is worthy of his hire. If commercial pressures hurt him, or in the end destroy him, we should question not the commerce in his life but the forms of commerce that society has imposed.

I have dealt so far with some of the economic effects and consequences of the Ulysses factor in society, and of the influence of these effects on manifestations of the factor in the individual. Its non-economic effects are at least as important. Often they are more so. Manifestation of the factor has always been related to family, tribal or national prestige—Knox-Johnston's feeling that a Briton should be the first to sail around the world non-stop, and that he wanted to be that Briton, is characteristic. This aspect of modern manifestations of the factor is so interesting that I devote the whole of the next chapter to it.

XXII

Nationalism

AT a ticklish moment the first Ulysses said to his son:

> Telemachus, when you find yourself in the thick of battle
> I am sure you will know how not to shame your father's
> house. In all the world there has been none like ours for
> valour.

John Ridgway, setting out with Chay Blyth to row the
Atlantic in a 20-ft dory wrote afterwards:

> We made good progress through the little harbour and I
> know that both of us had a great feeling of pride that we, a
> couple of Britishers, were doing this thing.*

Joshua Slocum, making Devonport, Tasmania, in 1897, recorded:

> The *Spray* was the first vessel to bring the Stars and
> Stripes to the port.†

When Eric Tabarly won the second Singlehanded Transatlantic Race in 1964, the newspaper *Paris Jour* wrote:

> Thanks to him it is the French flag which triumphs in
> the longest and most spectacular race on that ocean which
> the Anglo-Saxons consider as their special domain.

These are reflections of national and tribal pride over some
three thousand years. The Ulysses factor in man is an attribute making for survival of family, tribe or race, and in-

* *A Fighting Chance.* † *Sailing Alone Around the World.*

dividual achievements prompted by the factor are felt instinctively as enhancing the prestige of the group to which the
individual belongs. This instinct is as strong in the individual
himself as in the response to him. Maurice Herzog, making
his dash to the summit of Annapurna, wanted this mountaineering achievement for France, as much as—if not more
than—for his own party. Horie, making his singlehanded
passage of the Pacific, regarded his effort as a form of service to
Japan. When he reached the longitude of Midway Island, off
which the Japanese fleet was defeated in one of the decisive
battles of the Second World War, he wrote:

> Facing south towards the island I bowed my head in
> silent tribute... I had no flowers to offer those gallant sea-
> men who slept in the depths of these seas. I promised my-
> self that for me this would be my springboard of victory for
> the successful crossing of the largest of all oceans, and that
> if I should make the Golden Gate Bridge, winning my
> victory in this singlehanded challenge of the Pacific Ocean,
> that victory would be my tribute to them.*

Nationalism is not necessarily arrogant or evil. We are born
into our own families, we feel part of our own people, we
want them to do well, to help if we can. This is an instinct as
old as man. We survive because our remote ancestors survived, and the factors which helped them to survive are still
in us. The first Ulysses, inspiring his son to fight well, was
concerned that the Ulysses family should go on. At moments of
despair many a man has given himself new courage by the
thought that his struggle is not for himself alone but for those
who come after him. These are honourable instincts. They are
not 'racial' in the sense that they imply any disrespect of other
family groups: to want one's own team to win is not to pretend that the other team has no virtues, or is composed of
inferior beings. To commemorate one's own dead in battle is
not to glorify war. It may be the reverse, to feel in deep
humility that one must try to redeem their lives in achievements that are not war.

In studying the emergence of a common human factor over
a long period it is necessary to take account of changes in his-

* *Kedoku*, p. 146.

torical attitudes which affect individual action. In the time of the first Ulysses (around 1200 BC) war, or at least fighting, was the expected lot of man. There were no banks. Your wealth was in goods which you kept in a strong-room guarded by armed men. You expected that others would try to raid you, and you made your defences accordingly. You also considered it quite proper to raid other people not bound to you by ties of family or friendship. When Ulysses was discussing with his wife the inroads into his possessions made by would-be usurpers during his absence from Ithaca he said in the most matter-of-fact way, 'I shall repair the greater part by raiding on my own.'

The unit of society was the clan rather than anything like a nation in the modern sense. Ulysses was called a king, but he was really a sort of tribal leader. His clan and neighbouring clans on the mainland and islands who spoke Greek considered themselves to be more or less related (though this did not prevent them from raiding one another) and to be a people distinct from the rest of the world, the barbarians who did not speak Greek. Ulysses and his fellows came together in loose alliances to raid a powerful neighbour, as for the siege of Troy, acknowledging one of their number temporarily as Commander-in-Chief, but Agamemnon's Greek 'army' remained essentially a group of tribal contingents. When Achilles had a row with Agamemnon over a captured girl and withdrew his contingent from the battle it was considered a bit unsporting of him, but entirely within his rights. A man's main loyalty was to his clan, and within the clan to his own family.

The Ulysses factor in man, being genetically a survival factor, has naturally emerged in forms contributing to the survival, or increased prosperity, of the clan. The explorations of the first Ulysses were of fundamental importance to the expansion of the Greek-speaking community from the eastern Mediterranean to colonies throughout the Mediterranean world. As the power-groupings in human society grew larger and the concept of 'nations' came into being the factor in individuals worked to the material benefit of nations. Over the centuries of European expansion the most successful nations were those in which the Ulysses factor in individuals was most active, the Norse, the Portuguese, the Spaniards, the

French, the Dutch and the English. Various Italian city-states had periods of great prosperity deriving from the Ulysses factor in their citizens such as Marco Polo (1254–1324) and many lesser men, but their power groupings were rendered obsolete by other historical processes. Columbus, a Genoese, had to look to Spain for sponsorship.

Through this long period national aggrandisement was not considered in any way immoral, and those who contributed greatly to it were heroes, half-worshipped in their own countries, respected everywhere. The Spaniards respected Drake although they feared him. Sir Humphrey Gilbert, lost with his *Squirrel* during his search for the North West Passage in 1583, put patriotism first in his famous call to explorers published in his *Discourse* in 1576:

> He is not worthy to live at all that for fear or danger of death shunneth his country's service or his own honour; seeing death is inevitable and the fame of virtue immortal.

In my own childhood the glory of what used to be called the British Empire had dimmed, but not the inspiration of its heroes, Drake, Davis, Raleigh, Cook, Clive, Warren Hastings and the rest. We took it for granted that to do likewise, to add an island or a new patch of red to the map, was to secure 'the fame of virtue immortal'.

We have seen that with the eighteenth century the *primary* importance of geographical exploration in contributing to national prosperity diminished, and that the Ulysses factor underwent a philosophical mutation, recognising some *absolute* virtue in climbing untrodden peaks or sailing lonely seas. Nationalism, however, remained a powerful driving force. It was good for the soul of mankind that man should reach the South Pole, but in some way it would be better for England if an Englishman could get there first. Scott's death was felt as a national tragedy, deepened by the fact that he had lost the race to the South Pole so narrowly to the Norwegian Amundsen. Every Englishmen felt his heart lifted in 1953 when Everest was climbed by a British party led by John Hunt. True, the actual climbers were Hillary, a New Zealander, and Tensing, a Sherpa, but in that context both New Zealanders and Sherpas were honorary Englishmen. And was not the very mountain named after an earlier British explorer, Sir George Everest (1790–1866), who had been Surveyor-General in India when India was part of the British Empire?

Nationalism is still an immensely powerful driving force. The huge national effort of putting men on the moon has been kept going in the United States largely by American determination that American men should get there first. Whatever may be the scientific achievement of the Americans on the moon, one of their first actions there was to plant the US flag. I don't think that many people really felt anything wrong in this: a few commentators deplored it, but I doubt if their view was much shared. It *was* an American triumph, 'a leap for mankind', no doubt, but an American leap. Had Englishmen got there first the Union Jack would have floated over the Sea of Tranquillity. The instinct that gives an explorer some rights in what he discovers is as old as man, and so is the instinct to family or national pride. It is part of humanity's self-respect.

Since the Second World War that instinct has emerged in a significant way in relation to the Ulysses factor. The apparently needless exploit requiring great self-discipline and endurance is symptomatic of the factor in advanced societies. Since it is a common factor, one would expect its emergence to be roughly proportionate to populations. But it does not appear evenly. Over the past three decades the most frequent, and the most intensive, manifestations have been in Britain and France. Other interesting examples have occurred in small nations, Norway, Denmark, Holland, Switzerland, which enjoy advanced living standards but do not exercise great material power outside their own frontiers. Japan, which was defeated in war, has contributed some outstanding manifestations. Kenichi Horie I have discussed briefly in my study of him. Another interesting Japanese example is Ikuo Kashima, who sailed a 19-ft sloop (which he built himself) from Genoa to New York in 1965, trailed her across to the west coast of the United States and went on to further adventures in the Pacific. The United States has produced a number of manifestations of the factor, but in proportion to its population, and the income available to finance personal expeditions, far fewer than statistically might be expected. From Russia have come none at all.

It is as if the instinct for national survival in nations whose material power has diminished, or which are too small for the exercise of great power in modern terms, is expressing itself through individuals, substituting the conquest of Annapurna, of Everest or Cape Horn for imperial glory. This appears both in the individual initiative to undertake such exploits and in the national response to them. French national rejoicing when Tabarly won the Singlehanded Transatlantic Race in 1964 was out of all proportion to the apparent importance of the feat. On his arrival in the United States he was greeted with the news that he had been created Chevalier of the Legion of Honour, and throughout France enthusiasm was more in keeping with national celebration of some great naval victory than for one man's crossing of the Atlantic in a small boat. The response in England to the voyages of Chichester and Alec Rose was similar. Both were knighted. The crowds that assembled at Plymouth to meet Chichester and at Portsmouth to welcome Rose could not have been much greater had they gone to cheer the victorious homecoming of fleets that had saved Britain.

Exact statistical comparison is impossible because there are few statistics, and even where statistical information can be assembled, the differing nature of individual exploits makes conclusions hazardous. Still, there are enough figures to denote tendencies. The best recorded statistics are for the Atlantic, and these may reasonably be accepted as characteristic, for although conditions vary, the impulses that prompt men to sail the same ocean in small boats are at least comparable.

The clearest figures are those for the Singlehanded Transatlantic Race. Here the conditions to be expected were the same, entrants accepted the same rules and there was one common purpose—to try to win the race. I shall use only the figures for the first race of 1960 and the second in 1964, for in these races the impulse to adventure was unclouded, or almost unclouded, by other factors. The *idea* of singlehanded ocean racing was novel, and those who responded to it responded also to the challenge of the unknown. True, there was sponsorship, but so much remained unknown that money was not of direct importance. After 1964, when the race was established, other factors entered. It remains a fine human venture, but its publicity-value to manufacturers has become greater, and the importance in it of specialised design of boats and equipment has increased. For an assessment of the national in *personal* as distinct from the national in *sporting* or any other motives I shall therefore limit the figures to the first two races.

Of the five men who sailed in 1960, four were British and one French. Of the fifteen entrants in 1964, eleven were British, one Australian living in England, two French and one a Dane. There is fair comparability with statistics for the *Sunday Times*'s singlehanded race round the world in 1968–1969, again novel, challenging and unknown. Of the ten men who were announced as having entered for it, six were British, one Australian and three French. It may be held that since these races started from Britain there was a built-in statistical probability of British and French starters, but at least that cannot apply to Atlantic nations in a Transatlantic Race. British and French entrants had to reckon on sailing back from America to Britain or France—it would have been as easy for Americans to sail over to Britain to start. In a race round the world I doubt if the starting-point matters much.

In a work of devoted scholarship* Mr Humphrey Barton and his daughter Mrs Patricia Pocock have collected information about 137 voyages involving true crossings of the Atlantic ocean made between 1865 and 1961 in boats under 40 ft in length, and one singlehanded crossing in a boat 45 ft long. The limit of length is somewhat arbitrary: *Gipsy Moth IV*, for instance, in which Chichester sailed singlehanded round the world would have been excluded. But it is impossible to define a boundary between plain sailing and adventure, and as a rough working guide these figures will do. One of the voyages recorded was made by oars, 131 under sail and six under power. The power-driven crossings here are properly included, for they were at least as dangerous as ocean passages in small sailing boats—one was made in an amphibious jeep. The largest power-driven boat (45 ft) was taken singlehanded.

These Atlantic voyages in small boats were made over a period of ninety-six years. Omitting one or two obscurities, they were made under 106 skippers, some sailing with crews,

* *Atlantic Adventurers.*

some singlehanded—several of them made more than one crossing, which explains the apparent discrepancy in the figures. Analysis of the skippers by nationality is extraordinarily interesting. In a few cases it is hard to determine nationality as distinct from national origins, and where there is doubt I have tried to err on the side of statistical safety. An Englishman who became a naturalised American I have counted as American, as I have German Americans and Norwegian Americans. A French Canadian is Canadian, Australians, New Zealanders and Irish (even before 1914) I have counted separately and not included as British (I hope they will forgive this statistical nicety). The doubtful cases are not enough to cloud the main picture.

This shows 105 men and one woman (Ann Davison) over just short of a century, who created and led expeditions in small boats across the Atlantic. Sometimes they sailed alone, sometimes with others. The true picture is not quite so predominantly male as these figures suggest, for eight women sailed with their husbands and four more women took part in various expeditions as members of crews. But this is an analysis of the nationality of the leaders or skippers on Atlantic voyages, of those who (it must be assumed) felt the first impulse to go. In husband-and-wife teams it may be that the driving force was as much in the woman as in the man, but this one cannot know. In any case, in an analysis of nationality it does not matter, for man and wife may be presumed to share one nationality.

The crude statistics show the nationality of these 106 prime movers in ocean adventure as:

British	38	Danish	2	Greek	1
American	21	Dutch	2	Italian	1
French	9	Australian	2	Swiss	1
German	5	Canadian	2	New Zealand	1
Norwegian	4	Irish	2	South African	1
Latvian	3	Israeli	2	West Indian	
Polish	3	Finnish	1	(Trinidad)	1
Swedish	3	Estonian	1		

But this is the crude analysis. If one looks at expeditions in relation to their dates these facts emerge:

Leaders of Atlantic Expeditions Before 1914
American   British   Other
   13   2   2

Leaders of Atlantic Expeditions 1919–39
British   German   French   American   Other
   6   4   3   1   7

Leaders of Atlantic Expeditions 1945–61
British   American   French   Other
   30   7   6   24

(*Note.* These figures are one short of the crude total because that includes a voyage made by four Norwegians in a pilot cutter from Norway to Newfoundland during the war. It was a magnificent voyage, but it can also be considered an enforced, or partly enforced, adventure. There were other heroic small-boat voyages during the war, but they are not relevant here.)

The pattern is clear. In the period before 1914 the United States was a rising power, and the Ulysses factor expressed itself in confident bold adventures. Almost all the great Atlantic voyages before 1914 were American. The first known attempt to cross the Atlantic in a small boat was made by William Hudson and Frank Fitch in 1866, in a ship's lifeboat converted to sail. They sailed from New York to Deal, covering some 3,260 miles in thirty-five days—a fine passage. In 1876 an American, Alfred Johnson, made the first single-handed passage of the Atlantic in the 20-ft *Centennial*. In 1877 the New Englanders Thomas Crapo and his wife crossed from Chatham, Mass., to Newlyn in Cornwall in a 19-ft whaleboat rigged with two masts. In 1892 another New Englander, William Andrews, crossed from Atlantic City to southern Portugal in *Sapolio*, canvas-covered and only 14 ft 6 in long. Andrews established a record for the smallest boat to make an ocean passage which stood for seventy-three years until his compatriot Robert Manry broke it with *Tinkerbelle* in 1965. Andrews was a mechanic by trade, but in his day you could not live in New England without learning about the sea. He was a soldier in the US Army for four years and made at least one voyage as a fisherman to the Grand Banks. He was 49 when he made his voyage in *Sapolio*, but it was not his first small-boat Atlantic crossing. With his brother Asa Andrews he had sailed from Beverley, Mass., to Mullion in Cornwall in the 19-ft *Nautilus* in 1878. He attempted another voyage at the age of 61, setting out with his wife from Atlantic City in a 20-ft boat bound for Spain. They were not heard of again, and were presumed lost in a severe gale that they encountered about one week out.

Between 1895 and 1898 Joshua Slocum made the first singlehanded voyage round the world. In 1897 the New Jersey oystermen George Harvo and Frank Samuelson, Americans of Norwegian extraction, rowed from New York to the Scillies and on to France in an 18-ft open boat, establishing another record which was to stand for some seventy years. Harvo and Samuelson were the only men to have rowed across the Atlantic until John Ridgway and Chay Blyth performed the feat in 1966. Indeed, these nineteenth-century Americans may be said to hold the record still, for their time of fifty-five days for an Atlantic passage by rowing has not been nearly equalled, let alone beaten.

These are but a sample of American exploits during the nineteenth century and the opening of the twentieth. I have concentrated on the Atlantic because of the unique material available for statistical comparison, but the drive of the Ulysses factor allied to national self-confidence was sending American men and women to adventure all over the world. By individual energy and imagination the vast North American continent was opened to cultivation and commerce as leaders of families pushed their national frontiers westwards. In 1909 Robert Peary got to the North Pole. In China and in the Pacific American men and women found new fields for missionary enterprise, the Ulysses factor in them sublimated to the service of God, another typical manifestation of the factor in vigorous nations.

American national energy in the nineteenth and early twentieth centuries was similar to that of the English in the sixteenth and seventeenth. There had been, however, a historical change of attitude that deeply affected individuals. In the sixteenth and seventeenth centuries much of the world was still unexplored, claims to sovereignty were often nominal and the enslavement of conquered peoples was considered almost as natural as in the time of the first Ulysses. There were few checks to physical exploration, or to the gains to be extracted from primary geographical discovery. Drake, Hawkins, Frobisher and their fellows could serve their country and enrich themselves. Piracy was respectable or frowned upon largely according to its degree of success. The successful pirate could come home to found schools and almshouses, to die with a fine inscription on his monument. It was the incompetent or unlucky who got hanged.

In the nineteenth century the seas were policed by the Royal Navy. Piracy had been generally outlawed a century earlier. In the nineteenth century the slave trade was abolished, and although primitive people did not enjoy the protection of a social conscience that is a powerful world force now, there were the stirrings of such a conscience. More important, perhaps, the sovereignty claimed by the great powers was real, to be infringed at peril. A man could no longer get hold of a ship, recruit a band of followers and expect much success from freelance adventuring. The driving force remained; the form of action changed. The factor that sent Drake to sea in the *Golden Hind* moved William Andrews to embark in *Sapolio*. Drake would bring back the richest cargo of booty that any ship previously had carried to England: Andrews would cross an ocean in the smallest ship that had ever made the passage. The philosophical change that widened the scope for manifestation of the Ulysses factor by conceiving an absolute value in travel to remote or difficult places came about in Western Europe, substituting an accepted *personal* purpose for actions that formerly had helped to express a national purpose. The Americans made practical application of this by deriving national satisfaction from the apparently 'useless' individual 'record'.

The First World War brought another mutation in the emotional significance of the Ulysses factor expressed in national terms. A world weary of war had temporarily no use for signs of national virility. The United States was established as a great power, and American national consciousness needed no reassurance of greatness by individual acts of courage and endurance. The rising power of Russia was clouded by revolution. The Ulysses factor in man, however, had to find outlets, and for a time obtained a satisfying emotional response in exploits of man-allied-to-machines. In the Western world the war had taken millions of men from their homes for work in factories and offices, and there were widespread feminist demands for opportunities for women to demonstrate 'equality' with men. Alliance with machines released the female Ulysses factor from some of its old restraints: in an aeroplane or at the wheel of a motor car a woman could adventure as freely as a man.

The air was still a new element, and the exploits in the air of Alcock and Brown, Hinkler, Lindbergh, the early Chichester, Amy Johnson and other pioneers met a general emotional need for enthusiasm over something that seemed clean and hopeful. The shadow of the bomber came with the later thirties. The exploits of the pioneers in air adventure were felt not only as national triumphs but as genuine steps towards new freedom for mankind. They were 'useful'. The philosophy that found virtue on mountain-tops and in lonely seas become unfashionable. The term 'escapism' came into use to express disapproval of those who were moved to go off on their own in ways that seemed to offer no practical advantage to anybody.

The two decades between the wars were bitter and confused. For much of the time national and individual lives were corroded by the world slump. Then the tide of war began to rise again in Germany. Instincts of national survival needed more than small-boat voyages to reassure them: the satisfaction obtained by individuals from such exploits was 'escapist'.

Nevertheless, the early philosophy, though temporarily out of fashion, was not universally abandoned. Men continued to want to climb mountains and to adventure in small boats, and their books inspired others. Both poles of the earth having been reached by man, the ascent of Everest, earth's highest mountain, remained a supreme physical goal. Some might question the 'use' of expeditions to attempt to climb Everest, but there was no lack of recruits for them—and great mountaineers were heroes to many, if not quite national heroes. There were Everest expeditions in 1921, 1922, 1924, 1933, 1936 and 1938—perhaps they failed to stir the world in quite the same way as expeditions to the poles before the First

U

World War or feats of adventure after the Second, because none was successful: the world prefers success. But there were other reasons; the world was preoccupied with other forms of nationalism and the fear of war.

George Mallory and Andrew Irvine died on Everest in 1924. In 1934 a strange attempt to climb Everest singlehanded was made by another Englishman, Maurice Wilson. His attempt was related to a mystical belief in purification by asceticism, and although he was not an experienced climber, he believed that by asceticism he could acquire the physical strength needed to achieve the summit. He reached a height of some 20,000 ft, but died on the mountain. He was 37, and his memory is still revered in Tibet.

There were few great sea-adventures between the wars, but enough to keep alive the tradition. Much of the initiative here was French. In 1924 Alain Gerbault made a single-handed crossing from Gibraltar to New York in *Firecrest*, and went on to sail round the world. Another Frenchman, Jean Gau, sailed singlehanded from New York to Spain in 1936. In 1933 the British Commander R. D. Graham made the first singlehanded crossing of the Atlantic from east to west with a remarkable passage from Bantry in Ireland to St John's Newfoundland in the 30-ft cutter *Emanuel*.

American individual enterprises at sea of the kind that had been so heart-stirring before 1914 almost dried up between the wars. This was not because there were no American small-boat sailors. They were numerous, and good, but they devoted themselves on the whole to conventional yachting. Consistent American success in beating off challenges for the America's Cup maintained national prestige at another level. The Ulysses factor enters into all forms of sailing, as it does into many other human activities, but the conventional is not its full development. The factor in its traditional manifestation continued to emerge, however, and an interesting American example between the wars was in W. A. Robinson. He was an engineer who went from college to a job in a textile mill near New York, but boats on Long Island Sound had his heart. He saved $1,000 and bought the 32-ft ketch *Svaap*, in which he sailed round the world between 1928 and 1931. His later career is difficult to assess. As he himself has put it, 'I fell victim to what might be called "island disease", or, in this

case, more specifically "Tahiti disease".'* The Ulysses factor
may send a man to the South Seas, but to fall in love with the
Pacific and to make one's home there involves other springs of
human action. W. A. Robinson is a magnificent seaman and
has made some outstanding voyages, both before and after the
Second World War. To what extent these can be considered
Ulysses type voyages I am not sure. His post-war vessel
Varua, 70 ft overall and displacing 50 tons, is a big ship by the
standards I have been discussing, and her voyages, although
enterprising, seem more in the nature of big-yacht cruises
than Ulysses-type adventures. Another American, Thomas
Drake, sailed from Charleston, South Carolina, to Spain in a
35-ft boat in 1926. His boat was wrecked off the Dutch coast,
and later he went to the Pacific. He was drowned in the
Pacific in 1936.

One of the more interesting manifestations of the factor
between the wars was in a young Estonian, Ahto Walter. He
was born in 1912 and served as a boy in merchant ships. In
1930, when he was just over 17, he bought the hull of an
ancient 29-ft boat for £15, rebuilt and rigged her, and with
his brother Kou Walter sailed from Talinn in the Baltic to
Torquay and on to Miami, via Madeira and the Canaries.
From Miami he went on to New York, and from there sailed
back to England, where he sold his boat for £200 and went
back to Estonia to buy another. In his next boat, slightly
smaller (27 ft), he made three more Atlantic crossings, visiting, among many other places, West Africa and sailing thence
(from Gambia) to New York. His companion on some of
these voyages was an Englishman, P. C. Barber, who sailed in
company with Walter in the 32-ft cutter *Enterprise*. Barber
sailed *Enterprise* from Gambia to New York with Walter in
Ahto II. They left Bathurst, Gambia, on the same day in
1933. Walter took forty-eight days on the passage and Barber
fifty-two.

Most of these expeditions between the wars got some publicity, but the attention they aroused was not remotely comparable with that given to Herzog, Hunt, Hillary, Chichester,
Rose, Knox-Johnston and one or two others since the Second

* W. A. Robinson, *To the Great Southern Sea*. Peter Davis 1958.

World War. There are several reasons for this. Emotional response to the Ulysses factor has undergone another mutation,
and a most interesting one. Instead of expressing the self-
confident, aggressive pride of nations rising to power, it now
reflects *defensive* national pride, the feeling 'Well, we may
not have an empire, but at least we can climb Everest—sail
singlehanded round Cape Horn—walk across the Arctic...',
whatever the exploit may be. Britain is the greatest modern
power to have suffered historical eclipse, followed by France.
Theoretical reasoning would suggest a heightened manifestation of the Ulysses factor among both British and French
people since the Second World War. This is exactly what has
occurred. The Atlantic statistics show an overwhelming preponderance of British initiative in Ulysses-type adventure
since 1945. Between 1945 and 1961 Britain, with a population
little more than one-quarter that of the United States (5.5 : 20),
produced 4.5 times more Atlantic adventurers than the
United States. The figures for France are nearly as remarkable, though they do not show so obviously. On a population
basis (5 : 20) the French might have been expected to produce
one-quarter of the American total. In fact, the French proportion is six to seven, and my statistical basis does not show the
intensity of French activity. The figures are of *people* who
have created and led expeditions involving an Atlantic crossing, and they do not distinguish between voyages limited to
the Atlantic and those of which the Atlantic passage was only
a part. French marine adventure tends to be particularly intense. Marcel Bardiaux, for instance, who crossed from West
Africa to South America in *Les Quatre Vents* in 1951, went
on to make a singlehanded passage round Cape Horn in
winter, and over the next seven years visited some 500 different anchorages, completing a circumnavigation of the world.
Jean Gau, who made his first Atlantic crossing in 1936 and
who therefore does not figure in the French statistics post-
1945 (I have counted no one twice), has since sailed round the
world alone *three times*, financing himself by working ashore
between voyages as a chef. The US magazine *Yachting* describes Gau as a Frenchman, but for some years his base—if so
far-wandering a man can be said to have one—has been in the
United States. I am not sure whether Jean Gau should be
counted now as French or American. His origin is French.

When the figures are carried beyond 1961 the preponderance of British and French initiative is even more striking. The American Slocum Society helped in the organisation of the Singlehanded Transatlantic Race, but *all* entrants in the first race were British or French, and the sole exception in the 1964 race was a Dane. Looking more widely than the Atlantic, Tilman, Chichester, Rose, Lewis, Knox-Johnston, Ridgway and Blyth, Sheila Scott, Wally Herbert and the Vinlanders are all British; Tabarley, Herzog, Moitessier, Lionel Terray, Fougeron, Lacombe, Bardiaux and Gau—by one reckoning—French. This cannot be statistical chance. The emergence of the factor as an expression of national spirit after the collapse of former imperial power can also be seen in Japan.

The behaviour of the factor in Germany since 1945 is of particular interest. Germany was defeated in war, and a simple application of the Ulysses theory would suggest that national pride would re-express itself in heroic individual adventures. The five years immediately after the war brought one notable example. In 1949 an elderly German named Paul Muller decided to sail to South America with his 18-year-old daughter Aga, in a converted lifeboat only 16 ft long which they named *Berlin*. They had trouble with bad weather in the Channel and again off Ireland, when they were rescued by lifeboat and taken to Waterford. They repaired and reprovisioned their tiny boat and set out again. They were approaching the north African coast when Paul Muller became ill. They closed the coast and managed to make a desolate beach, where he died. His daughter kept her head and was fortunate to find help after a hard journey along the coast.

After this the impulse to this type of adventure in Germany seems to have petered out—there are no German equivalents to Chichester and Tabarly. Looking more deeply, one sees some fine German mountaineering and small-boat sailing, but it is more in the form of sport than of intense individual activity. Relating this to modern German life, it is apparent that there is no particular need for individual expression of German national survival: the economic triumphs of the German people are sufficient assurance of this. The factor, therefore, expresses itself in more private and personal ways.

The voyages of Dr Hannes Lindemann in 1955 and 1956

are possible exceptions, but they are difficult to classify in terms of national self-expression. In 1955 Lindemann was working in Liberia for an American company when he made an adventurous voyage along the Liberian and Ghanian coasts in a 23-ft canoe, only 2 ft 6 in wide. He fitted the canoe with a sail, and later in the same year crossed the Atlantic from the Canaries to the West Indies, reaching St Croix in the Virgin Islands. He went back to West Africa by more normal shipping, and in 1956 set out again from the Canaries to sail to the West Indies in a 17-ft folding boat. He made the Leeward Islands after a passage of seventy-six days—a truly outstanding voyage. The extent to which these voyages may reflect national consciousness as well as personal initiative is hard to say. I have included them in the statistics, but draw no conclusions from them.

The emergence of the factor among small nations is also interesting. Heyerdahl is Norwegian, Axel Pedersen, who sailed, mostly singlehanded, from New Zealand to Denmark in the 28-ft ketch *Marco Polo* in 1958, joined David Lewis for his Iceland adventure in *Rehu Moana* and then went on to sail *Marco Polo* singlehanded to America in 1964, is a Dane. One of the first men to make a small-boat crossing of the Atlantic after the war was Swiss. He was Hans de Meiss-Teuffen, and he sailed the 33-ft yawl *Speranza* from Kingston-upon-Thames to New York in 1946. *Speranza* was then 43 years old.

Refugees are more likely to be driven by desperation than a need for adventure, but the Ulysses factor in man has contributed to many remarkable escapes. One such was in 1945 when a party of Estonians who did not want to live under the Russians sailed from the Baltic to Norfolk, Virginia, in a sixty-year-old sloop called *Emma*. She was only 36 ft long and in dreadful condition, but seven men, five women and four children crowded into her. They were afraid (for political reasons) to go down Channel, so they made for Scotland, went through the Caledonian Canal into the Irish Sea, and after calling at Dun Laoghaire went on to sail to America via Madeira. Their voyage lasted just over eighteen weeks. They were short of stores, their ancient boat needed constant pumping and they were horribly crowded. But they stuck to it with heroic determination and reached the United States safely. Their adventure has been recorded by two of their

number, Voldemaar Veedam and Carl B. Wall, in their book
Sailing to Freedom. In this exploit, as in all journeys by
refugees and escapes by prisoners of war, one cannot say to
what extent the impulse to escape derives from the Ulysses
factor, for other powerful motives are at work. But the factor,
being a survival factor, has a part, sometimes perhaps, a decisive one, in determining why one man will make repeated
efforts to escape, while others, in whom the factor is less strong,
remain more acquiescent in their lot. Survival here need not
be simply physical survival—one may have a better chance of
physical survival by remaining a prisoner of war or continuing to live in an occupied country. The man or woman compelled to escape in an effort to survive is consciously or unconsciously trying to preserve certain qualities which have been
important to family or nation in the past and which seem
threatened by existing circumstances. The *emotional* response to this manifestation of the factor may also be national-
istic, the feeling: 'My escape is not so much a triumph for me
as an expression of the determined will of my people.'

The Ulysses factor was not absent in Britain and France at
the height of their power. It inspired philosophical mountaineering and many great journeys of exploration. It tended,
however, to manifest itself in ways that were, or could be felt
to be, deeply serious, serving knowledge, religion or science.
The emergence of the factor in rising nations is often impudent. Drake's raids on the possessions of then all-powerful
Spain were impudent. William Andrews's crossing of the
Atlantic in the smallest boat ever to attempt the passage was
impudent as well as brave. This characteristic of impudence,
of a sort of cockiness, is characteristic of many manifestations
of the factor in its most modern, defensive, mutation. For
Chichester and Hasler to agree to race each other singlehanded across the Atlantic for half a crown was splendidly
impudent. For Ridgway and Blyth to tackle a seventy-year-old
record for rowing across an ocean was impudent. There is impudence in the idea of a singlehanded race round the world.
There was heroic impudence in Maurice Herzog's dash to the
summit of Annapurna. The first Ulysses showed precisely this
quality of impudence when he was imprisoned in a cave by

the giant Cyclops. He escaped by telling the giant that his name was Mr Nobody, so that when he managed to wound the Cyclops and the giant called for help from his neighbours all he could say was 'Nobody has hurt me'—which they naturally ignored. It is an attractive human quality in this context, at once brave and gay. It enhances the emotional response to national heroes, giving a lift to up-and-coming nations, inspiriting those whose power has declined. It is an expression of zest, and it has been apparent in all manifestations of the Ulysses factor that have come from Britain and France, and from small nations, since the Second World War.

By contrast, the emergence of the factor in the United States now manifests a seriousness of purpose similar to that which characterised it in Britain before the First World War. Manry's remarkable voyage in *Tinkerbelle* was marked by idealism and high purpose, not impudence. He wanted to get away from 'trivialities', to be able 'to stand back away from human society ashore, and look at life for a little while from a new perspective'. He hoped that his voyage might have done something 'to make me a better person'. The American space programme, which reflects some Ulysses characteristics though it is not in itself a manifestation of the factor, is dedicated to the advancement of science.

What of Russia? No known manifestation of the Ulysses factor in the forms that it has taken throughout history has occurred in Russia since the revolution, but this means lack of information, not lack of initiative. The factor is common to mankind and must emerge in Russia as it does elsewhere. Its expression has certainly been masked politically: manifestations of the factor are by nature individual, and a political system based on collectivism will give neither publicity nor recognition to exploits that satisfy an intensely individual need. Moreover, Russia and Soviet Asia cover an immense area, and there is much room within their confines for satisfaction of the human instinct to explore. Russian expeditions have done interesting work in the Arctic, and there must have been many individual expeditions over the past fifty years in Siberia and Central Asia. Mountaineering is a recognised sport in Russia, and the Russians have their own summits to reach and great ranges to explore. Even so, it is puzzling that no Russian has set out in a small boat to cross the North Pacific. Perhaps he has, and we simply do not hear of his adventures. There is more to it than this, however. In periods of intense national preoccupation the individual has little scope for contracting out of the herd. During the wars of 1914–1918 and 1939–1945 survival, both individual and national, was a problem so direct over large parts of the world that the instinct for survival needed no special expression. Russian history from 1917 to 1945 was largely a collective struggle for survival. Men and women with enthusiasm for the revolution had all the excitement of feeling that they were helping to create a brave new world; those without enthusiasm still had to eat, and that was preoccupation enough. After the German invasion of Russia in 1941 the whole nation was inspired by united determination to resist and to defeat the invader. The years immediately after 1945 were preoccupied with making good the ravages of war and political consolidation of the 'Soviet bloc' in Eastern Europe.

It is at least half a generation since that period ended. Russia has emerged as one of the two greatest powers on earth, rivalled only by the United States. One would expect the Ulysses factor in Russia now to manifest itself in adventurous expeditions throughout the world, each characterised by some high scientific or moral purpose. They have not appeared. Such Russian activities—at least outside Russia—are still clouded by politics. If a singlehanded Russian sailor turned up at an American port and said that he had crossed the Atlantic or Pacific he would almost certainly be held for interrogation: what would happen to a Russian in, say, Leningrad who announced that he proposed to sail singlehanded to New York, I do not know.

The Russians, like the Americans, have a gigantic space programme. They have lost the race to put a man on the moon, but are only marginally behind the Americans—if they are behind—in the exploration of space. Russian political philosophy no doubt sees in this vast collective effort a proper expression of man's urge to adventure. The Russian cosmonauts *have* become national heroes, given the same kind of publicity and acclaim that greets such exploits in the west. A cosmonaut himself (or, in Russia, herself) must have many Ulysses qualities, but neither in Russia nor anywhere else can exploits in which the individual is little more than an extension to a computer permanently satisfy man's need for *personal* physical adventure. That the Russian system does not meet all human needs may be seen in the 'defections' that take place from time to time when Russian citizens seek political asylum outside Russia. Here again one cannot draw conclusions. The motives that prompt a man to exile are complex and often sadly contorted. But it may be that if a Russian *could* sail a small boat to Martha's Vineyard simply because he *wanted* to sail to Martha's Vineyard there would be fewer defections. There might even be none at all.

Note for students of statistics: The Atlantic analysis 1865–1961 in this chapter is based on material collected by Humphrey Barton and Mrs Pocock, but my figures will be found to differ slightly from theirs. This is because we are dealing with different things: their totals relate to voyages, mine to people. In a few cases I have assessed obscurities in national status differently. The main effect has been that I have slightly under-rated what could fairly be regarded as British participation, but this is what I mean by erring on the side of statistical safety.

XXIII

The Future

I HAVE traced briefly the influence of the Ulysses factor on man from remote pre-history to modern times. It can, I think, be accepted:

(i) That there is in a man's genetic make-up a factor impelling him to firsthand physical discovery.
(ii) That it is a survival factor.
(iii) That it is present in all human beings, but highly developed in relatively few.
(iv) That it expresses both an individual and family—tribal–national need.
(v) That it mutates, philosophically and materially, influencing trends of social development and in turn being influenced by them.
(vi) That it is indestructible.

Intense manifestation of the factor in people of British and French stock since the war is not chance. Both Britain and France have enjoyed imperial greatness in still living memory, neither has had the economic success that has enabled Germany and Japan to recover national self-confidence after national catastrophe. Institutions in Britain and France have, in a sense, failed: national consciousness has yearned for individuals to demonstrate somehow that national greatness can be found beyond new frontiers. The individuals have emerged. The emotional response to Knox-Johnston, Tabarly and the rest is different in kind as well as in degree from demonstrations to welcome a victorious football team. Success in sport goes some way towards restoring national morale, but it is not enough. The contemporaries of the first Ulysses passionately enjoyed athletic games, but they remained games. Ulysses expanded the Greek world. Man's instinctive reaction to material loss is to look for something else. When food-gathering failed in primitive society the Ulysses factor prompted individuals to cross rivers, seas and mountains to find new land for survival. That cannot now be done, at least it cannot be done without war and political upheaval which other survival instincts in mankind try to prevent. A mutation in the Ulysses factor has substituted achievement in physical adventure for material gain. The great adventurers have found new frontiers to cross, of loneliness, of endurance, of man's will. Their compatriots recognise this and respond to it. The returning Knox-Johnston is greeted like a victorious admiral because he *has* achieved a naval victory. It has hurt no one, it has added no new territory to anybody's map, but it has extended national frontiers just the same. This gives deep national comfort. Everybody feels in his heart, if he does not say so, 'Well, the nation that can produce a Knox-Johnston can scarcely be written off.'

National response to Ulysses-type exploits is, however, curiously uneven. It is instinctive rather than rational. Why do some exploits win instant acclaim while others, perhaps greater in themselves, get polite applause rather than an ovation? National instincts are fundamentally simple, and if they are to respond quickly to achievement it must be achievement that can be comprehended simply: it does not have to be understood, but it must be comprehended. Every schoolboy (the overworked phrase is relevant here) has heard of Everest, the North Pole, Cape Horn, the Atlantic ocean. To climb Everest, get to the North Pole, sail a small boat round Cape Horn or across the Atlantic—these are (or seem) decisive events, like examination questions that can be answered 'Right' or 'Wrong'. The courage, endurance, physical adventure are self-evident. Tilman's voyage in *Mischief* to the rim of the Antarctic is among the greatest sailing feats of this century, but it has had little national recognition. It achieved nothing immediately obvious, and so attracted no immediate response. A more recent example of undervalued achievement is Wally Herbert's great Transpolar journey of 1968–1969. It was an immense undertaking, a wonderful example of British national initiative, and yet the nation did not wait breathlessly for news as it did at various stages of Chichester's

or Rose's or Knox-Johnston's voyages. Again, the achievement
was not immediately obvious. The expedition got to the North
Pole, yes, but people have got there before, and it was not
specifically a journey to the Pole—its objects were, in fact, far
greater, and even more difficult of achievement. Such exploits
filter into national consciousness rather than strike it. There
is *too much* to comprehend. They are no less important in
national self-expression than exploits which arouse instant enthusiasm; indeed, they may be more important. But their
effect is long-term.

This has a bearing on space-adventure, which, as I have
explained, is not a substitute for individual physical adventure. There are too many people involved, there is too much
to take in. The Ulysses factor may be highly complex in individuals, but the response is simple: it is the response to an
attempt by a man, or a few men, to do something sufficiently
out of the ordinary to bring wonder, but not so far out of the
ordinary that wonder becomes bewilderment. When Herzog
climbed Annapurna the French triumph was to have been the
first men in the world to reach a summit over 8,000 metres
(roughly 26,000 ft). Few were concerned with the technical
difficulties of the mountain—and of getting to it—which
made the reality of achievement far greater than the mere
height of its peak. Tilman's climb on Nanda Devi was a
triumph because he got to the top: men had in fact been
higher on Everest, but they had not got to the top and had,
therefore, in some sense failed. Men have got to the moon,
which is an obvious triumph, but they have neither walked,
nor swum, nor sailed there: the huge industry of technology
which got them there is as emotionally meaningless as a
cement works. The achievement of *men* on Everest and
Annapurna can be *felt*. They walked. You do not have to be
skilled with an ice-axe to know that ice is slippery. You do not
have to know anything about the *technique* of climbing to
feel your own fingers clench a little as you think of a man
scaling a rock face.

Extreme manifestation of the Ulysses factor in individuals
is rare, but at lower levels of performance the factor can be
satisfied quite simply—the dinghy, the rough hill walk in new
country, can bring deep personal fulfilment. Man does not
live by bread alone, but we do not really know what else we

need for survival, and we can be restless and unhappy—even become ill and die—without knowing what it is we lack. In advanced societies primal needs for survival—food and shelter —are mostly met more or less automatically. Social organisation provides employment, widespread distribution of food and material goods for wages to buy, and even insurance against the accidents of life. Yet the Ulysses factor remains active: it has not become a vestigial remnant of something that the ancestors of man once needed but that modern man has no use for, like the tailbone. The factor still is needed. Why?

It is a survival factor, and therefore acts as a protection against developments that threaten human survival. We do not necessarily know what these are: we do know that there are hostile forces in our environment against which we must protect ourselves, and we can say that the factor must, in some way, aid protection. One hostile development in modern industrial society about which little is known is zoological 'crowding'. This does not mean the discomfort of a crowded commuter train in the rush hour: in the zoological sense 'crowding' can be lethal. It occurs in different species of animals and plants when some threshold is crossed beyond which individuals are unable to live in one another's presence. Some species, ants and various grazing mammals, for example, can survive in enormous hives or herds. Others cannot. In nature the availability of food and prevalence of disease tend to keep the size of animal societies within bounds safe for each species, but if for some reason a community multiplies beyond its threshold of 'crowding', then, even if food is available, biological disaster threatens.

What the threshold of crowding is in man is unknown. Man is to some extent a herd animal, but his ancestors did not live in large herds, nor do his closest relatives among the primates now. Some primitive human communities have died out for no very obvious reason simply because they grew beyond a certain size when brought into contact with more advanced social organisation. Modern man has clearly adapted himself to survive a high degree of crowding in urban societies. Are there limits to this? Are some advanced societies near a point at which the lethal threshold of crowding may be reached?

The American anthropologist, Professor Carleton S. Coon,

has devised a new theory of evolution in which human adaptation to crowding has been of cardinal importance to survival. He observes:

> Although we do not know how our ancestors lived in the days before speech and tools, it is unlikely, on the basis of comparison with primates, that they constituted large bands or troops. The social unit was probably a small one, consisting of one or more family units ... Even when human beings had become able to tolerate the presence of several hundred other individuals, usually in small groups, but occasionally in large ones, adaptation to what zoologists call crowding did not end... In the Bronze Age came cities and the extreme crowding characteristic of urban communities ... The Iron Age brought empires and the Industrial Revolution spawned slums. Today vast armies, huge corporations ... channel the interaction patterns of millions of human beings.

He goes on:

> In rodents, rabbits and hares, as well as in other animals, social pressure—an amount of interaction greater than the animal can tolerate—stimulates the part of the brain known as the hypothalamus, and this organ sends information to the anterior lobe of the pituitary, commonly called the master gland. The pituitary in turn reduces its secretion of growth hormone and of gonadotropins ... The end product of this neuroendocrinological chain of events is stunting ... increases in susceptibility to diseases, and a higher rate of mortality. When animals die as a result of this sequence of events it is usually through a rise in the cholesterol level accompanied by arthero-sclerosis. This has been shown by Ratcliffe* in his autopsy studies of animals that died in the 1950's in the Philadelphia Zoo, despite an ideal diet... Like the overcrowded wild animals studied by Christian† and others they succumb to endocrine disfunction.‡

* Carleton S. Coon, *The Origin of Races*. Cape 1963.
† M. T. I. Cronin and H. L. Ratcliffe, *Changing Frequences of Arterio-Sclerosis in Mammals and Birds at the Philadelphia Zoological Garden*. 1958.
‡ J. J. Christian, *Phenomena Associated with Population Density*. EFP1.

Put simply, this means that however well fed and well off in a material sense an animal may be, the stress induced by social pressure, or crowding beyond a certain point, is liable to be destructive. This applies to man as much as to any other animal; indeed, crowding may be more of a threat to the survival of man than of other species because of man's ability to control his own environment and food supply.

Human communities have survived and flourished by adaptation to crowding, by the interplay of other factors in man to counter its evil effects. There can be no doubt but that one of these protective attributes is the Ulysses factor. In earlier times it provided a direct physical counter to crowding by impelling exploration to find room for families, tribes and nations to expand. But crowding is not merely a direct bodily threat: the obscure glandular disfunctions which it produces can stunt personalities and kill by psychological disorders as well as in more obvious ways. The philosophical mutation of the Ulysses factor has given man a psychological defence.

Advanced social organisation and technical skills enable modern man to crowd huge populations into limited living space, with security of food supplies and a high degree of medical protection against the smallpox, typhoid, cholera and other physical diseases that were once the outcome of proximity. The mind or soul of man has been less protected: the fever hospitals are empty, the mental hospitals are full. Urban man feels sub-consciously that he has lost a dimension. The Ulysses factor may help him to regain it. Of course, not everybody wants to follow Manry to find prophylaxis in mid-ocean in a 13-ft boat. Such extreme manifestations of the factor will always be rare. The fame of the first Ulysses has lasted for three thousand years because of his unique combination of human qualities. There will not be another Tilman this side of—who knows when? But biological survival is brought about by particularly efficient adaptation in *the individual,* whose qualities gradually permeate the group. These rare individuals open windows for mankind. They enable two-dimensional man to breathe back a third dimension into himself.

The range of the factor's manifestation is infinite. For every great exploit that gets into the papers there are thousands that only individuals know about. Achievement begets achievement. Haarvo and Samuelson seventy years ago. Ridgway and Blyth in 1966 rowed little open boats across the Atlantic, two men in each boat. In 1969 Tom McClean rowed a dory *alone* from Newfoundland to Ireland, and John Fairfax rowed *alone* from the Canaries to Florida. Chichester and Rose sailed singlehanded round the world in 1966–1967 and 1967–1968, each with one stop for human refreshment in Australia. In 1968–1969 Robin Knox-Johnston sailed round the world not just alone but without putting in anywhere, or calling on anybody for water, food, repairs or comforting. Technical achievement in these high-level adventures constantly increases, what is more important is that each gives new inspiration to low-level adventure. The lasting achievement of all the Everest expeditions is in the men and women who find solace and fulfilment on lesser slopes from the Peak District to the Caucasus.

There is more to it than this, however; crowding is only one development of modern society potentially hostile to man. Social organisation, in itself, may contain elements hostile to the individual. No sane man would want to go back, even if it were possible, to the conditions accepted as the lot of humanity before the concept of general responsibility for the welfare of all began to affect political and social systems. Yet there is evidence that over-cosseting by the State, by trade unions, by large industrial corporations, by any other agency which transfers responsibility in life from the individual to some faceless 'they'—however benevolent in intention—is inimical to the individual. The grape that has too sheltered an existence does not produce good wine: the great vintages are from vines on exposed hillsides that have to struggle to survive. What is true of viticulture is true of human society: the over-sheltered individual does not thrive.

The Ulysses factor in man deliberately seeks exposure—to the elements, to difficulty, to personal responsibility. There is no masochism in this. The first Ulysses enjoyed a good meal and a comfortable bed, but he came to both with heightened enjoyment because physically he had earned them. This is not a matter of mere pleasure in repose after physical exercise. A round of golf or a brisk walk home from the station may give a man an appetite, but in those dark moments of self-communion that come to everyone, when a man asks himself,

x

'What am I existing *for*?' neither golf nor the walk from the station is sufficient answer. If you can say to yourself, 'Well, I climbed the Beerenberg on Jan Mayen,' that may be enough, even thirty years later, to feel that you 'can bear to die'. But most of us will not be able to say this. It does not matter. It will often be enough to feel, 'I was alive when men climbed Everest, or Annapurna, or Nanda Devi, or sailed single-handed round the world', and then to feel 'And I have sailed a boat in a Force 8 in the Channel, and I have climbed Kinder Scout and seen all the valleys of Nepal in Edale.' It may even be enough to feel that you have understood, perhaps momentarily, why men *want* to climb mountains or to cross oceans in small boats. There are many kinds of window to the room of the human spirit. All that matters is that a man should be able to open *some* window. The Ulysses factor is the impulse to open it.

In man's continuing adaptation to society, then, is the continuing need for the exercise of this fact in him. But there is more to it even than this. Man is born into tribe or nation, and tribes and nations, like individuals, have an instinctive will to survive. The achievements of individuals that add to national self-esteem and assist national survival are properly hailed as national triumphs. But Shipton, Tilman, Herzog, Tabarly, Knox-Johnston and their fellows also belong to mankind. Theirs are victories that every nation can cheer without the least fear that they threaten anybody else. That is another element in man's survival on this planet, and perhaps not the least important.

An Index to Twentieth Century Adventure

In this book I have sought first to identify the Ulysses factor in man, next to follow its manifestations in the broad stream of history and then to examine in more detail its occurrence in individual men and women in the decades since the Second World War, the opening years of the second half of the twentieth century. Some imbalance in this pattern is inevitable; to bring the foreground into focus has meant leaving the background rather misty. I have accepted this hazard because of the importance of the foreground in our own lives; the influence of the factor on our contemporaries, and so on us, has seemed to be particularly worth analysing because of its bearing on the development of our own society. But background and middle-distance are important, too. No foreground exists in isolation—it is what it is by reason of the total landscape that helps to form it.

The historically distant background I have attempted to sketch in earlier chapters. Here I am concerned with the middle-distance, the period immediately before the decades of our own era, and its direct links with the individuals whose lives are manifestly influenced by the Ulysses factor now. The field is vast, and any attempt to portray it requires compromise. One must begin somewhere, and my starting-point is arbitrary—the year 1900. It is not, however, quite so arbitrary as it may seem. New centuries are not in themselves new periods of human history, but they are not wholly without scientific merit in defining periods. A century covers roughly four human generations, which is about the limit of *personal* contact between generations. Men who were alive in 1900 will continue in some measure to have a personal influence on others throughout most of the present century. Personality is a diminishing influence, of course (the influence of action and of writing is another matter). But personality is important, and in some sense the lives and feelings of all who live in this latter half of the twentieth century will continue to be influenced by the personalities of those who were alive at its beginning. That is one valid reason for the choice of 1900 as a starting-point for a survey of this sort. Another is that it is also historically convenient: it allows a reasonable continuity with the nineteenth century past before the cataclysm of the First World War fundamentally changed human society. It allows a similar continuity with the physical past before the fundamental changes brought by modern technology (changes accelerated by war).

So much for my starting-point. Preparation of the index itself, a summary of the exploring factor in individuals over some seventy years, presented problems many times more difficult. The need for physical limitation is obvious: but what limits, and how formed? The solution here is again arbitrary. After consultation with my publishers I decided to limit the index to a round figure of about 100 names. In fact, this figure has been exceeded slightly, but that does not matter. There is no virtue in any precise number of entries; all that matters is the scale of selection, and that was the scale chosen—to select about 100 individuals living after the turn of the century whose actions show some significant influence by the Ulysses factor. (Living after the turn of the century, of course, does not mean *born* after 1900. Many of those who have contributed most to the development of the twentieth century, in all walks of life, were *born* before it began.)

The scale is therefore arbitrary; what of the selection itself? All selection to some extent involves subjective judgment—even the impartial computer must be influenced by the subjective judgment of the programmer. All one can do is to make rules and then do one's best to abide by them. The criterion for inclusion in the index is to be or have been an individual 'whose actions show some significant influence by the Ulysses factor'. It must be emphasised that this implies no league table of merit—a man is not greater or less great as an explorer because his name is listed or omitted. And 'influence' requires interpretation. In most cases the 'influence' referred to here is personal and individual, from within a man rather than external to him. But not necessarily in all cases. Scott of the Antarctic is an interesting example of this. I do not think that Robert Scott was *initially* much influenced by the Ulysses factor *in himself* to go to the Antarctic. He was a naval officer, he was selected to command his first expedition by Sir Clements Markham,* who had met him by chance in the West Indies and been much attracted to him. It is the tradition of the Navy to go where one is sent. Scott, keen on his Service and ambitious, was eager to accept a command which offered an excellent chance both of excitement and promotion. At this stage of Scott's life the influence of the Ulysses factor was external to him—in the excitement generated around him by the *idea* of

* President of the Royal Geographical Society.

Antarctic exploration, and in Markham (though here rather in the sense of Prince Henry the Navigator, who worked through others instead of acting himself, see pages 52–53). Shackleton, by contrast, was almost pure Ulysses. But Scott is listed in the index because his actions *were* profoundly influenced by the Ulysses factor. Whatever private motives, or simple sense of duty, first sent him to the Antarctic, the Ulysses instinct in him was there awakened; the passionate determination of his second expedition to get to the South Pole was a powerful manifestation of it.

Such contrasts illustrate different aspects of the factor, its manifestation in primary and secondary forms. They are to be seen in differences of approach between Nansen and Amundsen, between Gerbault and Rose, in differences, indeed, between every individual influenced by the factor, even though their actions may seem to follow a roughly similar pattern. These differences are important, for they bring out the variety of individual response to the factor and demonstrate the *range* of humanity sensitive to its impulse.

Quality of achievement is another question raised by study of the index. Nansen's investigation of the North Polar Drift was of major geographical importance, Amundsen's dash to the South Pole achieved—what? In this context it does not matter. The index reflects seventy years of individual human endeavour; the quality of individual achievement cannot be assessed because it is immeasurable. Even relative values cannot be compared—there is no means of comparing a pioneer Atlantic flight with a sojourn among the pygmies of Central Africa, a journey in Greenland with a raft-voyage across the Pacific, a singlehanded circumnavigation of the world with the scaling of a peak in Patagonia. In mathematical terms the value of any product of the Ulysses impulse is perhaps best considered as a constant: where U represents the factor and I the individual, $UI = C$. And C can have any value you like. Both U and I are infinitely variable, but their product in any given case may be the same—a value relating to expression of the human spirit, contributing to human survival, but inexpressible in material terms. Results of great material value may derive from the Ulysses impulse, but often these will be indirect. Herman Watzinger, for instance, who accompanied Heyerdahl on the raft *Kon-Tiki*, was impressed by the abundance of fish-life in the Humboldt Current. After the expedition he went back to South America, developed a refrigeration industry to serve the fisheries of the Pacific Coast and established a Norwegian fishing industry based on Chile. This has brought major economic benefits to many people. Gino Watkins led an expedition to Greenland in 1930 to survey bases and to collect meteorological data for a possible Trans-Greenland air route from Britain to North America—on a globe the shortest route from Britain to North America crosses Southern Greenland. The increased range of aircraft soon made intermediate stops for Transatlantic flights unnecessary. But the meteorological work of Watkins's expedition became of unexpected value when war broke out in 1939. These achievements derived from the Ulysses impulse in Heyerdahl and Watzinger, in Watkins and his companions, but they are not the measure of their exploits. Comparative quality of achievement is not to be looked for in this index: it is a record of quite other things.

Comparison of motive, however, is proper, and of great interest. This is to be observed most clearly among mountaineers. Comparison of motives here reflects to some extent differences between generations, and this must be borne in mind—there are fashions in all things. But there are philosophical differences, too, and these are much more interesting. Longstaff, Tilman, Shipton and others in their tradition of climbing are primarily mountain *explorers*: they climb because they love the wildness of mountains and need to reach a summit; if, on the way to a summit, they meet a particularly difficult cliff they will use all their ingenuity to discover a route that outflanks it. Other climbers, mostly—but not all—of a later generation, climb *primarily* to surmount difficulties. If a route is even moderately easy they are not interested in it. And to overcome the difficulties of vertical or overhanging faces without handholds of any sort they allow themselves all kinds of artificial aids—drills to bore holes in rock, expansion bolts to fit into the holes, rope ladders to fix to the bolts. Christian Bonington, a leading exponent of this sort of climbing, describes an episode during his ascent of the North Face of the Cima Grande in the Italian Dolomites by a route called the 'Direttisima', a climb of exceptional severity:

> About fifty feet above, at the foot of a shallow groove, I could just see a tiny black ring protruding from the blank wall, obviously an expansion bolt. I slowly edged my way up towards it ... On reaching the groove I found some more pitons* and a couple of expansion bolts. They were all at extreme reach: climbing on pegs might be compared to going up an iron ladder with rungs six feet apart and rotting away with rust.†

The Italian Walter Bonatti, one of the greatest of all climbers since the Second World War, makes this observation:

---

* Metal spikes hammered into cracks in rock.
† *I Chose to Climb*, by Christian Bonington.

With the use of expansion bolts, or some other method of that sort, which is substantially the same as having spikes cemented into the rock, conditions are greatly changed. The sense of the unforeseen almost entirely disappears, and so too the challenge of the climb itself ... The balance between physical and spiritual effort is altered, giving absolute precedence to the physical. In such a way I would say that the spirit of the climb is killed. It becomes merely harsh and brutal, with no reason why it should be done at all.*

Which motive more truly expresses the Ulysses impulse: the desire to *conquer* a mountain face with the aid of whatever contrivances modern technology can devise or the desire to get to the top of a mountain by climbing there as nearly as possible by a man's own human resources? I cannot say. I think that both reflect *an* aspect of the Ulysses factor—to accept no physical boundary as insurmountable, *or* to attempt to surmount physical horizons by one's own human strength and spirit. I have touched on this in Chapter XIII, and conclude that the factor has undergone a slight but distinct mutation, matching the technological advance making what might be called the New Climbing possible. Certainly these artificial methods have achieved some astonishing ascents, including the North Face of the Eiger by a direct route in 1966. In that climb John Harlin, the American climber who planned and led a joint British–American expedition to tackle the face, lost his life. The climb was achieved after John Harlin's death on the mountain by Dougal Haston, a British member of the Harlin team, and by members of a German expedition led by Jörge Lehne and Peter Haag, who combined with the others during the ascent. This direct route up the North Face of the Eiger is now called the Harlin route, in John Harlin's memory.

Is such a climb useless? Perhaps. But it is neither more nor less useless than getting to the South Pole, or sailing round the world singlehanded, or reaching the top of Everest. Climbing the North Face of the Eiger by a route formerly held to be impossible has certainly extended a little the frontiers of man. And criticism of 'artificial aids' requires qualification; the aids themselves may be artificial, but a man has to get there to drive in his bolts. Nevertheless, there is a margin between motives here, though it is so far indefinable. It might be a magnificent piece of engineering to construct a lift to take passengers up the North Face of the Eiger, but the motives that sent tourists up in the lift would not have much to do with the Ulysses factor. That, however, is not yet relevant. Climbing some formidable mountain face by the most advanced

* *On the Heights*, by Walter Bonatti.

of modern techniques does not yet bear any resemblance to going up in a lift. It may demand the fortitude of an Arctic journey, with nights spent in hazardous bivouacs on tiny ledges in extreme cold. The index makes no discrimination between schools of climbing.

The physical frontiers extended by the New Climbing may be hard to define, but it has widened greatly the social bounds of mountaineering as an expression of the Ulysses impulse. Until the Second World War climbing and mountain exploring tended to be an upper-class activity. The reasons were primarily economic. The main areas of interest were in the Alps and Himalayas. Travel to either is expensive, and expeditions after the older pattern tended to be elaborate affairs. Between the wars young Germans and Austrians without much money began to develop techniques for assaults on difficult rock-faces, a form of climbing that required neither guides nor much in the way of organisation and offered almost limitless scope for personal initiative. They were encouraged in these activities by German military thinking. In Britain there were also devotees of rock-climbing and scrambling in the Peak District, Wales and Scotland, but such climbing was not regarded highly by the traditional 'alpinists'. After the war, with greater leisure for young working men and women, there was almost an explosion of interest in rock-climbing, bringing rapid development of techniques and artificial aids to climbers. This was assisted by more general social developments, increased official interest in physical education and the mobility brought by rapidly widening car ownership, making it easier than at any time in the past for parties of young people to go off for week-ends in the hills, by combining to travel in a car belonging to one of them, or by hitch-hiking. The result was a school of British rock-climbing eager to make use of every new technique, finding for itself a whole new world of adventure in the familiar hills of Britain. Industrial workers in Manchester found the gritstone ridges of the Peak District almost on their doorstep, and these rocks became the nursery of a new breed of mountain-adventurers, whose hero (deservedly) is Joe Brown, once a plumber, who acquired legendary fame by mastering climbs, first in Britain then in the Alps and Himalayas, before him held to be impossible. This New Climbing is classless, drawing people from every walk of life and inspiring youth over the whole range of society. It *makes* its own adventure. If familiar rocks begin to seem too familiar they can be tackled in winter, and new routes of exceptional severity by which to climb known faces can be sought. If this is not mountain-exploring in the older sense it is certainly exploring the physical powers of man in relation to mountains.

Sailing was never so limited in a social sense as mountaineering because the sea is universal, and a boy with a passion to explore could generally find some way of going to sea. And if he were sufficiently determined to cross an ocean for himself he could generally find some way of acquiring a boat. But the social range of sea-adventure has also widened since the Second World War. New techniques of boat-building, and, again, the new mobility of widespread car-ownership, have brought dinghy sailing within the reach of almost every boy and girl who wants to sail. Individuals who make long voyages in small boats remain exceptional—and will continue to be so—but the man who hankers after his own voyage is more likely to be able to make it than he has ever been. The singlehanded voyage, with the benefits of self-steering devices and radio aids to navigation, has something in common with the New Climbing. Both contribute to man's exploration of himself.

The index must be read against this background of social and technological change. The entries for its later decades reflect more *individual* exploits than those for its earlier years, but this is not because of any sudden flowering of human personality. The Ulysses impulse has always been an individual thing—by its very nature it must be. Nansen and Shackleton were exceptional individuals as well as exceptional leaders of others. Their conceptions were individual, but they required groups to carry them out. Over the seventy years covered by the index there has been increasing scope for individual performance, but it is interesting to see how important the expedition-group remains. Gino Watkins, who achieved real greatness in his brief life of 25 years, is remembered as much for the men he assembled for his Greenland expeditions as for his personal performance. But his powers of leadership and of selection were essential parts of his personal performance. What a splendid group he assembled for his Arctic Air-Route Expedition of 1930–1931! They included F. Spencer Chapman (*The Jungle is Neutral*), Augustine Courtauld, Martin (now Sir Martin) Lindsay, L. R. Wager (to distinguish himself on Everest) ... every member of that expedition served it and his generation well. Heyerdahl's companions on the raft *Kon-Tiki* were similarly a splendid band. So were the men of the expedition to Annapurna led by Maurice Herzog, of the team that climbed Everest, of the group led by Wally Herbert across the Arctic rim of the world. Increased scope for individual expression of the Ulysses impulse has not lessened the importance of the factor in inspiring leadership and group-loyalty.

Ulysses was not a tramp. This statement is necessary to dispel the illusion of adventure that may surround the occasional drop-out from society. The Ulysses impulse requires self-discipline in the attempt to achieve some precise end; it is not to be seen in the man who elects to wander simply to escape the constraints of responsible living. The man living in an old boat in some small tropical harbour, scrounging money or a meal where he can, is not animated by the Ulysses factor. He may sometimes seem romantic, but he is a sea-tramp rather than a sea-adventurer. The drop-out may or may not merit moral censure. His motives may be saintly as well as selfish. But he is not Ulysses.

This index is intended as a starting-point for further study. The foregoing notes explain its setting. Its limitations are obvious—in scale, in inevitably subjective selection, in range. Sporting activities as such are deliberately excluded. Crews taking part in the Fastnet Race, for instance, may have been influenced by the Ulysses factor to take up ocean-racing, but other influences are strong, too—the competitive spirit, the desire to achieve victory for a particular team, the *camaraderie* of yachting. An Olympic runner may be influenced by the Ulysses factor—but he is subject to many other influences as well. Manifestations of the factor are always complex, and the margin of motive between sporting instinct and the Ulysses impulse is sometimes hard to define. But sport is better considered as a field of its own, and *purely*, or even *primarily*, sporting exploits are outside the scope of this book. For all its limitations, however, I hope that this index does provide a fair sample of human endeavour linked by the thread that I have called the Ulysses factor over the years of this century.

A note on bibliography. Books by (or, in some cases, specially concerning) those whose names are listed in the index are given with the entries. This is intended as a reading-list; it does not purport to be in any way a complete bibliography relating to those concerned. Many of them have written books on scientific subjects in their own special fields—such titles are not given. The books listed are a selection of interest to the general reader. A brief bibliography of other works of general interest in the study of exploration and of the Ulysses factor in man is on page 351.

Abruzzi, Duke of (Prince Luigi Amadeo of Savoy). Italian. 1873–
      1933. Explorer and mountaineer. Led expeditions to Hima-
      layas, Central Africa and Arctic. Party (under Lieut Cagni,
      Italian Navy) from his Polar Expedition 1900 reached then
      farthest north (220 m. from North Pole). First ascents main
      peaks Ruwenzori range 1906.

Adams (formerly Sites), Sharon. American. First woman to sail singlehanded across the Pacific 1969, first woman to sail singlehanded from California to Hawaii 1965. (Chapter XX.)

Ahto, Walter. Estonian. b. 1902. Many long voyages in small boats. First Transatlantic crossing with elder brother 1930, when still only 17. Five Atlantic passages between 1930 and 1932. (With Tom Olsen) *Racing the Seas.*

Alcock, (Sir) John William. British airman. 1892–1919. With (Sir) A. W. Brown (*q.v.*) made first non-stop flight across Atlantic (Newfoundland to Ireland) 1919. Killed in air crash in France less than a year after flying Atlantic.

Allcard, Edward. British. Years of sea-wandering all over the world. Many remarkable passages, including singlehanded rounding of Cape Horn. *Singlehanded Passage* (1950), *Temptress Returns* (1952), *Voyage Alone* (1967).

Amundsen, Roald. Norwegian. 1872–1928. Seaman and polar explorer, in whom competitive instinct was strong. First went to Antarctic in 1898–1899 as mate of the sealer *Belgica* carrying Belgian Antarctic Expedition led by Adrien de Gerlache. Spent three years in Arctic 1903–1906, during which he forced North West Passage to the Pacific in 100-ton cutter *Gjoa* (equipped with auxiliary engine). This was the first achievement of the North West Passage. 1910–1912 returned to Antarctic in Nansen's boat *Fram* and reached South Pole on December 14 1911, beating Scott (*q.v.*) by five weeks. Pioneer of polar flying, accompanying Lincoln Ellsworth (*q.v.*) in flight over North Pole in 1925, flew with Ellsworth and Italian aviator Nobile (*q.v.*) from Spitsbergen to Alaska in 1926. Lost in seaplane during search for Nobile in Arctic in 1928. *The North-West Passage* (1908), *My Life as an Explorer* (1927), *Air Pioneering in the Arctic* (1929).

Anderson, William R. American. b. 1921. Officer of US Navy who commanded nuclear-powered submarine *Nautilus* in 1958 on first voyage under the North Pole. Remarkably able and courageous undersea navigation of Arctic Ocean, achieved partly by television scanning of underwater profile of surface ice. Anderson and his crew, however, could have no certain knowledge that they would not meet submerged cliffs or mountain ranges that would have wrecked their submarine in an instant. The cool determination shown by the expedition throughout voyage makes it an epic in polar history. *Nautilus 90 North* (1959).

Bardiaux, Marcel. French small-boat sailor. Built 30-ft sloop *Les Quatre Vents* himself, taking six years, and sailed round

ledge mountain people and Himalayas. Introduced Sherpas
(Tibetan people settled in Nepal) to mountaineering expedi-
tions. Made first attempt Nanga Parbat, explored with
Longstaff (*q.v.*) in Garhwal 1907. Lifelong interest in Mt.
Everest, probably due more to him than any other single man
that Everest became world goal of mountaineering. Led
Everest expeditions 1922–1924. *Twenty-five Years in the
Himalayas, Assault on Mt Everest 1922, Himalayan
Wanderer.*

Bryant, Leslie Vickery (Dan). New Zealander. 1905–1957. Mountaineer. Everest expedition 1935. Many climbs and new
routes discovered Southern Alps of New Zealand 1930–1946.

Buhl, Hermann. Austrian. 1924–1957. Mountaineer. Among very
greatest climbers post-Second World War. Nanga Parbat
1953. Died in climbing accident 1957.

Bunker, Robert D. H. British. b. 1936. Youngest entrant in Singlehanded Transatlantic Race 1964 in 25-ft sloop *Vanda Caelia.*
Broke bone in wrist, but carried on to finish passage to Plymouth–Newport, Rhode Island in forty-nine days.

Byrd, Richard Evelyn. American. 1882–1957. US naval officer who
specialised in polar flying. Flew from Spitsbergen to the
North Pole in 1926. Led air expedition to Antarctic 1928–
1930, discovering Marie Byrd Land and making first flight
over South Pole (1929). Led four more expeditions to Antarctic 1933–1935, 1939–1941, 1946–1947 and 1956. *Skyward*
(1928), *Alone* (1938), *Antarctic Discovery* (1936).

Cairns, Priscilla. British. Outstanding woman sailor. With Lewis
family on *Rehu Moana* 1965–1968.

Chapman, Frederick Spencer. British. b. 1907. Explorer and mountaineer. Expeditions to Greenland with Watkins (*q.v.*), Himalayas and Tibet. Remarkable exploits guerilla warfare in
Malayan jungle Second World War, described by first Lord
Wavell as 'story of endurance and survival beyond the normal
human capacity for survival'. *Watkins's Last Expedition,
Helvellyn to Himalaya, The Jungle is Neutral.*

Charcot, Jean-Baptiste. French. 1867–1936. Explorer and scientist
passionately concerned with finding out geographical facts of
the Antarctic and quite unconcerned with competitive race
to South Pole. Organised relief expedition 1903–1905 to look
for Nordenskjöld (*q.v.*), whose expedition had been trapped
in Antarctic ice. Nordenskjöld, however, was rescued by
Argentinians, and Charcot remained to explore Alexander
Land and Graham Land. Returned to Antarctic in 1908–1909
in his ship *Pourquoi Pas?* to explore and chart coasts south

and west of Graham Land peninsula. Discovered several new areas of land, including Charcot Land (an island) named after his father. Devised new equipment and techniques for mapping and travelling in Antarctic invaluable to later explorers. *Au tour du Pole-Sud.*

Chichester, (Sir) Francis. British. b. 1901. Pioneer aviator and singlehanded world voyager. *Gipsy Moth Circles the World* (1967), *Along the Clipper Way* (1966), *The Lonely Sea and the Sky* (autobiography) (1964), *Atlantic Adventure* (1962), *Alone Across the Atlantic* (1961), *Alone over the Tasman Sea* (1933, republished 1966), *Solo to Sydney* (1931). (Chapter XII.)

Cook, (Dr) Frederick A. American. 1865–1940. Anthropologist with Peary (*q.v.*) on expedition to Greenland 1892 and with Belgian expedition to Antarctic 1898–1899. Later travelled extensively in Arctic on his own and claimed to have reached North Pole on April 21 1908, a year before Peary's claim to have achieved the Pole on April 6 1909. After long controversy between protagonists of the two men Cook's claim was generally adjudged fallacious and Peary's accepted. An element of doubt, however, remains. *My Attainment of the Pole* (1911), *Through the First Antarctic Night* (1900), A. A. Freeman, *The Case for Dr Cook.*

Courtauld, Augustine. British. 1905–1959. Rich man's son who struck out for himself in Arctic exploration. Member of Gino Watkins's Greenland Expedition 1930–1931, manned meteorological station on ice-cap alone from December 6 1930 to May 5 1931 (was supposed to have been relieved after one month, but bad weather made relief impossible for five months). By self-discipline kept wholly rational through this long ordeal, took met. observations every three hours in appalling conditions, and although ran short of paraffin and candles, endured perpetual Arctic night philosophically and when relieved knew correct date. Ran out of tobacco (last pipe April 13, three weeks before relief) tried smoking tea-leaves (not enjoyed). Unique experience absolute solitude through winter on ice-cap, behaviour throughout a tribute to the highest qualities in man. Diary kept during this period in possession Scott Polar Research Institute, Cambridge. *From the Ends of the Earth* (1958).

Cousteau, Jacques Yves. French naval officer and pioneer of under-water exploration. b. 1910. Work of great importance in personal exploration of the world under the sea and in devising techniques and equipment for free-swimming under water. *Le Monde du Silence, Le Voyage de la Calypso.* Also in English translations.

Finch, George Ingle. British. b. New South Wales 1888. Scientist and mountaineer, FRS, president Alpine Club 1959–61. One of the great climbers and ski-mountaineers before and after First World War. His ascent of the North Face of Dent d'Herens in 1923 began the era of formidable 'face' climbs which were the most conspicuous new achievements in mountaineering of the 1930s and post-Second World War era in the Alps. Member of 1922 Everest Expedition and devised open-circuit oxygen apparatus, with which he reached 27,300 ft on Everest. This development was in advance of current thinking when many climbers still wore Norfolk jackets* on great climbs (though ice axes and nailed boots were used as well). Oxygen was considered 'unsporting' or unnecessary by many who attempted Everest in the next two decades, but Finch's judgment was vindicated in 1953 when Hillary and Tensing climbed Everest using open-circuit oxygen devices as advocated by Finch. *The Making of a Mountaineer* (1924), numerous articles in Alpine journals.

Fuchs, (Sir) Vivian Ernest. British. b. 1908. Geologist, educated at Brighton College and St John's Cambridge, where his tutor was Sir James Wordie (*q.v.*). Member Cambridge East Greenland Expedition 1929 and Cambridge Expedition to East African Lakes 1930–1931. Did important work on geology of Great Rift Valley. Leader of Falkland Island Dependencies Survey in Antarctic 1946–1948, and of Commonwealth Trans-Antarctic Expedition 1957–1958. (With Sir Edmund Hillary) *The Crossing of Antarctica* (1958).

Garrod, Reginald Austen. British. b. 1914. Traveller and small-boat sailor. London businessman with exploring instinct strongly developed. Deputy leader Vinland expedition 1966.

Gerbault, Alain. French. 1893–1941. Strange attractive figure who deliberately abandoned fame as international tennis champion for loneliness of singlehanded sailing. Aviator in First World War, lost many of his friends in battle, and this undoubtedly contributed to his later philosophy of loneliness and simplicity. Sailed 39-ft gaff cutter *Firecrest* singlehanded from Cannes to New York via Gibraltar 1924, spending 101 days at sea, went on to complete leisurely circumnavigation in 1929. Much voyaging in Pacific, whose islands he loved and attempted to protect from defilement of western world. *Fight of the Firecrest, In Quest of the Sun.*

Gill, Michael. New Zealander. b. 1937. Doctor and mountaineer. Outstanding among New Zealand mountain-explorers post-

* I owe this phrase to a distinguished climber who insists on anonymity.

Y

to all small-boat sailors. Sailing master of *Griffin* on Vinland expedition 1966 led by J. R. L. Anderson. *All Seasons Yachtsman, High Latitude Crossing* (1968).

Hayter, Adrian. New Zealander. Sandhurst, Regular Army officer (Gurkhas). Two singlehanded passages England to New Zealand, east about in 32-ft yawl *Sheila*, west about via Panama in 25-ft *Valkyr*, making singlehanded circumnavigation. *Sheila in the Wind* (1959), *Business in Great Waters* (1965).

Haugland, Knut. Norwegian. Army officer. Member Kon-Tiki expedition. Became director Kon-Tiki Museum in Oslo.

Herbert, Wally W. British. b. 1934. Led remarkable expedition by dog sledge across Arctic from Alaska to Spitsbergen 1968–1969. One of the longest and most formidable journeys ever undertaken—476 days in ice. *Across the Top of the World* (1969).

Herzog, Maurice. French mountaineer. b. 1919. *Annapurna* (1952). (Chapter XI.)

Hesselberg, Erik. Norwegian. Climber, small-boat sailor, artist. Member of the Kon-Tiki expedition.

Heyerdahl, Thor. Norwegian. b. 1914. Scholar of prehistoric navigation Pacific and Atlantic. Led *Kon-Tiki* raft expedition across Pacific 1947. *The Kon-Tiki Expedition* (1950), *American Indians in the Pacific* (1952), *Aku-Aku* (1958), *The Archaeology of Easter Island* (1961), and see *Senor Kon-Tiki*, biography of Thor Heyerdahl by Arnold Jacoby (1968). (Chapter VIII.)

Hillary, (Sir) Edmund. New Zealander. b. 1919. Climbed Everest with Sherpa Tensing 1953. Led New Zealand Transantarctic Expedition which completed overland journey to South Pole 1958 (in conjunction Commonwealth Transantarctic Expedition led by Sir Vivian Fuchs (*q.v.*)) New Zealand Himalayan expedition 1951. Cho Oyu 1952. *High Adventure, No Latitude for Error* (with Sir Vivian Fuchs), *The Crossing of Antarctica* (1958).

Hiscock, Eric. Hiscock, Susan. British. Three circumnavigations under sail in boats of 30 ft or under. Probably hold world record for husband and wife long-distance cruising under sail. *Around the World in Wanderer III* (1956), *Voyaging Under Sail* (1959), *Beyond the West Horizon* (1963).

Hoare, John. British. 1937–1966. Lost at sea with David Johnstone (*q.v.*) attempting to row across Atlantic. (By Merton Naydler) *The Penance Way* (1968). (Chapter XV.)

Horie, Kenichi. Japanese. b. 1938. Singlehanded Transpacific voyage Japan to San Francisco in 19-ft boat 1962. *Kodoku* (Sailing alone across the Pacific). (Chapter XIII.)

Howells, Val. British (Welsh). b. 1927. Merchant Navy officer, farmer, restaurant-keeper, splendid small-boat sailor. Fourth in first Singlehanded Transatlantic Race 1960 in 25-ft *Eira* (fifty-five days sailing time eight days Bermuda for repairs) third in singlehanded race 1964 in *Akka* (thirty-two days), much other adventurous sailing. *Sailing Into Solitude* (1966).

Hunt, (Lord) (Henry Cecil) John. British. b. 1910. Army officer, mountaineer. Led Everest expedition 1953 when mountain climbed by Hillary (*q.v.*) and Tensing (*q.v.*). *The Ascent of Everest* (1953), *Our Everest Adventure* (1954).

Irvine, Andrew. British. b. 1902. Mountaineer. Died (aged 22) with Mallory (*q.v.*) in attempt to reach summit of Mt Everest 1924.

Johnson, Amy (m. J. A. Mollison 1932, divorced 1938). British. 1903–1941. Learned to fly 1928. Two years later became first woman to fly solo from London to Australia. Record flight across Siberia to Japan 1931. England–Cape Town and back (new records) 1932. Broke London–Cape Town record again 1938. First woman to obtain Air Ministry Ground Engineers' Licence. Lost over Thames estuary while flying for war-time Air Transport Auxiliary 1941.

Johnson, Martin Elmer. American. 1884–1937. Johnson, Osa Helen. 1894–1953. Husband and wife who travelled round the world six times studying primitive peoples, making films. Spent honeymoon 1912 on 17,000 miles Pacific cruise in 35-ft boat. Borneo 1917–1919. Africa many tours 1921–1924. Spent nearly a year living with pygmies in Africa to make film *Congovilla* (1932). Osa J. *I Married Adventure, Bride in the Solomons*.

Johnstone, David. British. 1932–1966. Attempted row Atlantic with John Hoare (*q.v.*). Lost at sea 1966. (By Merton Naydler) *The Penance Way* (1968). (Chapter XV.)

Knox-Johnston, Robin. British. b. 1932. First non-stop single-handed voyage round the world. *A World of My Own* (1969). (Chapter XIX.)

La Borde, Harold. Trinidadian. b. 1933. La Borde, Kwailan (m. 1959). Long-distance ocean cruising in self-built 26-ft ketch *Humming Bird*. Atlantic crossing West Indies to England 1959. *An Ocean to Ourselves* (1962).

Lacombe, Jean. French. Small-boat sailor of great enterprise and courage. Several singlehanded passages Atlantic in very small

boats, including 21-ft *Cap Horn* in 1960 Singlehanded Transatlantic Race (fifth in race, sixty-nine days at sea) and 21-ft
Golif in 1964 race (ninth, forty-six days).

Lambert, Raymond Jules Eugene. Swiss. b. 1914. Aviator and
climber, skier. Everest expeditions 1952 and 1962. Member
Swiss aerial life-saving team. *Record a l'Himalaya.*

Larsen, Henry A. Canadian (Norwegian born). 1900–1964. Outstanding Arctic service with Royal Canadian Mounted Police.
Made North-West Passage twice in *St Roch* (104 ft) 1940–
1942 and 1944. *The North-West Passage* (1948).

Lee, Timothy Richard. British. b. 1937. Naval officer, adventurous
small-boat sailor. Navigator Vinland expedition 1966.

Lewis, (Dr) David. British–New Zealand. b. 1917. Singlehanded
sailor and pioneer of ocean cruising by catamaran. Important
practical research ancient Polynesian methods of navigation.
Children of Three Oceans (1969), *Daughters of the Wind*
(1967), *Dreamers of the Day* (1966), *The Ship Would not
Travel Due West* (1961). (Chapter XVI.)

Lindbergh, Charles Augustus. American. b. 1902. US Army officer
(Air Force). Pioneer long-distance singlehanded flight. Solo
air crossing of Atlantic (New York to Paris) 1927. America to
Copenhagen via Greenland, Iceland and Shetlands 1933. *The
Spirit of St Louis* (1953).

Lindsay, (Sir) Martin Alexander. b. 1905. After Wellington and
Sandhurst Regular Army (Royal Scots Fusiliers). Seconded
Nigeria Regiment 1927, notable journey across Africa (west
to east) through Ituri Forest and (then) Belgian Congo.
Member Watkins's Greenland Expedition 1930–1931, leader
British Trans-Greenland Expedition 1934. Distinguished war
service 1939–1945. Elected Member of Parliament for Solihull
1945. *Those Greenland Days* (1932), *Three Got Through:
Memoirs of an Arctic Explorer* (1947).

Longstaff, Tom George. British. 1875–1964. Mountaineer and explorer. Perhaps greatest mountain explorer of twentieth
century. Six journeys in Himalaya, five to Arctic, travels in
Caucasus, Rockies, Selkirks, much climbing in Alps. Explored
eastern approaches Nanda Devi 1905, climbed Trisul
(23,360 ft) 1907. Everest expedition 1922. Father of modern
Himalayan climbing, particular advocate of light, modest
expedition of the sort developed brilliantly by Shipton and
Tilman. *This My Voyage* (autobiography).

Mallory, George Leigh. British. Mountaineer. Important exploration of Everest massif 1921, member of Everest expeditions
1922–1924. Asked why he wanted to climb Everest replied,

'Because it is there.' Died on mountain with Andrew Irvine 1924 during attempt to reach summit. Just a possibility that he achieved summit and died on return, but unlikely.

Manry, Robert. American. Small-boat sailor. *Tinkerbelle* (1965). (Chapter XVII.)

Mawson, (Sir) Douglas. Australian (Yorkshire parent). 1882–1958. Physicist with Shackleton's first Antarctic expedition 1907–1909, with four companions made first ascent Mt Erebus, with party that reached South Magnetic Pole. Led own Australian expedition to Antarctic 1911–1914, taking an aeroplane to Antarctic for first time (not used, however). Discovered and named King George V Land. Led British–Australian–New Zealand Antarctic Research Expedition 1929–1931, did much important later work Australian Antarctic Territory. Perhaps Australia's greatest explorer, certainly one of most gifted and enterprising men in history of Antarctic adventure. *The Home of the Blizzard; the story of the Australian Antarctic Expedition 1911–1914* (1915).

Mermod, Michael. Swiss. b. 1936. Singlehanded navigator and long-distance canoeist. Learned to sail on Lake Geneva. Went to America aged 21, adventurous canoe expeditions Arctic Canada and Alaska. Travelled to South America, made singlehanded descent of Amazon in local narrow canoe (pirogue). In November 1961 sailed from Callao in 26-ft sloop *Geneve*, rebuilt by himself from old Norwegian clinker-built longboat. In December 1966 arrived Hyeres (Toulon) having completed singlehanded circumnavigation. Describes own philosophy 'Non pas une recherche de l'aventure, mais surtout une recherche de l'homme dans ses divers habitats'. *Des oceans pour voir des hommes* (1968).

Moitessier, Bernard. Moitessier, Francoise. French. Sailed 36-ft ketch *Joshua* from Tahiti to Spain 1966, creating record for non-stop voyage in small boat until beaten by Chichester 1966–1967 and Knox-Johnston 1968–1969. Francoise M. first woman to round Cape Horn in small boat. Bernard M. entered *Sunday Times* singlehanded round-the-world race 1968, but withdrew from race after sailing halfway round world.

Mudie, Colin. British. Yacht designer with important influence on small-boat cruising. Sailed in *Sopranino* with Patrick Ellam (*q.v.*). Attempted balloon crossing of Atlantic as member of crew of *Small World,* and when balloon came down in sea navigated 'basket' (designed by him as a boat) safely to West Indies. Designed David Lewis's catamaran *Rehu Moana*. (With Patrick Ellam) *Sopranino* (1958).

Annapurna expedition. Many distinguished climbs. *Du Mont Blanc à l'Himalaya, Entre terre et ciel, Etoiles et Tempêtes.*

Ridgway, John. British. Army officer, small-boat sailor. Transatlantic rower. (With Chay Blyth) *A Fighting Chance* (1966). (Chapter XIV.)

Roch, Andre. Swiss. b. 1906. (Engineer.) Climber and avalanche expert. Member Swiss Everest expedition 1952, expeditions to Greenland 1938, Garhwal 1939, Alaska 1950, Dhaulagiri 1953, Greenland 1956–1957–1959. Made Roch Run (ski-ing) Colorado 1937. *Les Conquêtes de ma Jeunesse* and many books on mountains and scientific works on avalanches.

Rose, (Sir) Alec. British. b. 1908. Greengrocer, who is outstanding small-boat sailor. Served Royal Navy (Atlantic convoys) Second World War, after war converted ship's lifeboat for deep-water cruising. Fourth in 1964 Singlehanded Transatlantic Race in 36-ft cutter *Lively Lady* (thirty-six days), sailed singlehanded round the world (318 days at sea, interlude in Australia) 1967–1968, making passage of Cape Horn. *My Lively Lady* (1968).

Russell, Robert Scott. British. b. (Kent) 1913, educated in New Zealand. Scientist and mountaineer. Notable climbs New Zealand 1931–1935 and Swiss Alps. Member Imperial College expedition to Jan Mayen 1938, Shipton's Karakoram expedition 1939. *Mountain Prospect* (1946) written while prisoner of war in Japanese prison camp is fine distillation of mountaineering philosophy.

Saint-Exupery, Antoine de. French aviator and explorer of sky-routes. 1900–1944. Most interesting and attractive man, who brought the instincts of primal exploration into flying. Many pioneer flights over Andes and in Africa. Philosopher of spiritual values in endeavour. Disappeared on war-time flying mission 1944. *Courrier-Sud* (1929), *Vol de Nuit* (1931), *Terre des Hommes* (1939) and charming children's story *Le Petit Prince* (1943). Most of his books also published in English translations.

Scott, Robert Falcon. British. 1868–1912. Officer in Royal Navy selected by Sir Clements Markham, president of Royal Geographical Society, to lead National Antarctic Expedition in *Discovery* 1901–1904. Led second expedition to Antarctic in *Terra Nova* 1910–1912 to attempt reach South Pole. This expedition turned into race with Norwegian Amundsen (*q.v.*), who reached Pole first on December 14 1911. Scott reached Pole on January 17 1912 and died on return journey with companions Wilson, Oates, Evans, Bowers. *The Voyage of the Discovery* (1913).

the hard way

Sites, Sharon. See Adams, Sharon.

Slocum, Joshua. American. b. (Nova Scotia, became naturalised American) 1844, lost at sea 1909. Master mariner, inspirer of all modern singlehanded sailing. First man to sail single- **?** handed round the world (via Magellan Strait) 1895–1898 in 36-ft sloop *Spray* (largely built by himself). Later lived at Martha's Vineyard. Several other singlehanded cruises in *Spray*. Aged 65 set off from Bristol, Rhode Island, for Orinoco River (Venezuela) and disappeared, presumed lost. *Sailing Alone Around the World.*

Smeeton, Miles. British. b. 1906. Regular Army officer. Smeeton, Beryl (m. Miles Smeeton 1938). Husband and wife who have sailed all over the world in *Tzu Hang*. On route Australia–Cape Horn with John Guzzwell (*q.v.*) as crew and Siamese cat as passenger capsized and dismasted in Roaring Forties. Made emergency repair at sea and worked boat some 1,400 miles to Chile, arriving safely with all ship's company, including cat. *Once is Enough* (1960), *Sunrise to Windward* (1966).

Smith, Stanley. British. Notable voyage with brother Colin Smith from Dartmouth Nova Scotia to Dartmouth England 1949 in 20-ft *Nova Espero,* one of the first post-war Atlantic crossings in very small boats. With Charles Violet (*q.v.*) sailed *Nova Espero* England to New York 1951. (With Charles Violet) *The Wind Calls the Tune* (1952).

Smythe, Francis Sydney. British. Mountaineer. 1900–1949. RAF (short service commission, invalided out 1927), RAF and Army 1939–45. Early climbing Dolomites and Alps, Kanchen-junga 1930, Kamet 1931, Everest 1933, 1936, 1938. When climbing high and alone noted feeling of friendly presence, as if roped to invisible second man (1933). *Camp VI, The Adventures of a Mountaineer, The Mountain Vision.*

Stark, Freya Madeline (m. 1947 Stewart Perowne). British. Travels in Arabia and Middle East. Many books, including *The Valleys of The Assassins* (1934), *The Southern Gates of Arabia* (1936), *A Winter in Arabia* (1940), *Beyond Euphrates* (1951), *Alexander's Path* (1958).

Stefansson, Vilhjalmur. Canadian (Icelandic extraction). 1879–1962. Anthropologist on various expeditions to Arctic 1906–1912. Learned to live with Eskimoes, practised Eskimo methods of travel and survival, and wrote many books extending knowledge of Arctic geography and life. *Autobiography* (1964), *North West to Fortune* (1958), *My Life with the Eskimoes* (1943), *The Friendly Arctic* (1921).

Tabarly, Eric. French. b. 1932. Naval officer. Won singlehanded

Transatlantic Race 1964 in *Pen-Duick II,* Plymouth to Newport, Rhode Island in 27 days 3 hours 56 minutes. Much conventional ocean racing. Brought up to sail by father and among greatest of modern French sailors. *Lonely Victory* (1964).

Tensing (Tenzing) Norkey. Sherpa. b. 1914. Mountaineer. Recruited as porter British Himalayan expeditions 1935–1938, became experienced mountaineer in own right. Reached 28,215 ft with Swiss Everest expedition 1952, climbed Everest (with Sir Edmund Hillary, *q.v.*) 1953. Director of Indian Government Mountaineering Institute.

Terray, Lionel. French. 1921–1965. Mountaineer and skier. Among the greatest Alpine and Himalayan climbers after Second World War. Climbed North Face of Eiger (with Louis Lachenal) 1947, with Herzog (*q.v.*) on Annapurna 1950, led successful Jannu (25,295 ft) expedition 1962. Several other expeditions Himalayas and Andes. *Les Conquerants de l'Inutile* (1961), in English as *Conquistadors of the Useless* (1963).

Thesiger, Wilfred Patrick. British. b. 1910. Explorer and traveller in Abyssinia, Upper Nile, Arabia. Two crossings of the Empty Quarter of Arabia. *Arabian Sands* (1959).

Tilman, Harold William. British. b. 1898. Mountaineer, explorer, small-boat sailor. *Mischief Goes South* (1968), *Mostly Mischief* (1966), *Mischief in Greenland* (1964), *Mischief among the Penguins* (1961), *Mischief in Patagonia* (1957), *Two Mountains and a River* (1949), *Mount Everest* (1938–48), *When Men and Mountains Meet* (1947), *Snow on the Equator* (1938), *Ascent of Nanda Devi* (1937). (Chapter X.)

Tschiffely, Aimé Felix. Swiss-born, lived much in Argentina. 1895–1954. With two horses travelled 10,000 miles from Argentina to Washington via Bolivia, Peru, Ecuador, Colombia, Panama, Costa Rica, San Salvador, Guatemala, Mexico. On Andes stretches of journey at times travelled at 18,000 ft. Journey took 2½ years 1926–1929.

Van De Wiele, Louis. Van De Wiele, Annie. Belgian. Husband and wife sailing partnership, world-wide cruising including circumnavigation in 45-ft ketch. (By Annie Van De Wiele) *The West in My Eyes* (1955).

Violet, Charles. British. Sailed with Stanley Smith (*q.v.*) in *Nova Espero*. (With Stanley Smith) *The Wind Calls the Tune* (1952).

Wager, Lawrence Rickard. British. 1904–1965. Mountaineer, Arc-

tic explorer and geologist (Prof of Geology, Oxford). One of
Cambridge school of young explorers in 1920s. Greenland
with Watkins (*q.v.*) 1930–1931, other Greenland expeditions
1932 and 1934. Member of Everest expedition 1933. Led (with
A. Courtauld, *q.v.*) British East Greenland Expedition 1935–
1936. Leader East Greenland Geological Survey 1953. Many
fine climbs in Alps.

Watkins, Henry George (Gino). British. 1907–1932. Epitome of
Cambridge school of young explorers between the wars. Army
family, not rich, but managed to get to Edge Island when he
was 20 and Labrador when he was 21. Vivid and attractive
personality inspired others to follow him, and succeeded in
getting financial support for expeditions. Thought up and led
British Arctic Air Route Expedition 1930–31 to survey air
route across Greenland from Britain to North America.
Average age of expedition 25. Valuable work done surveying
Greenland ice-cap and establishing meteorological station on
ice-cap, manned alone for five winter months by Augustine
Courtauld (*q.v.*). Discovered Mount Watkins. Experimental
work on diet for Arctic journeys major help to later expeditions. Drowned in accident on ice-floe while out in Eskimo
kayak, East Greenland at age of 25.

Watzinger, Herman. Norwegian. Engineer. With Heyerdahl on
Kon-Tiki raft crossing of Pacific 1947. Developed important
fishery industry Pacific coast of South America.

Wilkins, (Sir) George Hubert. Australian. 1888–1959. Aviator and
submariner. With Stefansson (*q.v.*) on Canadian Arctic Expedition 1913–1918. Trans-Arctic flight from Point Barrow
(Alaska) to Spitsbergen 1928. Antarctic flight 1928–1930.
Attempted to reach North Pole by submarine 1931—submarine 012 renamed *Nautilus* lent to him by US Navy.
Reached 82° 15′ N, but had to turn back because of damage to
submarine. Imaginative daring of this pioneer effort brought
out by fact that Pole not reached by submarine until twenty-
seven years later, on voyage by Commander W. R. Anderson
(*q.v.*) in another *Nautilus* (nuclear powered) in 1958. *Flying
the Arctic* (1928), *Under the North Pole* (1931).

Wordie (Sir) James Mann. British (Scottish). 1889–1962. Cambridge geologist. Went with Shackleton to Antarctic 1914.
Returned Cambridge after war and led numerous university
expeditions to Arctic 1919–1937. Became Master of St. John's
Cambridge (sometime tutor of Sir Vivian Fuchs, *q.v.*). Largely
responsible for idea of Commonwealth Trans-Antarctic Expedition 1957–1958 for International Geophysical Year. Important for his own work in Arctic and Antarctic and for his

General Bibliography

ALL books of history and travel ever written have some bearing on study of the Ulysses factor. I list here some of the general works that I have found particularly helpful in my own study.

Homer, *The Odyssey*. Translated by E. V. Rieu. Penguin, 1946.
Homer, *The Iliad*. Translated by E. V. Rieu. Penguin, 1950.
George Hourani, *Arab Seafaring*. Khayats, Beirut, 1963.
John Boardman, *The Greeks Overseas*. Penguin, 1964.
B. H. Warmington, *Carthage*. Penguin, 1964.
Herodotus, *The Histories*. Translated by Aubrey de Sélincourt. Penguin, 1954.
Zvi Herman, *Peoples, Seas and Ships*. Translated by Len Hertzen. Phoenix, 1966.
Leo Bagrow (edited R. A. Skelton), *History of Cartography*. Watts, 1964.
L. P. Kirwan, *A History of Polar Exploration*. Penguin, 1962.
R. A. Skelton, Thomas E. Marston and George D. Painter. *The Vinland Map and The Tartar Relation*. Yale University Press, 1965.
Magnus Magnusson and Herman Palsson, *The Vinland Sagas*. Penguin, 1965.
J. Kr Tornöe, *Colombus in the Arctic and the Vineland Literature*. Bokcentralen, Oslo, 1965.
G. R. Crone, *The Discovery of America*. Hamish Hamilton, 1969.
(Translated by) Cecil Jane. *The Journal of Christopher Columbus*. Blond and Orion Press, 1960.
(Edited by) J. C. Beaglehole, *The Journals of Captain Cook*. Cambridge University Press, 1955 onwards.
J. A. Williamson, *Cook and the Opening of the Pacific*. English Universities Press, 1946.
J. A. Williamson, *Sir Francis Drake*. Fontana, 1961.
Bjorn Landström, *Columbus*. Allen and Unwin, 1967.
John Edward Weems, *Race for the North Pole*. Heinemann, 1961.

Ian Cameron, *Lodestone and Evening Star*. Hodder and Stoughton, 1965.

W. H. Murray, *The Story of Everest*. Dent, 1953. (This was written before Everest was climbed by Hillary and Tensing. It is a most valuable record of earlier attempts on the mountain.)

Humphrey Barton, *Atlantic Adventurers*. Adlard Coles, 1962.

Charles A. Borden, *Sea Quest*. Robert Hale, 1968.

Bertrand Russell, *History of Western Philosophy*. Allen and Unwin, New Edition 1961.

H. J. Blackham, *Six Existentialist Thinkers*. Routledge and Kegan Paul, 1961.

William Barrett, *What is Existentialism?* Grove Press, New York, 1964.

Iris Murdoch, *Sartre*. Collins, 1967.

Carleton S. Coon, *The Origin of Races*. Cape, 1963.

Carleton S. Coon, *The History of Man*. Penguin, 1967.

William Howells, *Mankind in the Making*. Penguin, 1967.